PRAISE FOR
HIGH IMPACT
FEE NEGOTIATION AND
MANAGEMENT FOR
PROFESSIONALS

'One of the very few books that provides pragmatic guidance on how to raise assignment profitability at professional services firms.' **Gareth Hughes, EMEA Head of Pricing, LPM and Analytics, Reed Smith**

'This is a robust, research-grounded and above all practical guide, mixed with evidence from a seasoned professional in the field. A really useful addition for partners in any professional services firm.' **Mike Mister, Partner, Møller PSF Group Cambridge**

'Ori has been at the forefront of pricing and negotiation with PSFs for many years. He has a clear passion for, and understanding of, the complexity this area brings. This book will prove an invaluable guide to those seeking to navigate this increasing important area.' **Stuart J T Dodds, Director, Global Pricing and Legal Project Management, Baker & McKenzie Global Services**

'A thoroughly well-researched and comprehensive book that tackles the difficult issue of how Professional Service Firms and their clients can best negotiate and agree prices. Ori really understands the realities of achieving better fees and better client relationships.' **Kevin Doolan, Managing Partner, Møller PSF Group Cambridge**

'In increasingly challenging and competitive markets, this book provides professionals with invaluable guidance in a key – and neglected – area of their relationships with clients.' **Anthony Angel, Chairman, 4C Biomed Inc, and former Executive Managing Director EMEA, Standard & Poor's, and Managing Partner, Linklaters**

'Every partner and professional in a professional services firm should have a copy of this book and read it in detail.' **Hartmut Papenthin, Managing Director Operations, CMS Hasche Sigle**

'A must-have for any professional serious about managing the dilemma between building relationships and charging appropriate fees. I wish I had read it years ago.' **Anne Scoular, Managing Director, Meyler Campbell Coaching**

Second edition

High Impact Fee Negotiation and Management for Professionals

How to get, set and keep the fees you're worth

Ori Wiener

KoganPage

First published in Great Britain and the United States in 2017 by Kogan Page Limited

2nd Floor, 45 Gee Street	c/o Martin P Hill Consulting	4737/23 Ansari Road
London	122 W 27th St, 10th Floor	Daryaganj
EC1V 3RS	New York, NY 10001	New Delhi 110002
United Kingdom	USA	India

www.koganpage.com

© Ori Wiener, 2017

ISBN   978 0 7494 7738 7
E-ISBN 978 0 7494 7739 4

British Library Cataloguing-in-Publication Data

A CIP record for this book is available from the British Library.

Library of Congress Cataloging-in-Publication Data

Names: Wiener, Ori, author.
Title: High impact fee negotiation and management for professionals : how to
   get, set and keep the fees you're worth / Ori Wiener.
Description: London ; New York : Kogan Page, [2017] | Earlier edition: 2013.
   | Includes bibliographical references and index.
Identifiers: LCCN 2016053498 (print) | LCCN 2016058165 (ebook) | ISBN
   9780749477387 (pbk.) | ISBN 9780749477394 (ebook)
Subjects: LCSH: Fees, Professional. | Consultants–Fees.
Classification: LCC HD4964 .W54 2017 (print) | LCC HD4964 (ebook) | DDC
   658.15/224–dc23
LC record available at
https://lccn.loc.gov/2016053498

Typeset by Integra Software Services, Pondicherry
Print production managed by Jellyfish
Printed and bound by CPI Group (UK) Ltd, Croydon CR0 4YY

To
Ala – love of my life
and
Raphael and Gabriel, who continue to bring sparkles to their
father's eye – always

CONTENTS

ACKNOWLEDGEMENTS

Writing this book has been a major learning experience. A large number of past and present colleagues, clients and friends have been supportive of this project and I am very grateful to each and every one. Particular thanks go to John Morton for showing me how to deliver high impact negotiation support and for helping develop many of the concepts and ideas that can be found in this book. I am also indebted to John for his contribution to the chapter on gender issues. Stuart Dodds spent many an hour discussing key issues and principles with me, first as a colleague and later as a friend. I am particularly indebted to him for helping me articulate the 'get, set, keep' golden triangle. My Møller PSFG colleagues have been an invaluable source of ideas and support. Particular thanks go to Derek Klyhn for his input in the areas of procurement and for his feedback and advice in general. Kevin Doolan has provided valuable additional insights into the issues relating to pricing and matter management at law firms. Portia Hickey has been a godsend with respect to the research literature and the statistical analysis of our research data. My earliest clients deserve specials thanks for the confidence they put in me – confidentiality restrictions do not allow me to name them but thanks to H P / M L / H K / T K / P C / D H and A K nevertheless. Manju Manglani honed my writing instincts with my first articles on the subject. The team at Kogan Page were great. Liz Gooster's sense of purpose and enthusiasm were critical in the early stages of the first edition. I would probably still be working on drafts of the second edition if it were not for Amy Minshull's unique combination of patience and tactful follow-ups. Amy's editorial comments were invaluable. Nancy Wallace was a true gem in the production of both editions. I would also like to thank those who read early versions of the book and were unstinting in their feedback. My executive assistant Nadine Traughber has been a rock solid support throughout. My sons Raphael and Gabriel kept me focused on my delivery timetable for both editions, particularly when I threatened to fall behind. Without them I would no doubt still be working on the draft. They also taught me many invaluable negotiation lessons, and still do. Most of all, however, this book would not have been possible without the love, support, patience and encouragement of my wife, Ala, who is by far the best negotiator in the family.

Introduction

Everything is, so to speak, commerce or negotiation in life. (ANTOINE PECQUET, SENIOR FRENCH DIPLOMAT, 1737)

In all negotiations of difficulties, a man may not look to sow and reap at once; but must prepare business, and so ripen it by degrees. (FRANCIS BACON, ENGLISH PHILOSOPHER, 1597)

The rising importance of fee management

No skills are as critical to the career of a professional service provider (lawyer, accountant, consultant, etc) as those involved in handling clients. Most professionals are focused on the quality of their 'technical' skills and are, at best, 'blissfully unaware of their incompetence' in the non-technical areas, especially fee negotiation (Thompson, 2009). This works to their detriment as, for reasons I shall outline in this book, most clients take quality as a given and choose professional service providers on the basis of non-technical attributes.

When professionals do consider non-technical skills, those involved in winning new clients are generally seen as the most 'sexy', followed at some distance by those involving retaining existing clients. Those involving pricing, negotiating and project managing are mostly ignored, or worse still avoided like the plague. Yet these are the skills that will have the biggest impact on the financial performance of that individual as well as that of his or her firm. I used to call this collection of skills 'fee management'. A client of mine prefers to use the term 'value management'. As value management is a key driver of what great client service and this book are all about, I have decided to use this term as well.

Value management, ie the set of skills involved in pricing, negotiating and managing fees during the course of an assignment, is highly relevant on a daily basis. Those professionals best able to apply these skills will have daily opportunities to strengthen their relationships, win more work and improve their financial performance. Value management has been and still is badly neglected within many professional service firms (PSFs) and by individuals. Peter Hill, in his excellent book *Pricing for Profit* (2013) demonstrates how pricing is the single most important influencing factor on any firm's profitability and how, with relatively simple measures, profitability can be increased without necessarily providing clients with a worse deal. PSFs, along with many other firms, simply do not invest the time and effort required to establish truly optimal pricing processes or structures.

There are many complex reasons for this but all too frequently one is resignation that little can be done about it. Such pessimism is misplaced, as the results of our work with many PSFs have shown over the years. As a consequence of this neglect, PSF firms either do not bill fees commensurate with the value they deliver, or their clients are unhappy with the fees they are charged. Either way, relationships between PSFs and their clients fail to reach their full potential in economic, professional and personal terms.

Some consider this just an unfortunate aspect of the complexities of commercial life but the ramifications for individual professionals can be dramatic in terms of both professional and personal life. Professionals frequently have to 'defend' or justify their fees to their clients. These professionals are often poorly supported by their firms, have received little or no training to help them deal with such situations, and anyway find the concept of having to defend the merits and value of their work abhorrent and akin to engaging in the 'mentality of the bazaar' (probably more indicative of their 'mentality of the bizarre'). Engaging in market-style haggling is something most observers consider diametrically opposed to the typical personality profile of a professional.

As a result of this and because of the 'dilemma of goals' (Rubin and Brown, 1975) between getting a good fee and risking the client relationship, something we will refer to in Chapter 7 as the 'love versus money conflict', many professionals will try to avoid proactive value management. When avoidance is no longer an option these professionals become incredibly stressed when having to discuss fees with their existing or prospective clients. This stress will affect their personal health and the way the negotiation is handled, further undermining the client relationships (Hardy, 2008).

It is a curious paradox that many professional service firms and professionals are not at all professional when it comes to managing their own businesses. The contrast between their approach to 'billable' client work and 'non-billable' activities such as strategy, pitching, marketing, client management and everything relating to pricing, negotiating and invoicing is even more curious when considering that these activities would, if properly undertaken, help professionals become more successful, win more work and get paid better.

Of all the non-billable activities, most professionals find value management, ie setting, getting, keeping and collecting the fees they are worth, to be the toughest and most discomfiting. The most important reasons why this is the case relate to the need for professionals to build trust with clients when being selected for the work. Not surprisingly many find this a challenge at the best of times, never mind in the context of a potentially contentious fee negotiation. This book will explore these and other reasons for professionals' reluctance to engage constructively and with energy in fee negotiations and, more important, provide the reader with strategies and techniques to mitigate these challenges.

PSFs and professionals looking for support and ideas in the broader fee arena can find a plethora of materials on pricing, dealing with procurement, matter or project management and fee negotiation. Unfortunately, little of this material is written specifically for PSFs or is not sufficiently detailed or helpful on the non-technical issues (Phillips, 2009) and some of it is actually not appropriate for a professional service firm, particularly in those professions that are subject to regulation or codes of conduct. PSF management and professionals consequently have had to find their own ways to adapt key principles and processes for their businesses – with varying degrees of success.

This book addresses this gap and provides practitioners and PSFs with an overview of the key issues as well as practical guidance on how best to price, negotiate and manage fees. It will help you as a professional to become more profitable and effective in your dealings with clients.

Joining the dots – the 'golden triangle'

My colleagues at the Møller PSF Group and I have seen that few PSFs have found ways to connect the dots and create an aligned approach to value management, ie bring pricing, structuring, negotiating, project management and profitability management (including controlling and finance) under one roof to provide a consistent framework. This failure to generate a coherent approach has become particularly apparent in the post-2008 environment where clients have become increasingly keen to get value for money from their professional advisers and more sophisticated in getting it. This begets the question 'Why?' Why have PSF management not been able to get their houses in order? I believe that one of the fundamental reasons is that few professionals and their management teams have fully understood the connection between all elements of value management and the skills required by professionals to deliver them.

To understand how this can be achieved it is useful to think of fee management as three connected but distinct areas:

1 *setting* the fee (price and structure);

2 *getting* the fee (negotiation); and

3 *keeping* the fee (project fee management).

This is preceded by activities required to *win* the work and followed by activities to *get paid*. I refer to this model as the 'golden triangle'. *Setting* is concerned with determining what an appropriate fee for a particular piece of work should be and will depend on many factors. This is covered in Chapters 2 to 4. *Getting* is about engaging with the client to reach agreement on the fee and the framework that governs it; this is covered in Chapters 7 to 12. *Keeping* is about implementing the fee arrangement and managing it when projects or matters take on a life of their own (which most invariably do). This is covered more extensively in Chapter 16.

The critical point is that these activities are distinct but also heavily interdependent. Pitching for work, without pricing, is a form of madness. Asking for work without knowing what it will cost and how much the clients should be paying will inevitably result in difficulties and disappointment further down the line. There is no point setting a fee if there is a snowball in hell's chance of agreeing this with the client. Why bother engaging in a protracted fee negotiation when at the first instance of change everything has to be renegotiated or, worse still, unmanaged scope creep is allowed to kill the profitability of a project? On the other hand, why fight hard for a high headline rate (and risk losing the instruction) if you are very confident that the project will change over time, creating the opportunity to charge additional, higher margin fees?

Experience has shown that solid fee negotiation skills serve as the lynchpin holding the triangle together. There are a number of reasons for this. They include the tendency of many professionals to quote low to win the business. By so doing they give up potential profit as well as weaken their hand for when there is additional work from the client. Another reason is that a lack of confidence in one's abilities to engage and negotiate constructively with clients reduces the chances of exploring opportunities for delivering better work or being more creative. Finally, the same techniques needed to agree a fee at the start of an instruction are needed to manage an ongoing project or instruction. Again, confidence and competence in handling clients in this respect will greatly contribute to generating a positive outcome for all involved – including the client.

Figure 0.1   The broader context of the golden triangle

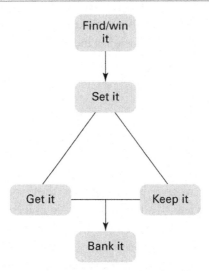

Readers of this book should expect to gain a greater understanding of the key principles involved in fee management and how to apply them. Although the book cannot replace experience gained from practice or attending programmes such as the Møller PSFG High Impact Fee Negotiation Workshop, it will help readers and their firms gain valuable insights and improve their personal and collective performance. I hope the book will also contribute to the personal and institutional wellbeing of professionals and their firms and help build better, more robust client relationships.

The world of PSFs is changing

We live in an age of increasing transparency and faster communication. Technology, the internet and social media are rapidly changing established working practices and the way in which service providers and clients or potential clients work with each other.

Increasingly, commercial success will not just be determined by those able to deliver the best work (quality) but also by those best able to deliver the work (efficiency). Both require professionals to be highly competent in communicating with existing and target clients. This communication will not just be a question of telling but also of understanding counterparts, responding and knowing how to best convey messages rather than just focusing on their content.

This book, in particular the chapters covering fee negotiation, will demonstrate how fee negotiation is just another, albeit more challenging, form of client communication and that those able to develop their fee management skills will reap a number of key benefits including:

- better rates and profitability;
- more work;
- raised client appreciation of the work delivered;
- better client relationships through better expectations management; and
- improved joint problem solving.

Many professionals worry about applying these skills, especially with important clients, for fear of antagonizing them and ending up with neither the business nor the relationship. This is often because they confuse haggling and arguing with robust and constructive negotiating. This book seeks to demonstrate that a professional can get both 'love' (the relationship) and 'money' (profitable rates). In fact the book will demonstrate how a well-conducted fee negotiation is likely to strengthen relationships, as both sides will know clearly what the future will hold and what will happen when circumstances change.

Swimming with dolphins or sharks

Another way in which the world of PSFs is changing is that clients have become increasingly proactive, some would say aggressive, in managing their professional service costs and relationships. As I will show in Chapter 1, clients have taken a number of different institutional routes to this, with some focusing their efforts on building strong relationships with a small number of providers and others looking to commoditize and dis-intermediate the provision of professional services. I also believe that there has been a change at the personal level in the way that individual clients work with their professional advisers. Individual clients can increasingly be divided into two broad categories (with some variations in between): dolphins and sharks.

Dolphin clients may be shy to start with, tend to be careful what they say or promise and take their time to get used to a service provider. Such individuals will take care of their advisers, helping them when help is needed. They can be trusted when making promises because they genuinely value their professional service relationships.

Dolphins still have their needs, ie they will still need to see good value, want to get the best prices, want their advisers to deliver quality work and meet deadlines and budgets. They will want clarity about the rules of engagement otherwise they won't work with you. One can, however, openly discuss mutual interests with dolphins, have sensible conversations about the long term and take risks in terms of upfront investment or short-term concessions in return for medium- or long-term benefits. Dolphins are worth their weight in gold. Unfortunately dolphin clients are a declining breed with the rise of procurement and greater sophistication of client buying processes. If you have a dolphin client I strongly recommend protecting and cherishing such a relationship and doing everything to nurture it. Dolphin clients are not as rare as unicorns but are a lot less common than many professionals would like to think.

Sharks on the other hand are very happy to get into the water with new advisers, in fact the faster the better. They do so not because they enjoy instructing new advisers but because they enjoy taking a bite at the first possible opportunity (or sooner), just for the fun of it or to test their adviser's mettle.

Shark clients will become even more exited if they smell blood, ie get concessions just from grumbling. With some this can easily lead to a feeding frenzy where they become even more demanding, outrageous and unreasonable simply because they can – ie their professional service providers let them. Shark clients tend not to care about the long-term impact of their actions on their adviser relationship because they don't care for one. For sharks, advisers are a penny a dozen and should be used and abused as much as possible; that is what they are there for – besides, it's fun. Really good sharks have perfected the art of making their first or early bites painless or even giving the impression that the professional is gaining major advantages; by the time they are done, however, their constant sniping, hammering and nibbling will have caused real damage to the service professional or firm, usually in the form of haemorrhaging profits and goodwill. A great description of the shark's perspective on negotiation can be found in Jim Camp's *Start with No* (Camp, 2002), in which he takes ideas such as win-win and integrative negotiation apart.

Any hopes a shark can be converted into a dolphin through great client service are illusionary. Sharks will revert to type sooner or later and usually sooner – after all they had a great time, enjoying the snapping and usually generated (short-term) benefits for themselves or their firm.

I cannot overemphasize the need to know your client and be clear on whether you are about to get into the water with a dolphin or a shark and to prepare accordingly. If you are about to swim with a dolphin, enjoy it but work at it. Protect the relationship, engage in give-and-take and look at the long term, building trust, taking calculated risks and engaging in joint problem solving.

If you are about to swim with a shark (and we all have to at some point) be careful. Don't expose yourself or your firm to unnecessary pain and risks. Be ready to snap back and don't feel guilty about this. Remember it is about survival of the fittest or most disciplined. The only way to deal with sharks is to remind them of the benefits you can deliver and the consequences for them of not working with you. With sharks we advocate taking every penny you can get, because they will try to take every penny they can from you and, anyway, future business will go to the adviser they can most chew up or that will deliver the most service or value at the lowest cost.

Sometimes it is easy to tell the dolphins and the sharks apart. Often it is not and their true nature may only become apparent as a project develops. It is worth remembering that procurement individuals are not automatically sharks and that in-house contacts are not automatically dolphins.

I believe that there is also a third type of client. Those readers interested to know what I call this can contact me via the book's website (www.psf-fees.com) and I will be happy to share my views.

Structure of the book

This book provides the platform for bringing order to the chaos and confusion surrounding fee management and will help professionals and their firms understand the key elements and actions needed to manage this area better.

Chapters 1 to 6 provide an overview of the broader issues and look at institutional factors such as drivers and contributors to profitability; pricing and value; structuring alternatives; dealing with procurement processes and how to embed good fee management practices and processes within a PSF.

Chapters 7 to 12 cover the individual perspective, including how to prepare for a negotiation; how to open the negotiation process with credibility and confidence; how to trade concessions and how to bring a negotiation to an effective close. These chapters also look at how to add more value by applying a creative approach to negotiating. A solid basis in negotiation techniques will facilitate creativity on pricing structuring and matter management and will in the process also strengthen relationships. Chapters 13 and 14 look at the impact of the individual (style) and of background norms (culture and gender). Chapter 15 reviews commonly used tactics, the selection of which will be driven by the issues raised in the preceding chapters. Chapter 16 looks at some of the issues that will help manage PSF projects profitably. Chapter 17 provides data, gained from our field research, illustrating the impact of good preparation as well as differences between a number of cultures and firms.

Tips for using the book

The chapters have generally been written on a standalone basis but to avoid too much repetition I have cross-referenced where a relevant but not central issue is covered in greater detail:

- Those looking to prepare for specific pending negotiations should start reading Chapters 7 to 15. Chapter 5 looks at dealing with procurement, an ever increasing negotiation challenge for professionals.

- Those looking for help with their approach to pricing should look at Chapters 3, 4 and 5.

- Those with management responsibilities seeking some ideas on the institutional aspects of fee management will probably want to start by taking a look at Chapters 2 to 6 and 16.

- Those looking to understand the influence that individuals and contextual backgrounds will have should look at Chapters 13 and 14.

- Those looking for quantitative data on the potential benefits of investing in value management and fee negotiation capabilities will be interested in the data presented in Chapter 17.

Additional resources and information can be found on the book's dedicated website: www.psf-fees.com. Readers can subscribe to a blog that provides thoughts, ideas, updates and insights on a fortnightly basis.

This book will help professionals and professional service firms regain the initiative in managing their client relationship and profitability. I look forward to feedback from those who have applied the principles and techniques set out in this book.

Note on language used in this book and sources referenced

I have used the terms 'practitioner' and 'professional' interchangeably to help with the flow of text. I don't distinguish between the two terms and both refer to the individual facing the challenge of fee management. Likewise the terms 'partner' and 'senior manager' should be taken as synonyms. Broadly speaking, and unless stipulated otherwise, I have in mind the individual who is answerable to his or her client and his or her employing organization and who is expected and authorized to take decisions on fees and work assignments.

Finally, I am well aware that different professions have different terms for their work. Lawyers talk about matters or instructions, consultants about projects. For the purpose of this book I have used the terms 'instruction', 'project', 'assignment' and 'work' as synonyms. As discussed above, I also refer to fee or value management as the overall process of activities involved in setting, getting and keeping fees. Nevertheless, it will be helpful to understand the special issues common to PSFs; these are described in the following chapter.

For those interested in looking at some of the underlying research or alternative views cited I have either included original references or more recent ones I thought more readable or useful.

As a coach/consultant and trainer I greatly appreciate feedback and any experiences readers wish to share with me as a consequence of reading this book. I would also be interested to hear from any individuals or companies that would like to participate in the ongoing negotiation research. I can be contacted at info@psf-fees.com.

For additional resources go to www.psf-fees.com. Those interested in a regular, short update and prompt around fee or value management may wish to check out and subscribe to my fortnightly blog on www.psf-fees.com/blog.

What is different about buying professional services?

If you think it's expensive to hire a professional to do the job, wait until you hire an amateur. (RED ADAIR)

We are seeing a rapid change in many segments of the professional services world. Firms have for some time become more sophisticated and demanding with respect to their suppliers and the last two decades saw this phenomenon spill over into the PSF world. Hitherto quasi sacrosanct professionals are finding themselves treated more and more just like their clients' other suppliers – and they don't like it. The greater use of procurement as well as the availability of technology, in particular the internet, and the advent of artificial intelligence and natural language analysis capabilities, have resulted in an unprecedented assault on long-established PSF working practices and margins. Unfortunately, precious few PSFs have found ways to deal with this. A number of factors have exacerbated the impact of this trend. These include:

- The general nature and personality of professionals working within PSFs: most professionals see themselves as technical experts and specialists. They will have spent a decade or longer acquiring their technical skills and qualifications. Many may also have had to undergo some kind of apprenticeship before qualifying, reinforcing established working practices and perspectives and a 'we are different' mindset.

- Commercial skills, including negotiation, are simply not included in most professional curricula and play an insignificant role in either the route to qualification or in the early years of a professional's career development.

Many of the larger PSFs have recently realized this and it is noticeable that leading firms in a number of professional services areas have started to offer partners and associates such training and development.

● There is also something in the technical nature of the professions themselves that results in many practitioners wishing to avoid the commercial or relationship aspects of their businesses. Many professionals advance by focusing on technical issues, facts or techniques, as part of their professional development. Commercial issues, especially fee management, are not just about facts and figures but also about ambiguity, wants, needs and ill-defined limitations and sometimes about such subjective issues as emotions and fears. Most professionals are not equipped to handle these. In fact, many have taken up their professions precisely because they wanted to avoid having to deal with such issues.

There is, however, an even more fundamental difference in why so many PSF firms and professionals experience difficulties with the commercial aspects of their work. This applies in particular to winning work and negotiating fees. This issue is very closely tied to the very nature of a professional's work. To understand this, consider the purchase of a tangible product such as a car.

When planning to buy a car, prospective buyers will first define their needs or wants such as fun, commuting, carrying capacity, size, power, number of seats and other selection criteria (eg convertible, hatchback, colour, transmission type, fuel type). They will also consider any constraints such as price, available budget, annual running costs, financing, insurance, delivery dates or maybe the size of available parking space.

Having defined these more or less precisely the prospective buyer goes out and looks at available options. Once the options have been narrowed down to a short list of preferred models the buyer will engage with one or several dealers (if they haven't done so already as part of the broader selection process). In the course of these discussions the buyer will be able to test the various options (ie different cars) in terms of their attributes and in particular how well they answer his or her need. (The 'brand' also has an impact on purchasing decisions – for cars and for PSFs. Although very important, this will not be explored further in this book.) Finally a purchasing decision is made and, subject to some last minute negotiations, the car is bought and delivered.

Whereas a car salesperson may have been involved in the selection and purchasing process to a greater or lesser extent, once the car has been delivered the salesperson is no longer involved in the interactions between the owner and the car (leaving aside issues such as service). Although a car salesperson may influence the purchasing process (and certainly the final price) the decision to buy is heavily based on the attributes of the car, which can be tested in advance. The personal attributes of the salesperson involved (or for that matter the people who built the car) are of very little relevance to the decision on which car to buy and certainly don't matter once the car has been delivered.

Now consider buying a professional service such as legal or tax advice or an architect's services. Some readers, especially those who had to undergo a long and arduous qualification process, may argue that technical expertise and in particular the quality of their work will be far more important than any of the 'soft skills' in winning work. I constantly receive feedback, from a broad range of clients and professionals, confirming that in the vast majority of cases clients 'pre-qualify' potential service providers on quality, ie by the time an adviser is considered for an instruction, quality is a given. In fact, most clients find it impossible to distinguish between the technical qualification or competencies of their advisers, taking these almost for granted. What they can distinguish is how well their adviser understands their needs, how creative or reliable they are in meeting these needs and how good the 'service' has been. Quality has become a hygiene factor. To explain why this is so consider the following.

A number of issues are very different from here on when compared to the car buying example described above. To keep matters simple let's assume that a prospective client has a fairly good idea of the professional service they need or want. First of all, most professional services tend to be high impact decisions. Whereas the value of a car is more or less what we pay for it (at least to start with), the value of most professional services to the purchaser tends to be a multiple of the cost of the actual service. We may pay £10,000 for the drafting of a contract but the value of profits associated with this contract is likely to be a large multiple of the lawyer's fees. Likewise, whatever the cost of getting tax advice or architect's designs for a house, the total tax saved or the profits from renting or selling the house are likely to be a significant multiple of the cost of the work commissioned.

Second, most clients can't objectively assess the quality of work received. By the very nature of going to a professional the buyer is going to someone (who should be) more expert in that particular field. The buyer is therefore at a disadvantage in terms of judging the quality of the work and furthermore has little visibility of the quality of work processes going on in the background. Even when the work is delivered, as in the case of a contract, tax opinion or architect's designs, clients are rarely in a position to be able to judge the quality of the work that went into producing the 'deliverable'. It is often several years before the client finds out for sure if the contract was suitably clear and enforceable, the tax authorities agreed with the tax opinion or the architect's design did not result in cracks or other defects to the building.

Third, and probably most important, when buying professional services clients buy the service, ie advice, opinion or designs as well as the people delivering the work. Once a car has been purchased there is no need for any further contact with the car salesperson. The decision to mandate a professional is almost always the beginning of a relationship or series of relationships that may last months or even years.

Professional service buyers therefore not only have to address uncertainties about the scope and quality of the final deliverable but also have to take a view on the quality of ongoing service during the project as well as the personalities of the delivering team.

Ironically, car salesmen working for established firms get high quality negotiation training on a regular basis!

The implications for fee management and fee negotiation

Given the differences between PSF and non-PSF purchasing processes highlighted above it should come as no surprise that PSF fee management and in particular fee negotiations are different to other more conventional supplier–buyer negotiations:

1 PSF purchasing and selling is personal. Buyers will not just choose a provider on the basis of quality but also on the basis of the people involved. The implication for professionals is that they are not just being judged on their technical skills but also on their personality, their personal impact and issues such as perceived integrity. Given the comments above about the difficulties most buyers will have in judging the quality of work, it is not surprising that the personal attributes of the professional or team will equal or outweigh any objective quality criteria. The importance of quality is further eroded in many purchasing processes where buyers 'pre-qualify' potential PSFs and assume that any short-listed bidders will be 'good enough'.

2 Because of the importance of the personal attributes of the delivering professional or team most buyers will want to see and experience them

during the selection process. This usually means that they want to buy professional services from the people who are going to be delivering the work or at least lead the charge. It means that successful PSF professionals have to be both good producers and good sellers of their work.

3 Trust thus becomes incredibly important for professional services sales. As subjective attributes such as personality, character and integrity cannot be established 100 per cent during a selection process, buyers have to trust their prospective advisers will act and deliver in line with what they have promised during the selection process.

4 Given the importance of trust, anything and everything a professional service provider does before, during and after an instruction, including fee negotiations, must serve to strengthen the trust of the client in the professional and their team.

Many professionals know this instinctively. They often cite the importance of personal relationships and trust and emphasize how much theirs is a 'people business' when discussing an upcoming fee negotiation or pitch. However, many have not understood the full implications of the issues raised above and consequently tend to hide behind technical issues, especially at times of difficulties.

When it comes to fee negotiations and their objectives, PSF practitioners need to consider a series of connected 'success measures' such as:

● *Price:* What is the appropriate price? Is price the appropriate measure? Could there be other factors that are more important to them or their client in the long run, eg will the work generate other benefits, such as know-how, track record, training, relationships, contacts, reputation? How will the negotiation improve on what is already on offer?

● *Scope:* Is the scope of work clear? Is it appropriate and accurate? What will happen if the scope changes – do we have the resources to deliver on time, to budget? Will the client understand potential changes to the scope? Can we manage such changes? How could the negotiation help improve scope-related issues?

● *Time frame:* How quickly does the work have to be done? How much time can we spend negotiating? When should we call it a day and get on with it?

● *Build trust:* Will the negotiations help clarify issues? Will they help manage client expectations? How compliant do we want to be seen to be, how independent?

- *Capturing future work:* Will the negotiations help open up the client for future work? How much short-term profit are we willing to sacrifice in return for long-term work and revenues? How can the negotiations help 'lock-in' this trade-off?

- *Understanding of interests/objectives/constraints:* How can the negotiations help us get to a full understanding of the client and their interests, objectives and any constraints? Are the negotiations helping generate the two-way flow of information that we would want or need?

- *Impact on relationship:* Will these negotiations help build the relationship/make it more resilient against the inevitable bumps in the road or are we just antagonizing the client with little to show for it in return? This aspect is particularly challenging as recent advances in neuroscience suggest that giving large discounts can in fact destroy client loyalty (Murray and Fortinberry, 2015).

These are difficult questions to answer at the best of times. When work is being won on the basis of a competitive selection process it may seem impossible to address all of them – but that should not stop practitioners from asking themselves: why do I want to do the work? Are the terms and conditions acceptable? If not what needs to change so that they become acceptable?

The only way that this can be done is by combining well-honed fee negotiation skills with experience and knowledge of the relevant markets and the client. Although in my opinion it has always been a central aspect of professional work, client sophistication and commercial competition have grown in the last few years, both in relative and absolute terms. It is all the more surprising therefore that even now the average 'Avon Lady' and her modern day equivalent continue to receive more training in this than most professionals.

Clients have become savvier at putting professionals through their paces when looking to hire them. It is rare now that a major assignment is awarded purely on the basis of some personal contact or a historic relationship between client and PSF or practitioner. Cost management improvements and increasing competition in the global market have prompted management teams to be more demanding regarding value for money and to be more outspoken.

As part of this we have also seen the rise of the procurement department in the sourcing of professional services (see Chapter 5 for more details on this). As a result, professionals are being forced to spend more and more of their time responding to professionally managed purchasing or selection processes and are more frequently confronted by professional buyers leading or supporting the client negotiations. Life has become tougher for professionals and this is not likely to change.

Involvement of procurement will throw greater clarity and transparency on relationships and selection processes and professionals had better prepare to deal with the implications of these trends. One way is for professionals themselves to become more professional about the way that they source business and in the way that they negotiate terms and conditions, not just at the beginning of a project but throughout the life of the project. This is what fee management is all about.

To understand better the barriers to adopting good fee management within PSFs and by professionals we first need to understand the key workings and characteristics of PSFs and professional service fees. This is the subject of the following chapter.

Why professional service firms are different

02

The best augury of a man's success in his profession is that he thinks it the finest in the world. (GEORGE ELIOT)

A central tenet of this book is that professional services and professional service firms differ from more conventional industrial or other services organizations. It is worth understanding why.

What are professional service firms?

There is no single definition of what constitutes a PSF. One approach to this question (von Nordenflycht, 2010) identifies three distinctive characteristics:

1 *Knowledge intensity* – the services require command of complex knowledge and/or experience. The knowledge is likely to be embodied within individuals as well as in systems, processes and in databases (the use of which also requires individuals skilled at interpreting and applying the knowledge). This knowledge intensity does not only apply at the managerial level (as it would in most other organizations) but also at the 'front line' or 'producing' part of a professional firm's workforce.

2 *Low capital intensity* – the firm does not require significant amounts of 'non-human' assets such as equipment, factories, patents, licences or inventories (leaving aside office space). The increasing reliance on IT systems poses interesting challenges to PSFs.

3 *Professionalized workforce* – this refers to the workforce (at least the producing, ie non-supporting, part) subscribing to specific norms of conduct or behaviour (ethical codes, behavioural standards) and being subject to some form of (self-)regulation such as membership of a central association. Such regulation may be state-backed (ie mandated and protected by law) to enforce minimum standards of competence and behaviour.

Not all PSFs comply with all the three criteria equally, but these characteristics seem to apply to most PSFs in one form or another. Examples of PSFs (based on von Nordenflycht, 2010) include:

Accounting

Law

Management consulting (strategy; IT/technology; HR; recruitment)

Coaching

Engineering consulting/design

Surveying

Advertising

Architecture

Investment banking/Investment management/Financial research/Financial advice

Marketing/Public relations

Medicine

Education (teaching, universities)

The impact of partnership

A common feature of many PSFs, especially in accounting and law, is that they were historically organized as partnerships. Although there has been a recent trend to convert to various forms of limited liability organizations most of these PSFs still run themselves as partnerships.

The relevance to fee management of partnership organizations is that they typically preserve the autonomy of individual practitioners and tend to 'manage' in a non-directive way by guiding, nudging and persuading rather than by commanding (Malhotra *et al,* 2006). This has resulted in many partnership PSFs having relatively weak management processes beyond those involved in their core 'knowledge' or 'technical expertise' areas.

In terms of fee management it has meant that many PSFs continue to struggle to implement the necessary processes and develop these skills for their partners and other fee earners. This situation is typically reinforced by compensation systems that reward the volume of 'technical work' rather than profitability; reporting systems (usually monthly financial reports) that focus on (short-term) billable work rather than on other contributions to the (long-term) performance of a firm; and a general ethos that places a premium on technical competencies and autonomy rather than commercial and collective success.

Why are PSFs different?

It is also worth reflecting on the nature of professionals and the impact this has on PSFs. As would be expected from the definition of a PSF, professionals tend to:

- focus on expertise and amassing specialized knowledge in a particular field;
- belong to a recognized professional body with entry qualification criteria often regulated by law and subject to 'authorization' requirements;
- conform to standards of ethical and professional behaviour such as having higher 'duties' to clients such as privilege of confidentiality, a duty not to abandon the client unless justified or other duties requiring professionals to put the interest of the client ahead of their own.

Reaching prerequisite qualifications usually requires extensive studies or training, passing exams and often some form of apprenticeship. Professionals tend therefore not only to be academically inclined but also to be risk averse and typically prefer to deal with facts and precedents. These characteristics, combined with a tendency to be output-driven and success oriented, means that many professionals feel uncomfortable outside their areas of technical know-how and often lack confidence outside their core expertise.

Most (but not all) professionals have a very clear hierarchy of preferences in terms of their working activities. Top preference by a very long shot is their professional practice, ie dealing with the technical issues in which they have invested so much time and effort to acquire competence. This is because most professionals see themselves in terms of expertise and their ability to resolve technical problems or challenges. Another reason why so many professionals tend to be overly focused on their practice is that their income (and view of self-worth) is driven by the amount of fees they generate 'working the files' or on client projects. As we will see in Chapter 3, when this is combined with a time-based approach to charging or billing clients, professionals will increase their focus on direct 'billable work' to the exclusion of many other aspects of their work that may be relevant and important but less direct. This phenomenon is known as the 'producer manager dilemma' and is the subject of extensive research and work by a number of academics starting with Lorsch and Mathias in 1987, Maister in 1993 and more recently by DeLong *et al* (2007).

Many professionals claim to understand the importance of client relationships and client satisfaction. The truth is that many consider dealing with clients a bothersome annoyance and an unavoidable aspect of work, to be minimized as much as possible. It is probably fair to say that client service ranks highly for most professionals when asked, but many invest insufficient time and energy learning how to provide or deliver such client service.

Most professionals recognize that they need to engage in some form of business development, but this is where many try to avoid doing anything other than amassing qualifications. It never ceases to amuse to be told by learning and development representatives briefing me and my Møller colleagues in preparation of a business development programme that the word 'sales' should be avoided at all costs as the attending professionals do not wish to be seen engaging in such mundane practices. This is only topped by the regular requests from professionals to shorten any programme offered to one or two hours, no matter how important the topic or great the professionals' need.

When professionals do engage in business development their preference is to focus on raising their personal profile by, for example, writing articles, speaking at conferences or producing newsletters, ie activities that avoid direct, intensive, one-to-one or, as I like to think of it, 'eyeball-to-eyeball' interactions with clients in which the professional has to demonstrate an understanding of the client's business, the commercial problems they face and in which he or she allows clients to test the professional's personality.

Not surprisingly other non-billable activities such as project management, firm management and leadership, coaching and mentoring and general firm-wide duties and administration receive even less care and attention. This results in professionals rarely acting in a professional manner when it comes to running their own businesses.

Why professional service fees are different

As described in the previous chapter, PSFs face the challenge that their 'output' or deliverables are, by definition, intangible services. The previous chapter covered the implications of the incredible impact that the individual has on the selection process. The intangible nature of services also carries a number of other implications. These include:

- The specifications of the output to be delivered cannot be defined exactly and often change as the work is being carried out.

- Buyers have to trust their service provider to deliver what has been ordered.

- The 'deliverable' is often a combination of ideas, recommendations, opinions or similar as well as the process of getting there, ie often the main 'value' of receiving the service lies not in the answers that emerge at the end but in the process of getting there.

- Many professional services tend to be delivered in relation to projects or long-term assignments. Both often develop a life of their own, which makes it difficult to predict at the outset how complex the provision of the service will be or how long it will take, ie how many resources will be required and hence the final cost of delivery.

- Buyers cannot easily determine the intrinsic quality of what they are buying, if at all, and often only after considerable time has passed.

- The cost of the services provided often has a significant value impact on the buyer's business, ie there is a multiplier effect arising from these services.

- It is not unusual for clients to have difficulties in quantifying the benefits and hence the value of the services received in absolute terms.

- Given the difficulties of differentiating on quality it is not surprising that clients also struggle to assess the relative benefits of using one service provider compared to another.

As mentioned, clients often struggle to quantify the value of a professional service. In some cases the service may even be considered a necessary evil due to regulatory requirements to use such a service (eg auditing, legal, engineering), and buying top quality will not always be a priority. Clients may have some minimum quality requirements to comply with regulations or statutes but many will struggle to construct a business case for buying 'premium' advice for the majority of their professional service requirements.

Clients are increasingly likely to engage in some form of 'pre-qualification' process to generate a short list of two or more potential providers all of whom will be good enough. They will then typically proceed with a selection process (some more formal than others) in which they will try to select the provider giving the best value for money. The criteria to do so are likely to be a mixture of 'technical deliverables', 'softer' issues such as personality match, trust in the team, reputation of the firm, and fees. These softer selection issues are amongst the reasons why a firm's reputation, track record and brand can have such an important influence on its success. Given that there are few tangible and objective criteria by which clients can determine in advance what they will get, they rely on recommendations and other indirect indicators of performance.

This is also why word of mouth and personal recommendations play such an important role in many professional service sectors. Clients will use peers or other users to find out what their service experience was in previous assignments and projects. Given the importance of the individual in delivering these services it is also not surprising that clients will often pay attention to all of the members of a team, even the relatively junior ones, or that this interest in the individual can often outweigh any considerations given to technical attributes, know-how or reputation of the firm employing the team.

These issues also set different marketing challenges to PSF firms depending on their size and resource base. On balance, big firms would be best served focusing their resources on building their reputation, as this way they can capture additional profits from premium pricing for the total range of services provided by their professionals. Smaller firms would be best advised to focus their limited resources and efforts on building the reputation of specific departments, service lines or teams to be able to compete with the bigger firms more effectively.

Challenges of pricing a service

Pricing is a major challenge for most firms in all sectors of the commercial world. A recent discussion document of a major international strategy consultant (Burns *et al*, 2016), for example, highlights the pricing challenges faced by the chemicals industry. Many of the challenges and issues raised in that document are similar to the challenges faced by PSFs. It should come as no surprise that pricing an intangible service of indeterminate quality and uncertain specification is especially challenging. The key dilemma for the professional is that if the service is perceived as too expensive it is likely to lead to losing the business and maybe even the client. The latter risk arises if the professional is consistently thought to be pricing too high and the client is no longer interested in wasting time and effort (Sodhi and Sodhi, 2008). Acquiring a reputation for being too expensive can have a long-term impact. Please note that there is a difference between a high or premium price and being expensive – all are questions of value for money. It may be perfectly fine to position oneself or one's services in the premium segment, but should be a deliberate strategy rather than an accident.

On the other hand, if a professional has priced too low he or she is unlikely to be able to recover lost profits on this and subsequent instructions as prices are 'sticky'. It is tough to get clients to agree to an increase for a service that they have had cheaper before. Something very substantial will have to change to justify a significant increase. Worse still, if a particular professional within a firm has 'under-priced', clients have been known to hold this price out to colleagues from the same firm, saying that if this professional can charge fees that are that low, so should other members of the same firm. Under-pricing can thus also cause serious long-term damage to a firm or connected professionals.

In addition, many clients use price as a signal of quality. Coming in too 'cheap' could be construed rightly or wrongly as a sign of lower quality. The key issue is that pricing should be the function of a deliberate, well-thought-through strategy incorporating a broad range of issues rather than something decided on pure 'gut feelings' or on a case-by-case basis. The issues of price and value are explored further in Chapter 3.

Professionals are historically not particularly sophisticated when it comes to the financial management of their firms. In fact many professionals do not understand the drivers of their own firm or current project profitability particularly well. Most professionals, for example, do not know the relationship between discounts given and changes in profitability. Many believe that a 10 per cent discount will result in a 10 per cent reduction in profit and that to compensate for this one need only work 10 per cent extra. In fact this is not the case for most professional service firms, as illustrated in Figure 2.1.

For the purpose of the illustration let's assume that a professional expects to work 1,000 hours at an hourly rate of 500. Direct costs associated are 350, ie gross profits are 150 per hour, or 30 per cent gross margin, generating a gross profit of 150,000. Applying a 10 per cent discount (ie 50) reduces the hourly rate to 450. If costs are not reduced gross profit falls to 100,000, ie a 33 per cent fall. To generate 150,000 of gross profits the professional would now have to work an extra 500 hours, ie 50 per cent more, at the reduced rate.

Figure 2.1   The impact of discounting: the 10:30:50 rule

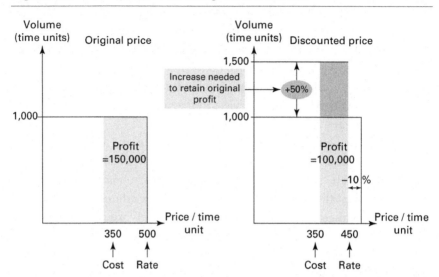

10% discount = 30% profit loss and requires 50% revenue increase to compensate

NOTE Based on illustrative hourly rate of £500 and gross margin of 30%.

© Møller PSFG Cambridge 2017 – Ori Wiener

Table 2.1 shows the impact that a discount has on profit for different levels of firm margins. The table demonstrates that the lower a firm's gross margins the more sensitive the firm's profits are to any discounts. This means that the lower the margins the harder professionals have to work to compensate for any discounts granted. Simply getting practitioners to understand better the drivers that influence their profitability will make a significant contribution to better fee management.

Impact and importance of strategy, market position and business development

Just as in a game of football where a good attack is firmly founded on a great defence, good fee management is supported by effective business development (a polite way of saying 'sales' in many PSFs) and marketing. Firms where business development is aligned with the firm's strategy typically do best in this respect. This is because a firm that has a strategy and

Table 2.1 The impact of discounts

	Loss in profit margin				
	20%	**25%**	**30%**	**35%**	**40%**
Change in fees					
−25%	125.0%	100.0%	83.3%	71.4%	62.5%
−20%	100.0%	80.0%	66.7%	57.1%	50.0%
−15%	75.0%	60.0%	50.0%	42.9%	37.5%
−10%	50.0%	40.0%	33.3%	28.6%	25.0%
−5%	25.0%	20.0%	16.7%	14.3%	12.5%
Additional hours needed to recoup profit					
−25%	Loss making	Loss making	500.0%	250.0%	166.7%
−20%	Loss making	400.0%	200.0%	133.3%	100.0%
−15%	300.0%	150.0%	100.0%	75.0%	37.5%
−10%	100.0%	66.7%	50.0%	40.0%	33.3%

has been investing in and developing resources to support this strategy, such as marketing, branding and positioning, is best able to take advantage of its investments and to capture the benefits of such investments to help it find the kind of work that match the firm's 'sweet spot', ie the kind of work for which a firm or the professionals in it are best suited. An example of this is a firm's reputation (part of its brand) which may have been built over time and becomes instrumental in attracting work of a specific nature.

In addition to helping attract the right kind of work there is also a major benefit to a firm and its individuals if the work plays to collective and individual strengths. This helps resist the kind of pressures, especially psychological ones, involved in fee management and in particular in engaging with clients who have different and at times conflicting interests.

Strategy, business development, marketing and their alignment are major topics and areas of work in which the Møller PSF Group engages with its clients. They are critical precursors to fee management but beyond the remit of this book. It is, however, important to note that, a) these are important topics, and b) they overlap and interact with fee management – there are no clear dividing lines, contrary to the views held by some (Cassell and Bird, 2012; Gates, 2012) who advocate a clean separation between selling and negotiating. I believe that some of these differences can be explained by the differences between PSFs and other manufactured goods settings. The business development or sales process almost always involves pricing and negotiation and pricing options or negotiation strategies will be affected by preceding sales activities, in particular if any specific promises had been made or undertakings given. Likewise, it may well be during the process of negotiation that additional opportunities become apparent.

Good negotiators know that there are times when they have to 'sell' their proposals or concessions to the other side and that the negotiation outcome can often be improved by increasing the pie and getting the other side to agree to include additional services in the 'deal'. Interestingly there is also some evidence to suggest that good negotiation skills can actually help contribute to the process and formulation of effective and more robust firm strategies (Jarzabkowski and Balogun, 2009).

Invoicing and collecting

To continue the football analogy, there is no point scoring a goal if the score is not recorded. Likewise there is no point engaging with clients on fees and delivering the work if invoices are not sent to the client and payments not checked. There are many ways in which the invoicing and collection processes of PSFs can be managed and improved. The major issues involving these tasks are mostly a function of process optimization. Although I don't want to undervalue the importance of these processes I will not dwell on them much more as they tend not to be central to the challenges reported by professionals in relation to fee management. These challenges lie at the heart of the 'golden triangle' first mentioned in the Introduction (for more details see Chapter 16).

Navigating the golden triangle for greater profitability

As described in the Introduction, there are three essential elements to fee management: setting the 'right' price and structure, getting it agreed with the client (negotiation) and keeping the price agreed. Each activity requires different skills and resources but they have to be brought together and aligned to be able to optimize the fees that a professional or PSF can generate.

Professionals often encounter problems related to one part of the triangle but attempt to resolve these with solutions that belong to another. For example, I am often asked by professionals how they should negotiate in a situation where three of four competitors offer to perform work to similar quality at a 30 to 40 per cent discount. The answer to this is that you don't because this is not a negotiation problem but a pricing or structuring challenge. To address this, professionals will need to review their approach to pricing the work. This may include changing the price or it may include having to restructure their business model or processes to be able to deliver the work at a lower cost.

Likewise, professionals often have to deal with overruns or other low-profit projects where the cause of the reduced margins is not a low rate or fee quote but poor project fee management. This could happen either because the project team is not being managed in line with the fee structure or because scope creep is not being managed. Figure 2.2 provides additional details on the key components of the golden triangle as well as some of the issues associated with each element.

One of the best ways to capture the full benefit of the approach embodied in the golden triangle model is to think of it as a continuous cycle or iteration, ie a professional should constantly be switching attention from one

Figure 2.2   Fee management: the golden triangle

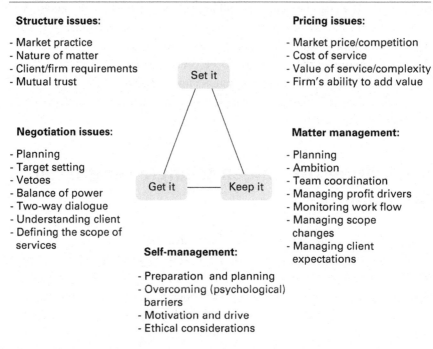

Structure issues:

- Market practice
- Nature of matter
- Client/firm requirements
- Mutual trust

Set it

Pricing issues:

- Market price/competition
- Cost of service
- Value of service/complexity
- Firm's ability to add value

Negotiation issues:

- Planning
- Target setting
- Vetoes
- Balance of power
- Two-way dialogue
- Understanding client
- Defining the scope of
  services

Get it ———— Keep it

Matter management:

- Planning
- Ambition
- Team coordination
- Managing profit drivers
- Monitoring work flow
- Managing scope
  changes
- Managing client
  expectations

Self-management:

- Preparation and planning
- Overcoming (psychological)
  barriers
- Motivation and drive
- Ethical considerations

part of the triangle to the other, seeking new opportunities to renegotiate when possible, re-pricing and constantly managing the client. This requires considerable self-discipline at first. Once professionals have started to apply this approach consistently most will see it as an invaluable tool to support and improve client relationships and raise personal performance.

Having looked at the broader context of PSFs and professional service fees and the relationship between set, get and keep as highlighted in the golden triangle, Chapter 3 will look in greater detail at the first of these – setting the price for a professional service.

The challenge of pricing PSF work

03

Price is what you pay, value is what you get. (WARREN BUFFET QUOTING BENJAMIN GRAHAM IN THE BERKSHIRE HATHAWAY 2008 ANNUAL REPORT)

What is a cynic? A man who knows the price of everything and the value of nothing. (OSCAR WILDE, *LADY WINDERMERE'S FAN*, 1893)

The two quotes above are surprisingly relevant to PSF pricing. For reasons to be explored further in this chapter many professionals find it challenging, to say the least, to understand the value their work contributes to their clients. Just about everyone has by now understood that a 'Marquis de Sade' approach to billing, ie 'bill till they scream' (Tolman, 1989) won't work. Clients may have a go at growling anyway – it might just get the bill down.

Many clients find it equally difficult to assess the value of the service received, but they instinctively know that they want to get as much 'value' as possible and pay as little for it as possible in return. Hence it is not surprising that professionals find it difficult to determine the 'right price' for their work and that they therefore resort to alternative means of setting and agreeing a price with their clients. This is graphically demonstrated in Figure 3.1, which shows just how intuitive and inefficient PSF pricing can be. The data, taken from a Møller PSFG client (with a reputation for good financial management) shows how similar projects within the same firm and specialist area were priced differently and how different the achieved margins were, ranging from a 50 per cent profit margin to a 20 per cent loss. This chapter will explore some of the underlying reasons for such a broad range of outcomes. Before diving into the details let's quickly review some basic concepts first.

Figure 3.1 Pricing is intuitive and inefficient

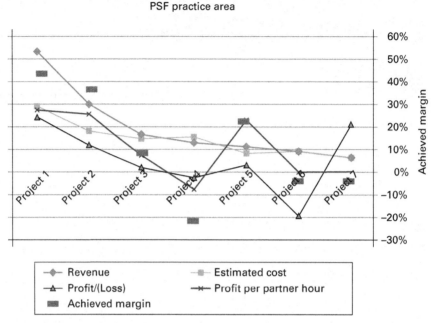

Comparision of seven similar transactions within a
PSF practice area

SOURCE Møller PSFG client data

© Møller PSFG Cambridge 2017 – Ori Wiener

The basic challenge of pricing PSF work – intangibility

Just about all professional service work is intangible, as discussed in Chapter 2. This makes PSF work similar to perishable goods, ie difficult or impossible to store. As PSF work takes 'time' to be delivered, time is one of the limiting resources for a professional and for PSFs. As we all know, we cannot stop or rewind time, hence professional service firms are forced to 'sell' their services continuously if they want to maximize their turnover and profits. Because the work is mostly intangible they cannot choose to store their work for sale at a later time. At best they can choose not to do client work but then they won't be generating revenues. (For more on this see Ron Baker's 2011 book *Implementing Value Pricing*.)

This is analogous to the yield management challenges faced by airlines and other transport companies – the revenues and profits of every unsold seat on a flight are lost forever. Airlines typically cannot wait until their planes are full.

They have to operate their flights to their predetermined schedule and once a flight has taken off you cannot allocate or use the empty seat on a subsequent flight or alternative route (Yeoman and McMahon-Beattie, 2011). PSFs are similar in that professionals cannot, within certain limits, compensate for non- or underutilization on one day by working extra-long on another.

The key dilemma facing both PSFs and airlines is that if they set prices too high, utilization (in airline terms – load factors) falls and less revenue will be generated. Given that these are fixed-cost businesses there is a disproportionate hit to profits. On the other hand, set prices too low and you reach full utilization but do not maximize profitability. What's worse, because prices are 'sticky', ie clients resist price rises, it is very difficult to raise prices (for the same work), compounding the dilution effect of low prices.

PSFs therefore face a constant challenge to manage their pricing so as to optimize profitability within markets displaying individual and at times unpredictable dynamics and lacking transparency – this is very tricky! Throw in the effects of competition and a professional's typical risk aversion (ie fear of not being busy) and it is easy to see another reason why professionals will try to avoid getting into an argument on price.

Intangibility brings with it another problem. Classic economic theory postulates that the price of a good or service is determined by the balance of supply and demand. If demand exceeds supply prices go up and vice versa. Although this basic phenomenon can be observed during periods of boom and bust it is impossible to be as accurate in connection with PSF work as in commodities markets.

Forecasting market levels of demand for PSF services is difficult but probably no more so than in other industries. Many PSF segments such as M&A legal advice or architecture conform to classic economic theories, seeing rates rising during a boom and falling during a downturn. The factors affecting supply, however, are not that straightforward. During a boom, lawyers, architects and other professionals typically will work longer hours or find ways to be more productive by, for example, using more leverage. Strangely enough, during a downturn professionals often make themselves even busier, as they cling to the type of work that would have been delegated to junior members of their teams in better times. A Møller colleague of mine refers to this as 'sticky finger' syndrome. Given this 'buffer' capacity, forecasting supply becomes a real art and anticipating pricing developments in the market therefore becomes very difficult.

A third and even more intractable challenge associated with intangible services is that it is often very difficult to specify the output of a service. As discussed in Chapters 1 and 2 clients find it difficult to know exactly what they will get at the end of an assignment and to assess the quality of the work or advice, etc. This brings us to the central challenge of pricing PSF work – value.

Delivering intangible services, however, can also bring advantages. Although by definition difficult to compare, some services can be replicated easily or with little adaptation. Smart service providers have figured out how to resell their services many times over but in such a way as to generate significant economies of scale. If priced correctly and if there is sufficient demand it becomes possible to generate a service that is highly attractively priced for clients but still highly profitable for the PSF.

This is typically the case where a service or process can be replicated easily and where the marginal cost of delivery can be kept very low. The ability to sell other value-added services on top of the core service can further increase profitability and even help differentiate the service. The key challenge here is that the upfront development of the service may require significant investment and that the service provider has to take the risk that there will not be enough demand for the service.

There is also a secondary challenge in that such services generally have to be process managed well to be profitable. This does not come easy to most professionals, who pride themselves on being 'experts' and who prefer to work on innovative or new challenges.

The value challenge however remains – if the service is priced too high it will not be attractive to the client, and if too low, value will have been lost to the PSF.

Theory of value/price

To get a handle on the value of PSF work it will help to get a rough idea of the drivers of value for PSFs. These can be summarized as follows (Hanohov, 2008):

- perceived quality;
- service performance;
- relationship management;
- confidence;
- trust;
- price.

A number of theoretical frameworks are used to provide PSF partners and managers with a broad understanding of the factors that go into PSF pricing. Unfortunately they tend to be of limited value to most practitioners and firms. The most frequently cited is the 'Cobb value curve' (Baker, 2011; Robertson and Calloway, 2008).

Cobb value curve

This curve demonstrates that the more complex or unique a service is the more it is likely to be worth. It also illustrates the trade-off between volume of available work and margin. It can be seen that there is an inverse relationship between complexity of work (ie high margin) and volume.

It is useful to think of different types of work in connection with this curve. Unique work would be at the extreme left hand, ie high margin side, reflecting the fact that there is very little work that is truly unique. The key criteria for this work is absolute technical brilliance and originality.

Less unique, but still high value, is work for which experience in dealing with this or a similar problem is required. This has been labelled 'experiental'. Whilst not unprecedented the capabilities of delivering this work are still only found with a relatively limited number of firms or professionals.

Lower down the curve, ie less complex but more volume, is work which has been labelled branded. This is work for which the reputation of the provider for being able to do a good job or getting it right is important. For this type of work clients see some value of going to a firm or professional that others will recognize as 'good'.

At the far right of the curve, ie the part that represents the most volume but lowest margin, is the work that would be considered routine. There are typically a large number of firms capable of delivering this work to a sufficiently good standard. Price and efficiencies are the key selection drivers. One of the implications is that most PSF work is low-to-middle margin work and not highly complex – despite what most professionals tend to think of their work.

The problem with this approach is that it says very little about the specific characteristics of a piece of work, or an assignment, to be able to locate it on the curve. This problem is compounded by the fact that most PSF projects tend to be a package with different elements of different complexities and hence different margins – one would need to price each element independently as well as factor in any potential synergies that can be generated when all work elements are delivered by the same practitioner or firm.

The value curve also says very little about what it is about the work that makes it 'unique' or value-adding. For example the curve does not provide help in determining the impact of urgency on value and price, ie the more urgent the higher the price ought to be. Experience shows that this approach may be helpful as a conceptual guide but does little to help practitioners establish the appropriate price for a piece of work.

Kano curve

A more useful approach is provided by the Kano curve (Ching-Chow, 2005; Kano *et al*, 1984), first postulated by Professor Noriaki Kano in the 1980s to explain the relationship between customer satisfaction and consumer product features. The principles can be applied just as well to services. It demonstrates that customers differentiate between products or services on the basis of two types of their features: those that are expected and those that are unexpected or new.

Clients will be sensitive to the absence or partial absence of expected features, ie they will be disappointed by a lack or partial lack of something they considered 'standard'. Relatively small shortcomings can have a disproportionate impact on customer satisfaction and hence willingness to pay. The curve also demonstrates that investment in such features will suffer from falling marginal returns above a certain level as customer satisfaction will not greatly increase with further investment. These features have become hygiene factors.

Figure 3.2   Kano curve

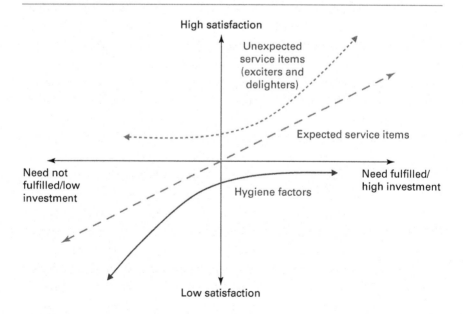

New or unexpected features that provide extra benefits or are perceived to add value, on the other hand, have the opposite effect. Even relatively small investments in new features will have a disproportionate impact on customer satisfaction and presumably willingness to pay. Hence these features are referred to as 'exciters/delighters'. The curve also demonstrates the impact of commoditization. As customers get used to new features or they become offered more widely, exciters/delighters turn into hygiene factors.

The reason this is relevant to PSF work is that it provides a basis for understanding the impact of different features of a service to clients. For example, given that technical know-how is a given, it is not surprising that most clients will take it for granted and find it difficult to become more excited about some incremental increase in a firm's or professional's technical competence. On the other hand some novel approach to client service can make a disproportionate impression on clients. Depending on the industry this can be quite varied. Over time these features lose their novelty or become widely available and have to be incrementally improved or replaced with new features to keep clients happy.

The Kano model therefore provides a conceptual basis for disaggregating a professional service or relationship into its component parts and for understanding what it is that clients will be willing to pay for. It also explains the, at times, vast differences in perspectives between professionals and their clients. Professionals tend to see their technical competencies as the core of their service whereas clients tend to look at the totality of the client experience. Figure 3.3 demonstrates that whereas the area of the diagram representing

Figure 3.3 Differences in value perspectives

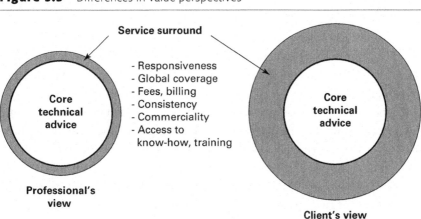

technical competence may be equally big (representing equal value) clients tend to assign equal and at times even more value to the surrounding elements of the client experience.

Given the high degree of heterogeneity of PSF work (intangible and not easily specifiable) and the relative lack of transparency, most PSFs are unlikely to have sufficient data to be able to apply the Kano model to price specific services and the model is therefore only of limited value. However, it is useful when trying to formulate strategic thinking regarding a firm's new product or service development and has also proven useful in raising professional service providers' awareness of the importance of non-technical innovation within PSFs.

Determining value

For PSFs working with commercial clients, in theory determining value is simple: figure out the present value of additional profits the client will be able to generate as a result of the work and take an appropriate proportion of that. In practice PSF pricing remains more an art than a science because of the following complex challenges.

Challenge 1: understanding the value of the service

Frequently professionals or their clients cannot quantify the additional profit resulting from the work delivered. For example, how much more profit will a firm generate by having a better accounting system or distribution contract? What will the incremental rental increase be from a more 'aesthetically pleasing' design? How much more money will a company generate by employing an executive search consultant to recruit the best candidate for a management position? How much more profitable will a business be due to its employees attending a particular leadership development course?

None of these situations is easy to address, but ultimately clients should understand how important this is to them and what the value is – otherwise they risk overpaying on the one hand or underpaying and getting a lower quality service on the other. Professionals are therefore well advised to engage with their clients in these sorts of discussions as early as possible. The benefits of such discussions include better awareness of the value of the service provided as well as potential explorations as to how to deliver the work in the most cost-effective manner.

Potential value drivers can include any of the following (and more):

- increased sales;
- reduced costs;
- reduced personnel turnover resulting in reduced costs (recruitment, training) or increased quality (know-how of products or services, better client service);
- better use of resources (efficiency);
- higher prices;
- reduced risks (bad debts, contractual defaults, poor investments, employee errors, criminal activities);
- greater quality of produce or services (leading to greater client loyalty and hence increased revenues or reduced business acquisition costs);
- lower levels of capital required;
- impact on reputation;
- impact on share price.

Robertson and Calloway (2008) provide additional details on these. A more technical and detailed approach can be found in *Pricing and Profitability Management* (Meehan *et al*, 2011).

Effective professionals will understand their clients and their clients' businesses and will understand how their services will help them. If they don't they had better learn quickly. Often clients will be more than happy to explain and discuss their businesses with their professionals so as to get the best possible service.

As highlighted at the start of the chapter, ultimately fees are driven by the perceived value of services offered (Weiss, 2008b). Professionals would be well advised to invest more time in establishing the value of their services in the eyes of their clients and establishing appropriate criteria for determining value delivered rather than focusing on 'bargaining' as most are wont to do.

Challenge 2: understanding the incremental value provided by professionals

Let's assume that a professional and the client understand the value arising from the professional service. The professional will still have to demonstrate to the client the incremental value arising from instructing him or her, as opposed to one of his or her competitors, assuming the client has a choice or is looking for alternatives. Here the professional has to determine how he or she or the firm can deliver the service or services better, faster or more efficiently compared to the alternatives open to the client. Please note that at this stage professionals should resist thinking 'cheaper' as price should be the output of the analysis – not an input.

In considering potential differences to their competitors, professionals will also have to explore with their clients to what extent these differences matter to the client. No point fretting about faster delivery when the client is not time-sensitive. Likewise, there will be times when clients will be happy with 'good enough' rather than 'perfect'. Other factors that will also affect a client's view on value received will include the reputation or brand of the service provider. Particularly for high-risk projects, clients will tend to go for leading firms or individuals so as to assure themselves or their stakeholders that they have done all they could to get the best advice from the best people. Here price is taken (rightly or wrongly) as a signal of quality. This is when competition will start to have an impact on perceived value and hence price. Clients will clearly want to instruct the cheapest provider if there were no other factors such as quality or personal chemistry differentiating the providers. This is how personal and institutional business development and marketing can impact the price that professionals can achieve.

Working with clients well ahead of the time that a service is needed is one of the most effective ways of pre-empting the competition. Many firms are willing to work for free or at a massive discount with clients during feasibility phases of projects or as a means of 'getting in' early. They know that clients will be reluctant to reopen issues with new advisers once they have gone down the road sufficiently far with the incumbent.

If, as is often the case nowadays, a client is forced to conduct some form of tender process the incumbent adviser or service provider can either influence the selection criteria or demonstrate superior understanding of the project to justify being appointed.

Challenge 3: determining the right share of value

As if the first two challenges weren't enough, one of the trickiest challenges in PSF pricing is to know at what percentage of value to price a service or project. Unfortunately there are no theoretical frameworks to provide an answer to this question. Ultimately the share of value a professional or PSF can claim for itself will be influenced by the relative negotiation strengths and capabilities of the professional and their clients, which are themselves influenced by competition and the availability of alternative business for the PSF.

Some PSF industries have established formal or informal guidelines in this area. Several countries have formal fee guidelines for legal services based on the value of the instructions. Investment bankers charge for M&A advice or capital raising (IPOs, bond issues) on the basis of percentages of deal value that are well known across the industry. Architects tend to charge a fixed percentage of work undertaken, which varies between countries. Executive search firms tend to operate to similar percentages of first-year compensation (but some firms differentiate themselves on the basis of a different fee model). Nevertheless, even in all of these cases, individuals still have the ability to influence the agreed percentage up or down and often underperform in setting an optimal price.

Moving from value to price

As the first quote in this chapter demonstrates, irrespective of what might be determined as the value of an assignment, professionals and clients need to agree a price for the service. Given the difficulties in determining value it is not surprising that many professionals and clients skip the value challenge and go straight to price. One contributing factor is the tendency for clients to ignore value as soon as they are able to identify a PSF's rate structure, eg billable time units such as hourly or daily rates (Weiss, 2008a). This backdrop and the wide usage of such rate structures add to a professional's challenges to focus fee discussions on value.

Four price perspectives

Practitioners tend to adopt one of four methods for determining the price for an assignment:

1. Simple value-based

As discussed above this is the least common approach. When a value approach is used it tends to be based on a crude percentage of the value of a transaction or project, eg the amounts of capital raised, the amount of costs or tax saved or the total expenditure in relation to the construction of a building. These percentages tend not to reflect any differences in quality of service or other differentiating service attributes.

2. Input or cost-based

Under this approach an estimate is made of the total cost of providing the service or project. In the case of most PSFs this means using some sort of time-based cost (hourly, daily or weekly rates) and adding a profit margin. This requires an accurate estimate of the volume and scope of work required. Many PSFs will apply different rates according to the level of skills of the professionals involved, particularly if leverage, ie the application of junior or support resources, is possible.

There are a number of issues associated with this approach, which are extensively covered in the literature, and some of them will be covered in the section on fee structure. The biggest problems with a cost-based approach to pricing are that it:

- provides relatively little incentive for efficiency;

- does not on its own pay attention to the benefits accruing to the client; and

- tends to limit the earnings capacity of the professional or firm to the total amount of resources available, typically time.

Some writers (eg Weiss, 2008a, 2008b) on this topic also suggest that this approach creates ethical problems in that any productivity improvement gained as a result of acquired expertise (ie faster completion) will lead to cross-subsidization from early clients, effectively paying for the learning curve in favour of subsequent clients. Others (eg Hill, 2013) point out that many professionals do not understand that the 'plus' in cost-plus includes a profit margin, usually set as the required profit margin to meet the year's budgeted profit and hence profit distributions. This leads all too often to excessive discounting on the wrongful assumption that a discount will still yield an acceptable profit.

3. Market-based

For many PSFs and practitioners the most common approach is to set a price in relation to the 'going' or 'market' rate. Under this approach, firms and individuals will set their price at a premium or discount relative to their competitors and will then attempt to negotiate with their clients based on perceived or actual differences in offers. In theory this should result in efficient pricing as the above listed factors would contribute to price determination. In practice, however, few markets are sufficiently transparent and few services sufficiently comparable to be able to guarantee efficient and fair pricing.

Under such a system the firms with the greater negotiation power and skills are likely to capture the lion's share of economic value. The issue here is that too many professionals take the price (assuming they can establish one) as a given rather than questioning how they could differentiate. This would require enquiring further into what clients would pay more for and why. Likewise the market price may not be acceptable to a specific client.

4. Last year plus

The fourth method found in almost all PSFs is to use last year's prices and add a bit. This 'bit' is usually linked to inflation and sometimes but too rarely to changes in the market. There are a number of problems with this approach. The first is that it perpetuates prior mistakes where prices have been based on cost or market values. The second is that clients may or may not be experiencing the same inflation as the PSF firm, so the disconnect between price paid and value received is likely to increase and prompt further resentment.

Pricing the work vs pricing the relationship

Another perspective to be considered is the overall relationship. Some pricing structures such as volume discounts or success/abort fees only make sense if there is a minimum number of projects in a given time frame. This allows risks to be spread out over the total number of projects, rather than be concentrated only on one. A success/abort fee may be too risky if applied only to one instruction (especially if it is material in size). On the other hand, assuming a reasonable spread of wins and losses, the risk of only applying the 'abort' part of such a fee arrangement is dramatically reduced when several projects are considered. For further details on the impact of pricing structures and AFAs (Appropriate Fee Arrangements) see the next chapter.

My view is that none of the above methods is sufficient on its own. Rather, my preferred approach would be to view pricing from a number of perspectives. I would, however, try to put as much effort as possible into the value perspective as this is, to my mind, the only way to generate premium value and to differentiate from competitors.

Pricing as a jigsaw puzzle

One of the most useful metaphors I encountered in working with PSFs on this topic has been to view pricing as a jigsaw puzzle in which the price is seen as the composite of a number of different and at times even contradictory factors. These include:

- the nature of the work (complexity, size, scope, scale);
- determinants of value from the core technical service (as discussed above);

- attributes of non-technical elements of the service valued by the client;
- input cost of providing the service;
- market/competitor pricing;
- alternatives to the service open to the client;
- perceived risks;
- timing issues;
- internal firm guidelines or standard (rack) rates;
- client expectations or prior experience;
- the quality of the relationship;
- pricing power of the service provider (reputation, track record, unique skills or expertise);
- purchasing power of the client (reputation, track record);
- regulations;
- negotiation competencies.

These factors can have different impacts on the price of a project or instruction. Figure 3.4 illustrates an example of how complex the considerations can be.

Figure 3.4 Factors affecting pricing

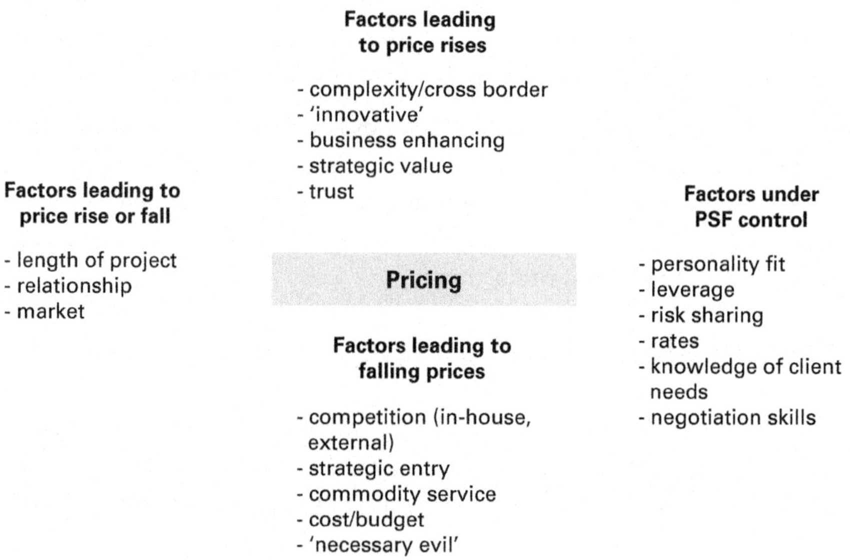

**Factors leading
to price rises**

- complexity/cross border
- 'innovative'
- business enhancing
- strategic value
- trust

**Factors leading to
price rise or fall**

- length of project
- relationship
- market

Pricing

**Factors leading to
falling prices**

- competition (in-house,
  external)
- strategic entry
- commodity service
- cost/budget
- 'necessary evil'

**Factors under
PSF control**

- personality fit
- leverage
- risk sharing
- rates
- knowledge of client
  needs
- negotiation skills

Table 3.1 Differences in pricing approaches between professions

	Self-confidence	Value orientation	Revenue orientation	Marketing and communication	Trust
Accounting firms		X	X	X	X
Actuarial services	X			X	X
Barristers	X		X		X
Consultants	X		X	X	X
Creative services	X		X		X
Investment banks	X	X			X
Law firms			X	X	X
Physicians					X
Risk management	X	X	X		X

SOURCE Hanohov (2oo8)

It is interesting to note how some professions are reported to differ from each other in terms of the relative contributing factors to pricing (Hanohov, 2008). Table 3.1 demonstrates that all PSFs are seen to focus on trust, for the reasons given in Chapter 2. The different approaches to marketing and communications are in part explainable by specific regulatory restrictions. Revenue orientation, ie the propensity to be particularly turnover-focused in their planning approaches, is probably due in part to relatively low financial sophistication.

A number of challenges associated with price, particularly those involving different priorities and perspectives on risk or timing, can be managed by the use of different fee or price structures. These will be covered in Chapter 4. A really great book on this subject, providing much more detailed insights, is Kevin Doolan's *Mastering Services Pricing* (2015).

Generating value with fee structures

04

We shape our dwellings, thereafter they shape us. (WINSTON CHURCHILL)

The quotation above is just as applicable to fee structures as it is to buildings. Most professionals pay little time or attention to structuring fees. Ironically, crafting a tailored fee structure for an assignment can be one of the most powerful ways to draw the connection between value and price and to bridge an otherwise insurmountable gap between client and service provider. Fee structures influence behaviours during PSF projects and thus can have significant long-term effects. Developing skills in this area can be an invaluable competitive advantage to practitioners as well as their organizations. All the more surprising then that most PSFs have not fully understood this and that the majority of fee agreements use standard fee structures.

I believe that there are three reasons why structuring has been neglected. The first is that professionals have simply not been given the required negotiation and other skills to be able to discuss and agree innovative structures with their clients. Secondly, many professions have, over time, become comfortable using 'standard' fee structures. Although these are probably helpful to establish a general starting point, precedents should not be allowed to stifle innovation and the ability to respond to special needs. Thirdly, most PSFs, particularly larger ones, cannot handle the complexities in terms of accounting and managing resources associated with non-standard structures. In fact many organizations are built around a particular approach to fees. The traditional law firm structure involving a seniority-based pyramid of partners and associates combined with a 'lockstep' compensation system would probably not survive if 'hourly rates' were to disappear overnight. That said, law firms with the most commonly found alternative compensation systems (known in the industry as 'eat what you kill') would also have to undergo radical changes in their internal operations in the event time-based billing were abolished.

I vividly remember a discussion with an executive search consultant who was able to describe losing clients and projects quite graphically because of his firm's centralized approach to fee structures. The firm in question was a global leader in its field and had a highly centralized accounting and reporting system that only allowed for one standard fee structure with very minor variations. The consultant's problem was that a number of competitors were able to offer fee structure alternatives that better suited the needs of the client, which did not necessarily result in a lower fee. As a result, a number of very significant instructions were lost to competitors. Worse still for the consultant was that his clients, who were willing to instruct him and who showed him the kind of structures they would like to work with, could not understand his firm's inflexibility. There is probably also an element of distrust involved here, in that larger organizations simply may not trust their professionals to reach 'good' agreements if allowed to deviate from centrally set standards – and why should they, if they have not given their staff the appropriate training and support needed to do so properly?

To understand the importance of structure one needs to reiterate that value to a client will not just accrue from a service provider's ability to deliver technical solutions but also from other aspects of the service such as certainty, budget predictability, risk or speed of delivery. It is helpful to apply a simple banking technique used to analyse financial investments to understand the range of options open for structuring fees. This involves looking at possible ways in which the cash flow of an investment product can be varied. Generally speaking this can be done by looking at the:

- amount, ie the total of fees to be paid;
- number of elements the total fee is broken into: milestones, up-front or balloon payments, completion;
- timing of each of the pay-outs: at start, at end, periodically, milestones;
- frequency: weekly, monthly, quarterly;
- risk in terms of the likelihood of each payment; and
- conditionalities that may affect the likelihood, timing or amounts of fees payable: conditions, bonus, performance fees.

Flexing each of these parameters or a combination of them will allow professionals to redefine potential structures. Co-designing these with the client is also a powerful basis for building a long-term relationship (so beware the sharks dressed up as dolphins). The analysis can be extended further by also considering the cash flows or contributions to be made by the professional service provider such as the nature of the service, size of team, timing and delivery of the service or components or other value-added services such as training, access to databases or similar.

The structure menu

There is almost no limit to the variations possible but a number of structures do tend to be used most frequently (Figure 4.1). These can be categorized into structures that:

- mitigate risk to the service provider;
- are focused on costs; or
- focus on value.

Risk mitigation structures

These structures are considered risk mitigating structures as they are 'input' (also referred to as 'times and materials') based on key cost components required to deliver the service. As the biggest resource constraint and cost item for PSFs tends to be time and staff cost, it is not surprising that a time-based approach to fees is frequently adopted. From a PSF perspective this makes sense as long as the time-based rates include an appropriate profit margin, utilization is high enough and clients are willing to shoulder the risk of overruns.

Time-based rates

This (and its variants, discounted, blended) is the single most commonly used fee structure for most professional service sectors. The basis for rates most commonly encountered is usually hourly or daily unless projects are particularly long.

Firms typically apply different rates depending on seniority, technical specialization and geography in an attempt to reflect differences in expertise, complexity of work and market levels. However, some firms work with single global rates or variations on the theme. There is usually some ability to discount from centrally set rates but most firms will have rules or guidelines on the approvals required if the discount offered exceeds defined thresholds.

Figure 4.1 The structuring 'menu'

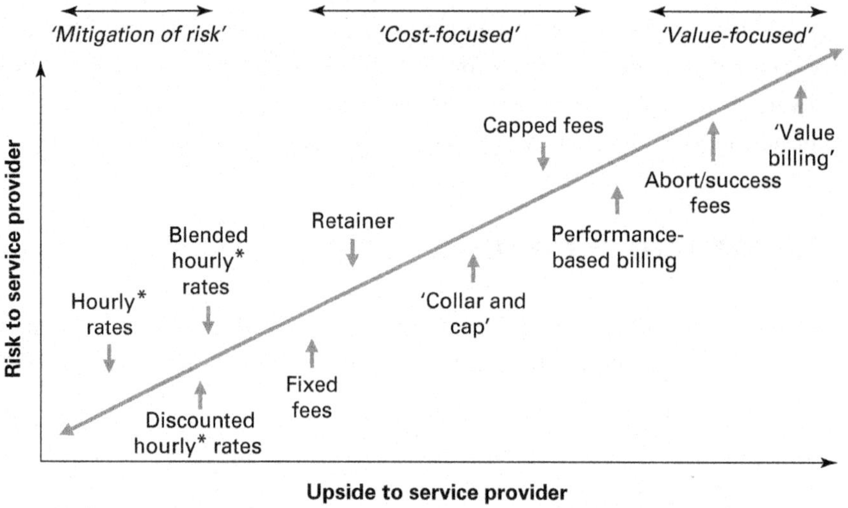

*This could also be daily or weekly rates

SOURCE Based on Dodds

© Møller PSFG Cambridge 2017 – Ori Wiener

Advantages

As discussed above, a time-based approach to fees provides PSFs with a number of advantages (Roch, 2010), the biggest being minimizing risk that they will not recover costs (ignoring the risk of default, etc). Furthermore, these approaches tend to be viewed as simple to calculate (time worked × agreed rate), straightforward to communicate to clients and easy to manage and monitor. The key component – time needed to perform given tasks – is something most firms track anyway using timesheets, so there is little by way of conceptual leap required to link the internal efficiency monitoring to invoicing. What would make this even more effective is firms collecting and analysing the time taken for discreet work elements to establish robust costing databases. Unfortunately few firms seem to be doing so effectively.

Disadvantages

There are a number of major disadvantages associated with a time-based fees approach. In fact, an entire industry has sprung up in recent years in the legal world proclaiming the evil of time-based pricing, the imminent death of the hourly rate and offering firms help in moving to alternative approaches. There have been a number of publications in this area (Lamb, 2010) mostly focused on the legal sector including guidelines issued by the Law Practice Management Section of the American Bar Association (Robertson and Calloway, 2008). Judging by current developments this is likely to be a generator of considerable consulting income (presumably not on a times and materials basis) for many years to come (Bodine, 2010).

The main arguments against time-based pricing approaches focus on the following key issues:

- They don't reward efficiency – practitioners earn more if they take longer or over-staff.

- They don't align to client objectives – clients pay according to what it took to deliver the service, not according to the benefit these services delivered.

- Lack of cost certainty – the cost of the service can vary as more time is required to deliver the work, making it impossible to define the total cost up-front unless the work required is extremely repetitive and predictable.

- Lack of transparency – how do clients really know how much time it took to deliver a piece of work and who is to say that this is the amount of time that it should have taken?

- They don't align with PSF objectives – a practitioner who has accumulated specialist know-how or expertise would not be able to charge for this (other than in higher rates) as the expertise is likely to result in the work being done faster.

- They don't differentiate between 'good' and 'bad' time – this means that practitioners are paid the same whether they are spending time on a high-margin part of the project or just on a routine aspect.

- They allow for simplistic comparisons between service providers – an hour/day is an hour/day. How can one differentiate between a firm that is providing great service and a firm that is just average? As we will see in subsequent chapters, many clients will deliberately engage in an 'apples and oranges' comparison to push rates down, and most professionals are unable to respond to this in any other way than to give an even bigger discount.

- They contribute to significant ill-health of time-based practitioners – a number of observers have reported on research demonstrating that firms that use time-based billing tend to impose higher targets for hours worked, resulting in higher levels of stress and ill-health. The hourly rate has also been attributed directly to increased mental ill-heath (Hardy, 2008).

- The adverse effects on the human body of chronic stress due to such factors as the use of the billable hours model, combined with the demands of a volatile working environment, have been graphically described by John Coates in his fascinating 2012 book *The Hour Between Dog and Wolf.*

In addition, some observers (eg Weiss, 2008b) have questioned the ethics of time-based charging as they point out that increased efficiency and hence lower bills (because the work can be done faster) would result in early clients (paying for the time to acquire the expertise) cross-subsidizing later clients (who benefit from the acquired expertise).

Despite all of these disadvantages, time-based fees are likely to remain a feature of many PSF industries for a long time to come for a number of reasons:

- PSF firms' operating models are so deeply built on time-based pricing that a major shift will take considerable time to implement and would require significant changes to the operating models and processes of such firms (costing, staffing, project management, profit accounting – to name just a few issues).

- Clients like them because they are either comfortable and familiar with them or because they have figured out that using alternative structures could result in paying more because the process would involve discussing issues such as value received.

- There are times when using a cost and materials approach may be appropriate simply because there are too many uncertainties connected with projects to be able to give a reasonable price on an alternative basis. These are usually projects expected to be long-running and with uncertain outcomes (eg litigation, new product or new market entry consulting).

There are a number of best practice guidelines that should be adopted in cases where time-based pricing is used. These include:

- setting milestones to review progress and cost either on a regular (weekly, monthly) basis or against pre-agreed project milestones or phases;

- ensuring active two-way communication between client and service provider to avoid surprises to either side; and

- trying to link the work to value where possible so as to ensure that both sides understand each other. This could also be linked to some kind of value bonus at the end of the project.

Cost-focused structures

Given the issues associated with the time and materials approach listed above, particularly from a client perspective, there are a number of structures that provide better 'cost control' for clients. These include structures such as day rates where hourly rates are the norm.

The basic concept is that a day rate is agreed based on, say, a six-hour day but the professional is expected to work eight hours. The rationale from the client's perspective is that the client only pays for the six most productive hours that a professional is working in an eight-hour day. The professional on the other hand benefits from being 'utilized' for the whole day. This approach basically applies the principle of 'hiding behind averages'. Clients should not be paying the same rates for productive or unproductive time and professionals should not be kidding themselves that they achieve rate X per hour or are utilized for X hours in the day when in fact this isn't the case.

Fixed/capped/collared fees

The most frequently encountered cost-focused structure is without doubt the fixed fee and its variants: capped and collared fees.[1] The basic concept is very simple – a client defines what service is wanted and the service provider quotes a single, fixed fee for providing the service. Usually, but not always, there are allowances for items such as expenses or third-party fees where relevant.

Advantages: Simply put – simplicity. Clients define what they want and PSFs quote a single fee. Clients can judge the fee against the value they perceive they will get from the work. The single price is easy to compare against offers from other potential providers. Budgeting and cash flow management are made easy for the clients and they believe they know what they get and the price they get it for. Clients can expect the fixed fee to be an incentive for efficiency.

Disadvantages: If only life were that simple! Many professional services cannot be specified accurately (remember the issues surrounding intangibility raised in the previous chapters), ie it is unlikely that the scope will be sufficiently accurate. Unless we are speaking of standardized, repeat type of work (and there is plenty of this) clients delude themselves if they think that they can scope a piece of work in such detail that they know what they are getting or that they can accurately compare the offers from competing service providers. The temptation to see every project or instruction as special and to treat them as one-offs is probably a greater impediment to standardization for many PSFs and practitioners than the specific instruction. Recent experience in the United States law sector has shown what can be done when firms (Quinn Emmanuel, Validatum) commit to a move to non-time-based fees.

Clients also run the risk that the pressure to perform work efficiently and to budget will have an impact on the quality of work. This can be a major conundrum for clients who may allow for a 'quality' premium to protect against the risks of contracting with someone who will not deliver to the required quality standard. In addition, many PSF projects involve intricate processes, judgement calls and multiple interactions between client, service provider and other parties. Projects often also change in mid-course in terms of depth and breadth required or timetable. The risks of a project changing scope in mid-course because of this are very high, unless we are talking about a very standardized, oft-repeated piece of work, ie commodity work. The only way a service provider can protect against such risks is to price the risk into the fee, ie the fee for delivering the work should be higher than on a comparable cost and materials basis. Clients may still consider this to be better value for money, if predictability of costs, etc is given high value.

Fixed fee approaches can on the other hand be attractive to professional service providers for a number of reasons (Shenson, 1990):

- Efficiency will generate extra profits.

- The use of junior resources and IT can increase efficiency and hence profit.

- There is no need to price individual fee earners and justify their personal rates.

- Value for expertise can be generated, ie a particular piece of work can be sold multiple times without having to charge less for work delivered faster. If service providers can sell a piece of work several times over they could offer the work at a lower price, thus increasing demand, and still generate good profits from the added margins.

A summary of price structures is shown in Table 4.1. It is important to remember that structures can also be combined to suit the requirements of clients and projects. Only extensive discussions with clients to determine their interests and constraints will yield the best structure.

Table 4.1 Summary of price structures

Price structure	Benefits	Drawbacks	Application	Key issues
Fixed and capped fees eg: £500,000 for advising on the acquisition of an asset or company	• Certainty of costs for client and PSF • Client can compare quotes • Promotes focus on efficiencies	• Dealing with fee issues surrounding change in work scope or timetable • Agreeing key assumptions • Difficulty of pricing embedded options elements	• Projects with clear scope • Projects with high certainty re complexity and length • Standardized projects	• Accurate scoping of the project before setting the fee • Availability of data on similar projects to assist with scoping and estimating costs • Fix in stages to allow reassessment at the completion of each stage
Abort/success fees eg: £75,000 charge if abortive, £125,000 if successful	• Aligns commercial interests with client • Applies fixed or capped fee • Quantifies cost range	• Can be unprofitable if most cost to service provider is incurred in early stages	• Projects where the client carries commercial risk, eg competitive auction process • Need regular deal flows to avoid unbalanced wins and losses	• Agree mutually acceptable risk reward criteria • Maintain independence of advice

(Continued)

TABLE 4.1 (Continued)

Price structure	Benefits	Drawbacks	Application	Key issues
Conditional fee arrangement The PSF firm's final fee is determined by the outcome of the project	• Partially aligns the professional's interest to the client's interest in the case	• Can only be used in limited circumstances • Overall cost still uncertain • Important to follow professional guidelines	• Contentious work selected on a case-by-case basis (typically in law)	• Identify the right type of project • Agree sensible commercial terms
Value billing Client and PSF firm agree fee in line with the client's commercial objectives	• Focus on delivering value • Align PSF fees to client interests • Cost can be reduced for unsuccessful projects selected on a case-by-case basis	• Potential disconnect between the scale and complexity of work and perceived commercial value	• On projects where relationship is underpinned by trust between PSF firm and client	• Transparency • Equitability • Combine with base level fees

Pricing model	Advantages	Disadvantages	Best used	Considerations
Retainer agreement A fixed monthly retainer to cover ongoing work	• Provides a monthly budget • Administrative ease of billing • Recognizes value of access to valued resources	• Requires complex unpaid for response if one-off enquiry • If retainer is not fully utilized	In managing the cost of regular support	• Creating a realistic estimate of requirements • Clearly articulate scope and how variations will be managed
Daily rates eg: £2,000 per day for a professional	• Certainty of cost • Client only pays for agreed number of hours per day and only the most productive time	• When the professional is regularly required to work late by the client	• Long-running or labour-intensive projects	• Key personnel • Change order management
Blended hourly rate eg: £320 per hour irrespective of which professional works on the matter	• Easy to apply • Encourages delegation • Avoids perception of over-resourcing	• No certainty of costs • Work may turn cut to be complex and require more senior professional time	• Simple projects • Standardized projects	• Selective use • Client comfort re use of junior resources

AFAs – Alternative or Appropriate Fee Arrangements

Client demand for fee structures other than input, time-based structures such as hourly or per diem rates has given rise to the use of the acronym AFAs – Alternative Fee Arrangements (Bodine, 2010; Lamb, 2010). This has become particularly established in the legal sector where requests for proposals (RFPs) quite regularly request fee proposals to also include AFA structures.

Of interest is the alternative usage of AFAs across the Atlantic. In Continental Europe and the UK, the term AFA is only applied to fee structures that are not time based, ie AFAs do not include hourly structures including blended or discounted hourly rates. In the United States, however, any fee structure that is not a full hourly rate was traditionally considered 'alternative' and so US AFA proposals commonly include blended and discounted structures.

More recently, I have come across a different interpretation of the acronym – Appropriate Fee Arrangements. I believe this interpretation is more reflective of the role and purpose of AFAs as it better reflects that different structures will serve different purposes and should be used appropriately, as discussed in this chapter.

The persistence of time-based rates

The most frequently used fee structures for many professional services such as law, training, coaching or consulting are time-based, the most common being daily or hourly rates. Given the problems associated with time-based rates (do not promote efficiencies, no direct connection to value, etc) it is worth reflecting why these structures have outlived many a report of their imminent demise and call for change.

The truth of the matter is that these structures persist because clients want them despite plenty of lip service paid to 'value-oriented' structures. This is because time-based rates allow for relatively easy and direct comparison between service providers. This in turn facilitates price competition amongst providers, irrespective of whether the price comparisons are fair and appropriate (they often are not). Time-based rates also frequently generate lower fees than if a value-based fee structure had been used.

Although many commentators (Lamb, 2010) argue that hourly or daily rates will soon be replaced by 'value-based' fees, I believe that we will see time-based fees continue to account for the majority of fees in many segments of the PSF market for many years to come. Irrespective of the structure or quantum of fees to be agreed, the key question in the mind of typical clients will always be 'for what', ie 'What am I paying for, what will these fees get me?' These questions lie at the heart of the selection processes driven by professional buyers also known as 'procurement'. How to define the scope of services to be provided and how to deal with procurement are the subject of the next chapter.

---

[1] Please note that fixed and capped are often used as synonyms. They are not, and represent totally different risk profiles. As such, fixed and capped fees should be priced very differently.

How to deal with procurement: the importance of scope

05

One of the features of professional services is that there can be a vast difference between the fees charged and the value created or destroyed.
(FIONA CZERNIAWSKA, PROCUREMENT SPECIALIST, IN CZERNIAWSKA AND SMITH, 2010)

Few phrases generate as much resentment or strike as much terror into the hearts of professionals as 'procurement is leading the selection process', 'our procurement department will be getting involved' or 'you need to talk to our procurement team'. In some cases such a reaction may well be fully justified, in some cases there may be some grounds for concern, but in many situations engaging with procurement actively and constructively may be a means of competitive differentiation. The latter will hold especially true if one's competitors continue to treat procurement non-constructively or approach dealing with them in an adversarial manner.

The increasing involvement of procurement can, if engaged with appropriately, become a major advantage under certain conditions. This chapter will attempt to provide some guidance for service providers and PSF management as to how best to engage with procurement, reap the benefits available and generate competitive advantage.

The involvement of procurement for the selection of professional service providers has gathered pace over the last couple of decades. Whereas procurement was traditionally involved in the sourcing of commodities, components, other material and labour, in the late 1980s engineering and architectural services started to be sourced using procurement. About a decade later came the involvement of procurement in sourcing advertising, PR and marketing services. Accounting and tax services were next to be hit in the mid-2000s and legal services started to encounter increased procurement involvement from around the late 2000s (Hodges, 2012).

Judging from recent developments and feedback from clients, it is highly likely that, unlike some other management fads that we have seen come and go, the involvement of procurement for sourcing professional services is likely to remain and become more established and sophisticated. Practitioners and PSFs had better get used to the idea and adapt to this development, which is also spreading geographically.

Before any misunderstandings arise at this point, let's be very clear – the involvement of procurement is inevitably going to result in increased scrutiny, efforts and greater resourcing on behalf of a PSF or professionals looking to win new work or retain existing work. This may be helpful for someone looking to get into a new client but is definitely going to discomfort incumbents. However, my colleagues and I strongly advise against a 'one size fits all' approach to engaging with procurement. The reasons for this will be elaborated on further in this chapter. The key challenge here, as it is in dealing with clients who do not involve procurement, lies in understanding what the procurement team or individual is trying to achieve, their motivations, incentives and the assumptions they bring to a specific project or selection process.

Is procurement really the enemy?

Let's start by looking at why so many professionals intuitively dislike the involvement of procurement. In 'pre-procurement' times, professionals would usually seek to establish relationships with their respective technical or expert counterparts (ideally the economic buyer) within a client's organization. Over time these relationships would become deeply entrenched, with both sides becoming comfortable working with each other. New instructions would often be assigned as much on the strength of the relationship and mutual familiarity as on the quality of the service or expertise provided. Fees, if ever checked in the market, would not typically be negotiated actively or aggressively – although some clients might expect some 'preferred terms and conditions'.

Such relationships often became cosy and frequently inefficiencies (and at times even corruption) started to creep in. This was observed by a number of strategy consultants such as Peter Drucker as early as the 1960s and in particular by Michael Porter in the 1990s, who pointed out that managing costs will have a substantial impact on a firm's competitive position and long-term success (Drucker, 1964; Porter, 1990).

With ever-increasing competition in the business world, senior management started to apply to professional services the same approaches that proved successful with sourcing goods, raw materials, components or equipment. The motives were originally no doubt to protect or improve margins that were typically thinner than most PSF margins. Over time, other motivations included minimizing supplier risk or generating other sources of competitive advantage.

To achieve these objectives, management mandated expert buyers (aka procurement) to start improving the sourcing of professional services and related processes so as to generate additional value and/or reduce the costs of these. The involvement of procurement is therefore intended to generate one or more of the following benefits for the buying organization:

1 reduce cost;

2 improve quality of service delivered/source the best qualified service provider;

3 reduce risks, eg improve dependability/reliability;

4 improve efficiencies of service provision or sourcing;

5 maximize value.

It is not difficult to see how any of these points, especially 1, 2 and 3 would cause many professional service providers heartache and would involve a review of those very cosy relationships which established service providers have invested so much time and effort building. Adding insult to injury in this case would be the fact that many of these objectives also involve professionals having, often for the first time, to respond to questions that in effect challenge their qualifications, their effectiveness or their suitability to provide a particular service to their clients.

These objectives also explain why the involvement of procurement is not only disliked or resented by service providers but also by their in-house counterparts within client organizations. Many specialists have invested significant time and effort building trusted relationships with service providers, often educating them in the needs of their organizations and processes. The involvement of 'purchasing' specialists who often (but not as often as is frequently portrayed) lack an understanding of the qualitative aspects of the service or advice needed can undermine or even destroy valued and valuable relationships.

To be fair to the professional service communities, procurement individuals and teams have also contributed their share of reasons for their unpopularity with professionals. Particularly in the case of 'semi-qualified' or poorly incentivized procurement individuals more harm can be done than benefits realized. Overzealous or badly briefed procurement individuals have applied tactics referred to as coming from 'procurement's standard playbook' (Burcher, 2012). These include:

- pretending that all bids will be treated equally, etc when in fact a provider has already been pre-selected;
- representing the selection as competitive with price the key factor;
- applying artificially short time frames, raising urgency;
- deliberately withholding available and important information to allow a considered proposal;
- proposing lopsided, arbitrary or capricious terms and making their acceptance conditional for being allowed to participate in a selection process;
- reopening negotiations when it suits the client even though agreement has already been reached;
- deliberate scope creeping with no intention of paying for extra work;
- bluster or 'my way or no way' statements made to bidders, conveying indifference;
- misleading representations that a bidder's proposal will only be competitive if terms are improved substantially;
- changing the terms or timetable of a fee negotiation at short notice with the intent of discomforting the service provider;
- sharing competitors' terms directly or indirectly (eg via auction);
- insisting a bidder match competitors' terms when in fact competitors had not offered such terms;
- refusing to allow personal contacts between service provider and end-user to prevent important information being exchanged;
- insisting on standardized responses;
- reducing all bids to one single parameter (fee, hourly rate, etc); and
- lying.

Whereas some of these tactics might be considered legitimate commercial practice, some definitely cross the boundaries of acceptable behaviour in most business environments. Some are outright unethical. These and several other tactics are encountered on an almost daily basis. There is an increasing body of evidence that demonstrates the damage to supplier/customer relationships from the use of coercive or other strong-arm tactics (Atkin and Rinehart, 2006).

In one particularly egregious example, a client of ours had been told during a protracted selection process that all competing providers were proposing six-figure fees starting with a five and that if they wanted their proposal to have a realistic chance they would have to match. This caused significant internal discussions as a rigorous analysis had concluded that a reasonable fee would need to be in the mid-700,000s. Eventually our client put forward a proposal in the high 500,000s. Several months later our client discovered (as part of their work) that they had been the only firm offering a fee below 700,000!

So how should a PSF organization or professional deal with procurement processes and procurement specialists? A first step would be to understand procurement. Two books provide very useful insights into the perspectives of procurement professionals: *Negotiation for Purchasing Professionals* (O'Brien, 2013), which interestingly talks about 'countering the seller's advantage' and *Legal Procurement Handbook* (Hodges Silverstein, 2015). This book is a compilation of articles from a broad range of legal services buyers and procurement consultants and consequently provides a very broad range of perspectives.

Understanding procurement

It would be helpful in understanding procurement thinking to apply an approach pioneered by Peter Kraljic of McKinsey in the early 1980s and explored further by Crocker, Moore and Emmett (Crocker *et al*, 2010; Kraljic, 1983). This approach basically analyses purchasing along two dimensions: the importance to the client of the services or goods purchased, and the complexity of the supplier market. These generate four basic categories which are illustrated in Figure 5.1 and can be described as follows:

a Low importance to buyer, simple to obtain: routine, commodity. These kinds of services don't add much by way of value and although needed are easy to obtain, usually because there are plenty of providers at similar and sufficient quality, ie switching costs are low. Not surprisingly buyers will, given the low importance and high availability, focus on price and

Figure 5.1   Kraljic matrix: areas of procurement focus

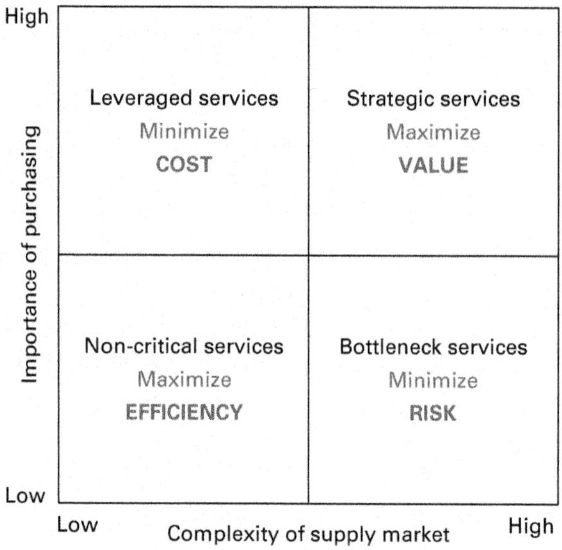

SOURCE Klyhn based on Kraljic (1983)

© Møller PSFG Cambridge 2017 – Ori Wiener

efficiency of service provision, ie they want it cheap and easy. This is a classic *commodity or routine service*. A typical service example would be industrial catering or cleaning.

b Low importance to buyer but not so easy to get. This could involve services that don't add much value but that cannot be easily found due to regulatory constraints (eg service provider has to be licensed) or where there are some switching costs. These could be thought of as 'bottleneck' services where buyers will still look for low prices but will also start to pay attention to issues such as security of supply, etc. These are often referred to as *critical services*. Typical examples might include healthcare.

c Where the value of the service is high but there are plenty of providers (as is the case for many professional services) and buyers will want to minimize cost. As switching costs are low these services are typically referred to as *generic or leveraged services*. Service examples could be logistics or simple property conveyancing.

d Where both the value to the buyer is high and appointing service providers is not easy because there may only be a limited number of suitably qualified organizations or experienced professionals available, buyers will focus on issues such as value added, creativity, reputation, etc. These services are referred to as *strategic* and would include specialist services such as senior executive search, high-end tax advice, big-ticket litigation or M&A advice.

The first challenge for many PSF organizations or professionals is to realistically assess which of the four boxes their services are in. Many professional service providers tend to overestimate their uniqueness and the relative importance to the client of their services. A simple rule of thumb against which to test the assessment is to consider who is leading the decision-making process. If the purchasing decision is taken by someone relatively junior or low in a firm's hierarchy the service is likely to be viewed by the client as a commodity service. Strategic decisions such as who to use defending a major law suit or designing the firm's new head office are likely to be taken by chief executives or members of the board.

Implications of the Kraljic matrix

The beauty of the Kraljic matrix is that it also helps service providers identify their strategic responses to procurement approaches. If a client is of the view that a service is a 'commodity' service, the best approach service providers should take is to focus on providing a low cost service and to emphasize aspects of cost savings, cost advantages, total lifecycle costs, etc. If on the other hand clients believe that they are looking for services in the 'critical' box then potential bidders should emphasize those aspects of their work that address the supply risk concerns the buyer organization may have – availability of team, dependability of services, spare capacity or similar.

'Strategic' services are best won by emphasizing the special value-added that the service provider can deliver. Discussions on providing this type of service are often best focused on understanding the true value-added that a client is looking for. Price is very rarely a top three factor.

Leveraged service providers have the biggest challenge in the professional service environment. Although their services are of great value to their clients, the existence of large numbers of alternative providers combined with low switching costs means that the purchasing decisions will often be influenced by price. One of my colleagues refers to service providers in this segment as 'stuck in the middle'. Providers in this segment have to balance a number of criteria such as quality of service, value-added services and costs. Regrettably the vast majority of professional service providers will find themselves in this box unless they are able to take appropriate action. One analysis (Czerniawska and Smith, 2010) suggests that organizations typically have very few strategic, trusted advisers. As the service becomes

Figure 5.2   Supply base segmentation

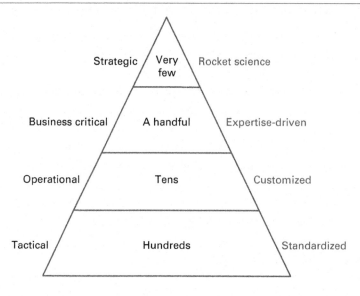

SOURCE Klyhn based on Czerniawska and Smith (2010)

© Møller PSFG Cambridge 2017

more commoditized (the polite phrase used by the writers is 'tactical') the number of potential service providers goes into the hundreds. Most PSFs will probably find themselves compared to about a dozen or couple of dozen service providers.

Dealing with procurement – effective counter-tactics

There are a number of effective approaches that can be taken to dealing with procurement. In reality a mixture of several is likely to be required and their usefulness will depend on a number of variables such as the service in question, the personalities involved and the buying organization's structure, culture and internal politics. The approaches include:

- Constructive engagement, ie accept that procurement will call the shots and work to their selection criteria.

- Reframing or differentiating, ie demonstrating that the service should be in a different one of the four boxes and hence the key selection criteria applied should be different or that you as service provider are able to deliver more value than alternative providers.

- Circumvention, ie engaging directly with end-users thereby either avoiding or circumventing the procurement team or process.
- Lifecycle management, eg exploiting opportunities that may arise between the time of purchase and the end of a project or assignment.

Constructive engagement

This approach basically accepts that a procurement process will be applied and seeks to understand the rules of the game. This is usually done by engaging the procurement team and proactively seeking information on selection criteria, constraints (eg budget, timetable), specification of services, and other decision factors. The more information is collected and understood the better.

Frequently a major obstacle to applying this approach is that procurement will not divulge additional information to that which is typically disclosed to all bidders as part of an RFP (request for proposals) or similar process. This is why it is usually best to establish good, ongoing working relationships with procurement departments. This way it is more likely that valuable information or insights into the thinking and decision making can be obtained.

Reframing/differentiating

Ongoing relationships are also essential for the second approach as this involves educating client organizations as to why particular services may not be as simple and comparable as the organization may have thought. Educating clients takes time and requires a good understanding of their requirements and a realistic assessment of the competitive differences between providers. This may take longer and require greater effort but may ultimately yield a good return on investment. In some cases it may be advantageous for certain providers to argue that the service is a commodity type rather than strategic. This may be the case when the provider has major competitive cost advantages (low wage environment) or more efficient processes (higher leverage or better use of technology).

Professional service providers therefore have to keep a constant lookout for potential competitors looking to 'rewrite' the rules by showing clients how they can get more for less. This process, referred to as 'commoditization', is generally inevitable but may sometimes come from unexpected sources such as a new entrant to the market.

Differentiation is the approach that most professionals will be familiar with, in which they try to identify service features of particular importance to a client and then proceed to demonstrate why they are best able to meet these needs. Sadly many professionals have not fully appreciated this process. This is why bidding teams will often bore their clients to death with overlong brochures or documents providing 'track records' or similar past assignment lists incorporating literally several dozens of examples in the hope to have thus demonstrated that they can do the job better than their competitors. Unfortunately all they have demonstrated is that they or their colleagues have been busy in the past without necessarily having demonstrated that they have understood the needs of their current client.

Circumvention

This approach is frequently attempted. Many professionals have succumbed to the seductive idea that their services are too important or too complex to be subjected to the vulgarity of a process best applied to purchasing hygiene

Figure 5.3   Circumventing procurement

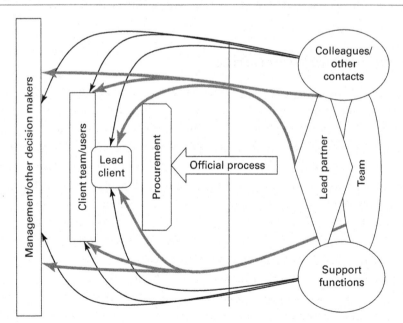

© Møller PSFG Cambridge 2017 – Ori Wiener

products or other run of the mill items or services. Most will have discovered, to their cost, that ignoring or circumventing procurement is a high-risk strategy, especially if the involvement of procurement has been mandated by top management.

This approach typically seeks to either undermine a procurement process or the procurement team by establishing direct relationships with key decision makers or end-users. It is most likely to produce positive results when the procurement team have failed to establish a constructive working relationship with the in-house end-users. Applying this approach indiscriminately can backfire, however. Establishing good working relationships with all stakeholders, a vital step in good customer relationship management, is essential for a reframing/differentiation approach to work. Figure 5.3 illustrates some of the complexities that can be involved. The figure also highlights that relationship building works best when there are a number of relationships at different levels between two organizations and when these are coordinated. The less procurement can 'blame' an individual for any undermining going on, the less likely they will be able to impose sanctions against the offending party.

Lifecycle management

This is probably the approach that lies at the heart of the most consistently successful strategies for dealing with procurement. It is also one of the better ways of managing clients and project profitability even when procurement staff are not involved. At the heart of this approach lies the realization that for most PSF projects management of the project or service delivery will have a substantial impact on profitability, client satisfaction and outcome. This is also part of the basis for the golden triangle mentioned in the Introduction to this book.

The reasons for this are many but the most important one is that many PSF projects take on a life of their own almost as soon as they have been started. Both exogenous and endogenous developments can affect a project or assignment and cause changes to the required output. How these changes are managed is critical. Once clients have realized that changes are required they ask their service provider to adjust to these changes which typically require additional work and effort on behalf of the service provider. Such changes usually involve more output, changes to the timetable, changes to the project plan or additional efforts involved in managing the team to accommodate the changes, etc. These changes are known as 'change requirements' and client requests for changes are referred to as 'change requests'.

How such changes are managed, especially within the context of fees, will have a major impact on all involved. On the one extreme there are service providers who comply with all change requests without changing the fee. The result is a decline in profitability or productivity as the additional time and effort are not compensated for by additional fees. This is not atypical for many advisory assignments, particularly where the service provider feels weak compared to the client. The reluctance of many professionals to query changes – after all they want to be known to their clients for their ability to deliver solutions – is sometimes abused by unscrupulous clients or procurement staff. The other extreme is found when any minor change in the project or assignment will only be actioned if a change request (from either side) has been agreed. This is not uncommon for major IT or software projects where even the smallest, uncoordinated change could have catastrophic consequences.

Therein lies the rub – the almost inevitable changes to PSF projects require careful management not just in terms of recognizing the changes needed but also agreeing appropriate fees for any incremental work. Once a project has started it becomes much more difficult or costly to replace the service provider. This raises switching costs and moves the balance of power in favour of service providers if they choose to use change requests as an opportunity to revisit the fees. Unscrupulous service providers could win an assignment by deliberately underestimating the work required and bid using low or reasonable fees. Then, during the assignment, as the client is forced to request more and more work to reach a required outcome, the service provider could demand excessively high fees for the incremental work.

Qualified and experienced procurement professionals are well aware of this trap and will often pay as much attention to project management issues as they do to the initial contract negotiation (Guth, 2008). One writer on this topic estimates that the source of value for simple projects is mostly (up to 90 per cent) driven by the original fee quote, whereas for complex projects as much as 80 per cent can be derived from ongoing management (Czerniawska and Smith, 2010).

Really sophisticated bidders also look for such opportunities. Tactics such as 'back loading', 'low balling' or 'clawbacks' are extreme examples of bidders deliberately quoting low at the start of a project in the expectation that the profit margins will be restored as a result of inevitable change requests. The IT and construction industries are notorious for budget and timetable overruns precisely because of the procurement dynamics involved.

PSF organizations and individual practitioners therefore need to become competent and comfortable managing their projects or assignments, constantly looking out for changes and being in a position to raise the subject of fees with their clients *as the changes occur* and not, as many are wont to do, at the end of the assignment, when the balance of power reverts to the buyer (see Chapter 7 for more on when to negotiate). This requires confidence and competence in project management and negotiation skills. One of the most important tools to master in this context is scope.

Why scope matters

Once a change requirement has been identified the first question to be raised will be, 'Is this in or out of scope?' This is usually asked ahead of any other questions such as 'Do we really need this?' The only definitive way to answer this question is to refer to the fee agreement or engagement letter or equivalent documents associated with an assignment. It is critical that all engagements or assignments are appropriately documented before or at the start of the engagement or project. Failure to do so not only exposes a professional or PSF to potential income losses but also, in the case of some professions' conduct rules (eg bar rules in most US jurisdictions), it may not be possible to withdraw from an ongoing mandate or assignment.

Defining the scope of an assignment is therefore a critical element in the early phases of a PSF assignment or project. Depending on the nature and complexity of the specific assignment it may even be that more time and effort are spent negotiating and agreeing the scope of a project than on discussing the fees. Both matter and should be given appropriate time and attention.

The exact content of a scope will depend on the specifics of the services provided and the project. At a minimum a scope should include:

- name of service provider (sometimes naming the team or team leaders);
- name of client and key contact points;
- objective of the assignments;
- description of the service to be provided including any deliverables at the end or during the assignment – ideally as detailed as possible;
- agreed timetable, including any interim milestones or phases and any associated deliverables;
- any specific or additional features to be included such as opinions, guarantees, warranties, etc;

- resources to be provided by the service providers;
- resources or other support (if any) to be provided by the client or other parties – this may include access to sites, data or key client personnel;
- critical dependencies.

Far too little time is usually spent defining the details of the work to be provided. The more detailed the scope, the less room there is for misunderstandings and disappointment for either side during and at the end of an assignment. Surprises, especially the unpleasant ones and disappointments are pure poison for a long-term working relationship between professionals and clients.

An extreme example is engagement letters or contracts in which the services provided are described as follows: 'all (insert appropriate industry) services related to X', where X is the overall project such as the construction of a major office complex, the search for a new CEO or a corporate transaction. Procurement would love to see wording such as this as it effectively allows them to say to a service provider: 'But it is included in the scope – see here' and then they gleefully point to the 'all services related to X' passage in the contract.

How clients use competitive pressures to undermine good scoping

Procurement practitioners will often try to use the competitive pressures of a selection or RFP process to negotiate scope in their favour. Particularly aggressive procurement processes will either try to limit discussions on scope using time pressure and deadlines or by threatening not to admit a service provider to the next stage of the selection process if it has not complied with the buyers' demands on scope.

Another technique sometimes encountered is when clients ask for binding fee quotes on the basis of a broad and vague project description and only allow access to detailed information after agreeing fees. Such clients will sometimes withhold important information in the knowledge that when the information surfaces and the scope needs to be adjusted (upwards) the professionals will not seek additional fees. This change in scope is referred to as 'scope creep'.

Scope creep often happens unintentionally, eg when genuinely new information has been discovered or unexpected developments have taken place. Such scope creep could also involve accelerating or lengthening a timetable. Sometimes, however, scope creep is part of a deliberate and detailed plan intended to generate additional profits for the (shark) client.

Needless to say, professionals need to be on the lookout against such practices and either resist them at the outset of a selection process or be prepared to engage in robust negotiation during the assignment. Either way scope creep is poison for PSF profitability (see Chapter 15 for more on managing project profitability).

Scope management techniques

Handling scope creep

The best way to deal with scope creep is to actively manage a project and monitor its progress against the original scope and to raise the issue of fees (ie more) as soon as the scope has increased. Really smart professionals will also mention a decrease in fees with clients where a scope has decreased. They will take the opportunity to demonstrate their ability to deliver extra value but will also try to retain some of the savings so as to increase their margins.

This approach does require confidence and competence in fee negotiations. There are a number of additional techniques; we refer to these as 'non-negotiation' techniques that can be helpful in this respect. They include the following.

Invoicing frequently, eg monthly and monitoring payment

Scope increases are likely to manifest themselves in higher than budgeted invoices. Professionals should therefore invoice frequently and in a timely manner. If clients pay but subsequently query the bills at least the professional is negotiating from a position of strength rather than running after the money. The latter is more likely to lead to agreeing further discounts or write-offs to at least recover some of the monies due. Alternatively the clients stop paying when the bills exceed budget. In this situation a practitioner is able to deal with the issue there and then rather than, say, six months later when the client has forgotten or chosen to forget why the extra work was needed in the first instance. The worst that can happen is that the practitioner does not reach agreement with the client and then stands down from the project. This is still preferable to doing the work and not getting paid.

Drawing up additional contracts for out-of-scope work

One of the most effective ways to anticipate client reactions to a final bill that is significantly higher than any pre-agreed quotes is to agree with clients separate contracts or fee arrangements for the out-of-scope work. There are at least two benefits associated with this approach. First, the total bill is broken into smaller, more digestible pieces and each bill (ie each piece of new work) is documented by an agreement the client signed. The second advantage is that the service provider is likely to deliver the in-scope work within or close to the original fee quote, thus demonstrating good fee estimation competence and improving credibility for the next assignment.

Specifying term limits to rates

Many PSF organizations and individuals find it difficult to review their rates in the context of long-running assignments. Although one cannot avoid having to discuss rates with clients altogether (unless one is happy to keep working on these), one way to make broaching the subject easier is to include in the original rate or fee agreement provisos limiting the time periods for which these rates are valid – usually one or two years. Although clients are likely to resist rates uplifts, at least they cannot complain that the issue is raised – after all, they had notice that this will happen.

Dealing with procurement effectively requires an institutional, aligned approach to fee management. The sole practitioner taking on the might of a procurement department is rarely likely to come out on top. There are also other aspects of the golden triangle (set, get, keep) that are best dealt with at an institutional level. The next chapter will cover the issues associated with raising the institutional fee management competencies of PSFs.

Preconditions for riding the scope creep curve

For all of these techniques to work properly it is critical that all members of the team, even the most junior, know what is 'in scope' or 'out of scope'. Furthermore, everyone needs to understand how best to handle any requests for out of scope work. If requests for additional work are accepted without giving clients notice that these requests may result in additional costs, and these requests are not immediately referred to the project leader, it may well be too late to go back to a client with a 'fee increase' by the time the project leader has realized that additional work is being done.

Chapter 16 provides additional insights into managing scope creep.

Raising the institutional game

06

Most, if not almost all, of our professionals have an idea of the fees but not the profit a particular instruction should generate. (EUROPEAN CLIENT, 2012)

Consider the following additional comments received from clients regarding profitability:

> Many of our professionals and those working for our competitors give discounts first and only think about the effects on profit second.

> If we could only get our fee earners to increase their recovery by £/€/$5 per hour our profitability and their take-home pay would increase by 12 per cent.

> Too many of our partners think nothing of authorizing €10,000 or £20,000 write-offs in relation to their projects. The impact on our finances is devastating.

> We end up discounting our standard fees on average 10 to 15 per cent as a result of sometimes tough negotiations but give away between 25 and 30 per cent in the course of working for our clients without so much as a single word exchanged with a happy client.

These comments and many similar ones received regularly are evidence that fee management in professional service firms is poorly executed despite the fact that management teams have realized the enormous impact this neglect is having on their firms and their potential futures.

Many of the key obstacles to raising fee negotiation competencies within an organization or partnership have their origins at the institutional level (Meehan *et al*, 2011). My colleagues and I often encounter situations in which fee negotiators (typically partners or senior executives) are left to negotiate their fees without being incentivized, motivated or supported by way of relevant financial training such as understanding their firms' profit drivers, or specific fee negotiation training.

Consider typical professionals such as lawyers or accountants at a typical firm who spend the first 10–15 years of their career honing their technical skills before becoming partner. They will have spent something in the region of 20,000 hours attending technical training (lectures, seminars, one-to-one sessions with mentors or team leaders) or practising their skills and honing their craft by focusing on billable work. By contrast, the very same individuals may during the course of those 10–12 years have attended a couple of workshops on client or relationship management and teamworking and some may have attended courses on project management. Very few if any will have received any serious negotiation training or if they have it will have been for a few hours or a day. The longest course we know of offered in the legal world (in Europe) lasted for two days and we know of only one firm that regularly sent partners to this programme (even this has now been reduced to one day).

In many professions and firms it is also a feature of the culture not to involve non-partners in any ongoing fee discussions, so by the time someone is promoted to partner (or an equivalent senior role) the number of days and probably number of hours that have been spent learning basic financial concepts and in particular developing fee negotiations skills can be counted on the fingers of one or at most both hands. Even when such individuals work in a finance-related area it is not unusual to see that they have spent precious little time understanding the drivers of profitability for their own firm or business area or had opportunities to get involved in fee-related issues. Given the technical focus of most professions it is not surprising that the lack of attention to these and related issues is also reflected in other aspects of a firm's operations and processes, particularly in areas considered incidental to the core profession, such as finance and profitability.

Attending negotiation programmes such as the one offered by the Møller PSF Group can be very helpful, with many attendees able to report significant improvements in their profitability. Of themselves, such courses are not enough if a sustained and significant firm-wide increase in profitability is the objective. Such a simple course-only approach is referred to within the learning and development world as 'sheep dipping' and is known to have only limited impact compared to a more systemic approach to addressing these issues.

In the case of fee management there is a need to link the key issues and tools introduced in a management presentation or training programme with the professional's daily working life. Initiatives need to be embedded by a constant flow of support and reinforcement of key messages. A fundamental root and branch approach should include the key elements discussed below.

Key elements

Understanding

We regularly discover that long-serving executives and partners of the firms we work with have a poor or incomplete understanding of the key drivers of profitability within their firms. We have noticed in recent years increased efforts by firms to raise the financial literacy of their fee earners; indeed the Møller PSF Group has generated a not inconsiderable amount of work helping clients address these issues. The fundamental problem is that many firms devolve responsibility for educating their fee earners on these issues to members of their finance department who, happy to become involved and to get a chance to show just how much this matters, proceed to bombard their fee earners with a deluge of densely written analyses and financial statements that could, at a pinch, serve as a powerful soporific.

More enlightened approaches (Hill, 2013) demonstrate the impact of changing key parameters using analytical tools similar to the one developed by David Maister, which in turn was based on an approach first developed by DuPont; see Figure 6.1. Even simple concepts such as the 'golden triangle' described in Chapter 2 help fee earners become better oriented and to at least better understand the source of some of their problems or challenges, which in turn would help them find the most appropriate solution or response.

Many firms have developed pricing tools for use by fee earners or support professionals. Take-up of such tools can vary significantly and few clients have reported take-up to be satisfactory across the whole of their firm. Many other firms are still struggling to develop tools that their fee earners or partners would find helpful.

More and more firms are beginning to develop databases in which information on work undertaken in the past is captured and made available to partners needing to take pricing decisions. Although no two deals will be identical, it is surprisingly helpful in many cases to look at similar deals to understand the range of fees and work required. These databases can also provide useful information regarding possible issues or challenges that have emerged in the past. There is a temptation for many professionals to

Figure 6.1   Tree diagram of law firm profitability

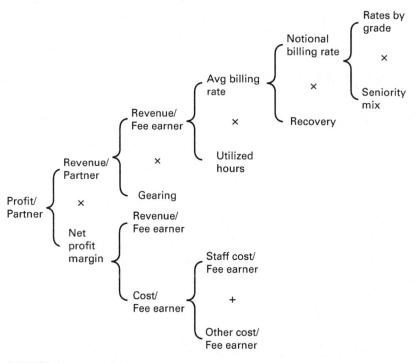

SOURCE Based on Maister

be overly optimistic when pricing a new transaction or project; comparing one's proposal against the firm's collective experience can be a useful reality check and help counter this tendency.

Other areas for attention should include project management with particular attention paid to the project fees and managing client expectations.

Internal information exchange

Regular discussions within business areas or offices regarding financial performance can generate major benefits, especially in creating a fee management culture. Such reviews should not just be restricted to partners but communicated more broadly across the firm. Emphasis should be placed on highlighting good practice and success stories focusing on understanding why it worked. Deal and pitch reviews are also helpful in this respect.

Although it is tempting to focus on deals that went wrong or pitches that were lost it would actually be more constructive to focus on success stories for a number of reasons. First, the reasons why things can go wrong or pitches are lost can be many and varied. Particularly with competitive pitches it is common that clients will not provide full and accurate reasons. Generally speaking clients will prefer to indicate that a pitch was lost on price rather than admit to other more subjective reasons such as personal chemistry, the fact that the other firm was always preferred and that the selection process was solely intended to 'keep them honest' with regards to a sensible price, or that there were strong personal relationships between the client's board and the competitor's team leader. Clients have an additional incentive to emphasize price as a reason for losing a pitch: they want to maintain pressure on the firm to keep prices down.

This discrepancy between the reasons given and the true selection criteria is demonstrated by the fact that in just about every survey that has been conducted over the last decade on why advisers are mandated, price is an important reason but very rarely if ever ranked as one of the top three. This is in stark contrast with the experience of professionals who report that the single most commonly cited reason for not winning an instruction was price.

Financial target setting

For partners and senior managers to be truly able to manage profitability we find that it is extremely helpful for them to understand and buy into the firm's financial strategy and its profitability targets. These emerge too often from a finance department or senior management without any efforts to achieve partner buy-in. Although this requires more effort and time to communicate and discuss, the returns are better cooperation and decision making on a day-to-day basis.

It is fair to point out that some PSFs have deliberately avoided introducing formal financial performance targets in an effort to maintain a focus on client service and collegiality. However, my experience, having worked with a few such firms, is that the pressures to perform and deliver financial results are just as great and even tougher to manage, given that there are no formal criteria against which professionals can monitor themselves or against which their managers or leaders can have constructive discussions.

New business acceptance criteria

One approach that has proven very helpful when introduced appropriately has been to use new business acceptance criteria so as to avoid dilutive work or accept poor conditions. One of the commonly encountered problems is that professionals tend, when in doubt, to accept instructions or projects at unfavourable rates rather than to reject them. As mentioned earlier, this is usually due to the fear of an empty desk or of being underutilized. To overcome this many of our clients have started to introduce some form of short checklist to ensure that taking on a new instruction or project makes sense from both an individual's as well as the firm's perspective. Typically these checklists for accepting a new mandate include the following:

1 Pays attractive rates/profitable – the most important reason for most deals.

2 Contributes to firm's track record – has to make a genuine difference or replace dated instructions.

3 Contributes to firm's reputation – must relate to important client or work in a particular field.

4 Contributes know-how – ie must cover new areas or relate to changing market practices.

5 Allows for new product or service development – there must be a reasonable expectation that other clients will be interested in this new product or service.

6 Allows for entry in new market or territory – again need to avoid one-offs, ie is the firm interested in these markets?

7 Allows for creation of new and important contacts – can be of real benefit if there is a clear follow-on strategy.

8 Provides option or opportunity to win bigger or more profitable work – one of the most abused reasons given, ie start small and get bigger. It is rare for instructions and relationships that are very technical or commodity-oriented to grow into bigger or strategic relationships. Such developments usually take several years and require a long-term strategy, implemented in a rigorous and disciplined way. However, it should be recognized that there are situations when clients will test a firm or a professional with a 'smaller' assignment. The key difference between these situations is intent. In the case of the 'test' there will usually be a clear plan on how to follow up on the initial assignment; this is often also echoed by the client. The former situation tends to be more often the case when the assignment or practitioner involved is very technical or specialist. Once a firm or individual is branded with a specific niche it is often very difficult to break out of this categorization.

9 Helps strengthen important and useful relationships – need to ask if these could not be supported in other, less costly ways.

10 Opportunity for 'paid' training – can be of use but should be used spar-
ingly otherwise firm's standing re quality could be endangered.

11 Makes other contribution to the firm's strategy – if so specify exactly
which.

These criteria don't have to carry equal weighting nor need all of them be
ticked, but if criteria 1 is not met, there should be several other good reasons
that stand up to scrutiny before a deal should be accepted. Also, some of
the criteria could be considered variations on the theme, for example reason
10, paid training, is a sub-set of reason 4, contribution to know-how. Each
firm will need to formulate its own list and develop its own criteria. The
most important point about using such lists is that everyone understands the
reasons for having them and the benefits of applying them, and that it will
encourage professionals to say 'No' to unprofitable or dilutive work.

Note that 'utilization' is not on the list. The reason for this is that being
busy on something dilutive or unprofitable is not contributing to the firm's
objectives and worse, takes up valuable resources (opportunity cost). It is
the factor most often cited by professionals and an extra effort has to be
made to ensure that it is not allowed to 'trump' the other issues.

Also, beware the use of 'strategic' reasons. There is a running joke that
firms have great deals, good deals, break-even deals, loss-making deals and
strategic deals. In this case strategic has become a euphemism for, 'I don't
have a clue why we should do this other than I want to be busy.' Our experience is that if a professional cannot specify exactly which benefits, other
than busyness, a new piece of business is going to contribute to the firm
the deal should in all probability not be taken on, and the firm's resources
would be better deployed elsewhere, even if that means taking time off.

Business termination criteria

Having struggled so hard to win clients, any clients, even non-profitable
ones, PSFs and professionals are loath to lose them. The truth is that most
PSFs will have clients on their books that do not generate profits. One way
to raise profitability would be to terminate relationships with loss-making
clients. Annual reviews and termination of the bottom 10 per cent of clients
(by profit) is one method advocated (Weiss, 2008a). The reason is that with
clients who have received a service at a particular price point, it will be hard
to persuade them to accept an increase (prices are sticky). Rather than fight
a losing battle it may be easier and a more productive use of time to just get
rid of these clients.

Use of 'firm' rates, eg notional or standard charge-out rates

Most professional service firms will have formal fee earner rates, ie hourly or daily rates for partners, directors, associates and other categories. These standard charge-out rates can have a number of different names. Firms can also vary greatly in the extent to which such rates are adjusted for geographies or practice areas, and some firms will have a single firm-wide rate for partners, etc. The use of such rates can vary from being rough guidance to formal prices that can only be changed with management approval.

The challenge with using such approaches is that they can be very inflexible and tend to discourage professionals from taking innovative or creative approaches to pricing. In those firms where discounting requires formal management sign-off it is usually difficult to get it if above a certain threshold. These procedural obstacles are poor substitutes for encouraging professionals to take a proactive and creative approach to setting fees with clients.

The best use of standard rates that we have seen is when they are intended solely as shortcut guidance for individuals to understand what prices are needed to meet budget or to cover costs, including an element of budgeted profit or opportunity cost.

Appointing a price or value champion

Some PSFs have started to appoint price or value champions (Baker, 2011) or have appointed committees or value councils. Their remit is to keep the topic of pricing at the forefront of thinking within the PSF and to help or motivate professionals to implement a more active approach to pricing and fee management. One of my previous employers recruited a pricing manager whose responsibilities included building a pricing database and improving internal pricing processes, helping partners to prepare for major negotiations and if requested to participate in specific client negotiations. This individual was probably the single most demanded person in the firm.

Monitoring market dynamics

Providing insights to professionals of current developments in the market with regards to price would also make a big contribution to helping ensure that fee management is given its appropriate attention. Understanding recent trends would allow professionals to anticipate competitor pricing and provide further input into the negotiation preparations. Providing professionals with accurate insights into the actions of competitors and reasons for these would be a major competitive advantage. Such information would further allow professionals to reach a better understanding of the current value of the firm's unique selling proposition (USP) to clients – and how to capitalize on it.

The biggest challenge tends to be the availability of accurate data within a meaningfully defined market. It may not be particularly helpful to be told that there has been a general price increase or decrease of x per cent in Europe in practice area A when a professional is about to prepare a proposal in a niche segment in, say, Germany or France in a totally different product or service area that is experiencing a completely different trend due to very different demand and supply dynamics.

Motivation

The reason why efforts to train fee earners or encourage them to use pricing tools tend to meet with limited success is that many fee earners fail to be motivated by money and hence fail to invest the necessary amount of time, attention and effort in these topics. This is often because these professionals believe that it is more important to be spending their time and efforts on billable client work or at least talking to clients. It also has to be recognized that many professionals took up their profession precisely because they were and are interested in the technical issues and challenges particular to their profession. Issues such as fees and profits tend not to have the same priority as they do for others. Many professionals also tend to consider themselves comparatively well paid, so why worry and waste time on activities that are uninteresting and possibly outside their comfort zone?

Firm managements therefore face a considerable challenge in finding ways to ensure that their fee earners are motivated to give this area its due attention. This needs to address the following specific issues.

De-risking

Many professionals consider fee negotiation to be highly risky for a number of reasons. First, many professionals worry about the possibility that a negotiation could risk or endanger their relationship. After all they are trying to be on the same side as their client in a project or they are striving for 'trusted' adviser status. How much would a client trust their professional adviser if they had to argue about such issues as money and fees? Many professionals therefore conclude that it is not worth the risk of losing an instruction or a client for the sake of a few extra thousand. There are probably fewer things that strike terror in the hearts and minds of professionals then the risk of an empty desk.

Furthermore, it is bad enough to lose a client due to money: it is even worse to have to explain this loss to one's peers, colleagues and management. Even admitting to weakness in this area and asking for help is pure anathema for many professionals who worry about their profile and ranking within their firm. The best ways for management to de-risk this topic is to set good examples, engage professionals in dialogue on this topic, celebrate 'good losses' and provide positive and negative incentives in relation to profitability.

Culture

This leads us to one of the core issues. Many firms simply don't have a fee or value management culture or a culture that would encourage fee earners and in particular partners to seek advice and support from peers, support specialists or management. Nor are they encouraged to welcome the occasional loss of instruction or client if the work or client was only to be had at unacceptable or unattractive terms.

Much of this cultural problem is also related to poor or weak performance management. Is it any wonder if fee earners or partners seek to maximize their billable hours at the cost of efficiency or profitability if the only metric their firm seems to be collecting is billable hours or revenues? This is certainly the case for a large swathe of firms in the legal and accounting professions and is not that different to the situation in many firms in other segments of the professional services world. Even in firms that officially use other measures we keep hitting the objection that the only measure that management really takes seriously is billable hours or turnover.

Another cultural aspect relating in particular to de-risking is the need for senior management or fee earners to go on record and share their experiences, particularly of failures and mistakes. Fee negotiation is risky: not even the most experienced and successful negotiator has reached his or her level of competence without making mistakes or failing to win all objectives. Why should fee earners with limited training and practice be different?

We found those firms that have been able to generate the biggest improvement in fee management competence to be the ones whose senior management have regularly engaged in dialogue with their colleagues and have shared their war stories and lessons learnt. This is after all one of the ways in which technical, proprietary know-how is passed on, so why not use the same method for this set of activities?

Competencies

In a sense, raising value management competencies is the easiest element of the institutional puzzle. Engaging a training organization or hiring an expert proponent to support fee earners in this area is relatively easy. The key challenge is getting fee earners to turn up to the workshops, seminars or lectures, to absorb the information and try to apply the lessons learnt or to consult the specialist hired. Again, a firm's culture and particularly the efforts made by management to support their fee earners will be critical in determining take-up. We also find that if training in these areas starts at junior levels there is greater likelihood that more senior people will get involved (reduced fear of embarrassment) and that individuals will feel more comfortable with the topic. It also reinforces the message that these activities are part of the core skill of a professional.

There is strong evidence (Kray and Haselhuhn, 2007) that those who believe that negotiation can be learnt perform better, ie achieve higher financial outcomes than those who believe negotiation competencies are innate and personality driven. Other research (Wong *et al*, 2012) suggests this is in part because those holding the belief that they can improve and learn from mistakes actually improve more and are more creative than those with a 'fixed' belief.

Individual firms will have different needs and selection criteria for recruiting specialist support executives so it is difficult to make generalizations. Management teams would be well served to consider the potential costs and benefits to firms from recruiting such specialists. One of the biggest dangers arises when firms recruit such specialists because professionals want to abdicate their responsibilities in this area. I would caution strongly against this. Nobody will be better placed to anticipate changing client needs and respond appropriately in terms of cross-selling and fees than the professional executing a particular piece of work for a client. Although specialists can make extremely strong contributions to the professionals and help them with these activities it will be rare when a professional can be fully replaced in this respect.

Common language

For me the most important contribution a management can make to their firm's institutional capabilities is to help create a common language for fees and fee management and to help partners develop a set of generally held believes about what is expected of them, including how to deal with difficult clients and how to seek and give each other support.

Having looked at the institutional perspective and the support that firms can provide their professionals, the next chapter looks at the preparations individuals should make in advance of a negotiation.

Preparing for fee negotiations

07

Failing to prepare is preparing to fail. (JOHN WOODEN, PIONEERING US BASKETBALL COACH)

Many fee negotiation problems can be traced to the following root causes:

- general mindset and perspectives;
- assumptions and inner saboteurs;
- lack of preparation.

General mindset

Approach to negotiating

For many professionals one of the most fundamental issues to recognize ahead of a negotiation is that a negotiation is a means of reaching (hopefully) agreement between two parties. Many commentators consider negotiations to be the art of making the other side choose what you want or at the least getting to an agreement that both sides think they won (Dawson, 1999). This will involve a highly dynamic process in which each side constantly needs to adjust to the actions or inactions taken by the other (Olekalns and Weingart, 2008). Others (Young and Schlie, 2011) talk of negotiations being like a dance in which the protagonists need each other to constantly interact and create a joint outcome.

In the context of a professional service fee negotiation we would normally assume that such an agreement will form part of a long-term relationship in which both sides intend to continue working with each other after a particular assignment or project has been completed. This need not always be the case but, as already demonstrated in Chapter 1, even when a particular project is considered a 'one-off', a working relationship will exist for the duration of the assignment and there may well be follow-up work.

This is one of the reasons why experienced negotiators try to avoid an adversarial, point-scoring approach to fee negotiation. The best negotiators see fee negotiations as an opportunity to create value by engaging constructively with the other side, even if the other side starts the negotiation from a position of 'No' (Ury, 1993). They also have a 'get more' approach in the sense of getting a better outcome than would otherwise have been achieved, rather than beating the other side (Diamond, 2010). Obviously they will try to claim as much of this value as possible for their side but they know that if they overdo it, the relationship and the opportunity to create more value in the future will be at risk. What is the point of negotiating the other side into the ground? They will renege on their commitments, not deliver as promised, cheat or go bust. Hardly the basis for a long-term relationship or for getting the service sought.

Mood is known to have an impact on planning and the course of a negotiation (Forgas, 1998). Research further shows that an optimistic personality helps reach better agreements. It has also been shown that mood can be primed. This means that a negotiator's mood has a double impact – once on the negotiator and secondly on the negotiator's counterpart (Kahneman, 2012).

Given that most negotiations start with a gap between the two parties (see Chapter 8 for more on this) either or both sides have to make concessions to reach an agreement. If neither side makes any concessions or if the concessions are insufficient we have reached deadlock.

So how do negotiators set about reaching agreement? Three different processes or modes are commonly used: enforcing unilateral demands, using logic, and trading (see Table 7.1). A fourth mode, used much too rarely, is creativity (see Chapter 12).

Unilateral enforcement, ie forcing the other side to do your bidding, is rarely seen in professional service situations as it is rare that a client can force a professional to work for him or her (on the client's terms and conditions) and even rarer that the professional can dictate terms and conditions to the client. And even if they could, if either side were to abuse their ability to force the other side to comply it would very likely destroy the long-term relationship. A variant of unilateral enforcement is when a disinterested third party is asked by the two sides to decide, judge, mediate, arbitrate or otherwise produce an answer both sides will abide by. Although such an approach is usually less damaging to a relationship, it may nevertheless not reach an optimal outcome and usually leaves one if not both parties feeling unhappy. This means that negotiation is far and away the most favourable means of resolving the gap between client and professional service provider.

Table 7.1 Approaches to negotiation

	Unilateral demands	Argument/logic	Trading
Description	• Making or imposing demands	• Using facts, logic and principle to argue the merits of the case	• Making concessions in order to get desired concessions in return
When to use	• When one side has the power and does not care about the long-term effects on the relationship	• When both sides can agree on the same principles, approaches, facts • When both sides want to be fair and trust each other	• When the situation is really about conflicting wants and needs, not 'the facts' • When the other side is trying to impose their wishes
Advantages	• Speed • Easy (if you have the power) • Unilateral/no need for dialogue	• Use of objective facts feels fair • Can lead to stronger relationship, improved trust, more business • Non-emotional • Technical • Meritocratic	• Most likely to get mutually acceptable agreement • Can result in good/better deal for own side • Develop understanding of the other side's needs and interests contributing to long-term relationship

(Continued)

Table 7.1 (*Continued*)

	Unilateral demands	Argument/logic	Trading
Disadvantages	• Does not allow for other side's interests and needs • Not likely to go down well/creates resentment/not acceptable	• Other side may not be interested in pursuing 'fair' deal but only in pursuing their own interests • Facts can be interpreted very differently • Can easily become repetitive exchange of views (at increasing volume or decreasing speed) rather than progression to end result (headbanging)	• Easy to do badly • Some willingness on both sides to move is needed • Cultural concerns about 'haggling' • Risk that optimal terms are not reached due to power-plays and counters • Requires preparation • Hard vs soft negotiator dilemma
Examples	• 'Take it or leave it' • 'We will only pay x per hour'	• 'Section x of the relevant Directive takes precedence in this case ...' • 'We have a more definitive/accurate interpretation of ...'	• 'If you agree to x, we will do y' • 'If you agree to a success fee we will agree to a discount'

The default mode of most professionals is argument/logic while the default mode of most procurement people is trading.

Using logic, in the sense of presenting rational arguments as to why your side is right and the other side is wrong, ie why our fees are fair and reasonable, is without a shadow of doubt the most frequently encountered approach to negotiation in general. For some professions such as law, it is the mode that the vast majority of professionals feel most comfortable with. The thinking here is that if both sides are rational (and fair) the facts will speak for themselves and applying logic ought to resolve the dispute. Unfortunately this is the approach that is least likely to work and does little to help build a relationship for a number of reasons:

First, arguments, in a negotiation context, are almost always about one side delivering their 'facts' or arguments with the other side inevitably responding by reciting theirs, resulting in significant time, effort and emotional capital being spent on arguing 'facts'. The problem with this is twofold. Any negotiator with a minimal amount of preparation time will assemble a long list of carefully selected facts to suit their position. Some professionals just love this and excel in their ability to do so, irrespective of the intrinsic merits of the facts. It has been shown, however, that adding an argument to an offer is likely to prompt a counter-argument and add to the challenges of reaching agreement (Maaravi *et al,* 2011). The other problem is that even if both sides can agree on the 'facts' they may well have different interpretations of what these mean. We often hear of situations in which an 'estimate' was given for a project, which the service provider treated as a rough indication of what the project would cost if all went according to plan, whereas the client would interpret the estimate as a pretty clear commitment regarding the size of the final bill. Even if both sides agree on the facts and apply the same interpretations to what they mean, these facts ignore or leave out the needs and wants of each side, which surprisingly frequently (and more often than most think) have no basis in rational, objective facts.

This leads us to the third method of reaching agreement, which is to *trade concessions.* Here both sides make and/or receive one or more concessions to reach an outcome acceptable to both (see Chapter 10 for more on how to do this). The trading approach to negotiation is well established in many industrial sectors and in many aspects of normal 'street' life. However, most professionals, probably as a result of their focus on 'technical' or 'professional' development during the early part of their career, have either never learnt or have forgotten all about this. It is also probably a by-product of a 'western' bias for a 'joint problem-solving' approach in which the optimal solution to a problem is reached by objective analysis of the facts and possible outcomes.

Beware 'compromise'

A frequent and dangerous misconception is that trading concessions means compromising. I usually hear three variants of this. The first sees compromise as an outcome in which both sides have made sacrifices of roughly equal size or equal proportion, ie all sides are equally unhappy ('equal or shared misery'). The second variant is where the compromise delivers a sub-optimal, lowest common denominator-based outcome (ie 'grubby compromise'). I do not advocate either of these and in fact the approach to negotiation recommended in this book is very much designed to avoid such outcomes. In most negotiations it is inevitable that one side will emerge better off than the other, either in absolute terms of value or in relative terms of concessions made, ie value split. When properly conducted, a negotiation will result in an outcome that will be better than would otherwise have been the case, ie the objective of a negotiation is to improve one's position, not to beat the other side.

The third interpretation of compromise focuses on a 'split the difference' approach (some would consider this a play on variant 1). This approach may be helpful in a highly limited, select number of circumstances – usually to bridge a last, small difference between the two parties. There is a danger in this approach that if a negotiator is known as a 'splitter' their counterpart, particularly if they are a shark, will inflate their own demands so as to artificially inflate the gap, thus shifting the 'middle' in their favour. This approach also reduces the likelihood that the negotiating parties will look for better outcomes (referred to in some negotiation research as 'Pareto optimal outcomes').

The mismatch problem

Many professionals enter fee negotiations with a very different mindset and perspective than their clients or negotiation counterparts; see Table 7.2. Professionals typically look at a future assignment in terms of complexities, challenges and potential surprises; after all they are hired as technical experts to solve these. Consequently they worry about the fee negotiation process limiting their options for tackling a project's challenges while at the same time maximizing their commitment in terms of time and resources and their exposure to liabilities or surprises.

Professionals expect and want to be valued for the quality of their advice and work and for the effort required to provide solutions. This also typically includes recognition for past investment of time and efforts including becoming qualified and accumulating know-how. This contrasts with the

Table 7.2 Differing perspectives of professionals and clients

Key criteria	Professional's typical perspective	Client's typical perspective
Scope of work	As defined as possible to ensure appropriate work is done	As broad as possible to avoid missing something important
Level of detail in the work	As detailed as possible to ensure answers or solutions are founded on all material facts or possible scenarios	Only as detailed as required to facilitate timely decision making or proceed with project
Outlook on certainty	Bias towards binary approach, ie black or white, win or lose	Commercial life is about managing risks and surprises
Costs/price	Preferably, as much as it takes to get the job done well. (Market conditions may have impact on this.)	As low as possible without risking quality of advice, service, deliverables, etc
Speed of response	Normally of lower importance than getting the result right	Typically high priority
Importance of technical issues (legal, accounting, process)	Very high	Necessary evil

mindset of typical clients or procurement buyers who usually look to get value for money and protect themselves against poor delivery and surprises.

Clients want to know they are getting value for money in terms of the solution or work they receive. As discussed in Chapter 3, many clients cannot judge the quality of either the work or the delivery processes and in many cases the quality of the solution or advice will only become apparent years after the work has been delivered, when a situation has arisen to test the professional's work.

These potential mismatches, set out in Table 7.3, often lead to mutual misunderstandings and hence conflict at the very outset of a fee negotiation and need to be addressed if the fee negotiation is to result in a satisfactory outcome for both sides. Professionals have to recognize these differences and engage with clients in a way that will allow all parties to reach a common perspective.

Table 7.3   Differing views on the purpose of fee negotiation

Key criteria	Professional's typical perspective	Client's typical perspective
To fix the fees	• Agree the highest fees acceptable or possible	• Agree as low as possible consistent with an acceptable level of performance • To minimize exposure to risk of overruns
Performance criteria	• Clarify incentives/penalties	• Get confidence in the professional competence of the provider
Definition of roles and responsibilities (on both sides)	• Clarity • Management of expectations • Limitation of responsibilities and risks	• Accountability • Limitation of scope of role • Fear of having to pay for something unwanted
The relationship	• Strengthens 'business partnership' and understanding of mutual interests • Clarity of agreement avoids 'nasty surprises' • Demonstration of commercial approach raises credibility	• We need to get to know these people so that we can feel comfortable that they understand our problems
Commercial terms	• Transparency	• Flexibility

The importance of information

As the section above highlights, understanding the other side is a fundamental prerequisite for a successful negotiation and the hallmark of top negotiators. (Chapter 9 will explain how to manage a two-way flow of information within the course of a negotiation.) There are two fundamental information concepts that are worth emphasizing here: the role of signalling and the difference between interests and positions (Fisher *et al*, 2011).

The role of signalling

Of the many 'styles' of negotiation that I encounter in our work, the one I inevitably find the least productive is the 'poker' style: it is the one that results in the most 'bust' deals in our negotiation master classes. Practitioners of this style typically try to avoid giving information or displaying any emotions or reactions to statements made by their counterparts. Whereas it is certainly helpful to be aware of one's reactions and to be very deliberate about what one wants the other side to hear or see, there are many problems with negotiating poker style. These include:

- lack of signalling the other side regarding progress;
- lack of feedback to the other side to promote constructive behaviour;
- does not build trust;
- does not exchange information needed to generate a better outcome;
- creates an adversarial atmosphere;
- often leads to ignoring signals from the other side.

Highly experienced and professional poker players are very good at hiding their emotions but are also very good at picking up even the faintest signals from their competitors. Average negotiators imitating this style in an effort to minimize signalling their emotions run the risk of cutting themselves off from the signals sent by their negotiating counterparts. As explained in other parts of this book, we strongly believe that actively exchanging information, including signalling one's reactions to the other side's actions and proposals, will contribute significantly to a positive negotiation outcome.

Understanding the difference between interests and positions

One of the most important contributors to successful negotiation is to differentiate between what people say they want and what they really want. Fisher, Ury and Patton, in their 1981 bestseller on principled negotiating *Getting to Yes,* wrote at length about the importance of separating the 'people' from the 'issues' (avoiding becoming personal) and of digging below the surface of what is often said during a negotiation, particularly at the beginning. A more recent analysis and description of how this can be done can be found in *Switch* (Heath and Heath, 2010):

Interests: what people really want

Positions: what they say they want

Untrained negotiators confuse interests and positions, all too often making demands or putting issues 'on the table' without making any effort to understand the other side's interests or communicate their own (see Table 7.4). The problem is compounded because once started, people find it more

Table 7.4 Interest vs position

Position	Interest	Issue	Alternatives
Client:			
• 'We want XY on this'	• Secure successful outcome of deal	• Worries about commitment of team or specialist	• Success fee
• 'I want daily reports on progress'	• Meet timetable/ manage delays/ control risk	• Method for information exchange is costly and inefficient	• Penalty for delay • Exception reports
• 'We want a fixed price for this at a major discount'	• Pay as little as possible in case of a broken deal	• Price structure	• Success bonus
Service provider:			
• 'We will need to charge 800/ hour'	• Raise profitability	• High headline rate	• Leverage and blended rate
• 'We would like to offer you a relationship discount'	• Additional instructions	• Expensive, price incentive	• Regular relationship reviews
• 'Going forward partner X will be working on this matter instead of partner Y'	• Conflicting demands on X's availability	• Client objects to changing partner in mid deal	• Review timetable, agree key dates

difficult to withdraw or amend their 'positions'. This can potentially lead to deadlock, headbanging and useless repetition, requiring additional effort to 'get out of the hole'.

Attention to interests is also likely to lead to more creative solutions acceptable to both sides. Recent research (Giacomantonio *et al*, 2010) has shown that negotiators achieve creative solutions trading off at the level of both the issue and the underlying interests.

How to understand their interests

I can't overstate the importance of asking questions and listening to the answers. The ability to ask good questions and be an active listener is one of the most salient characteristics of good negotiators. It has long been known (Raiffa, 1982; Shell, 2006; Thompson, 2008) that the best negotiators talk less and listen more than the rest, with the specific intent of finding out what the other side really wants and needs before – not after – putting a proposal on the table. Interests first – position second. This is more likely to enable us to come up with something that suits both sides. Here is a frequently cited example from *Getting to Yes* (Fisher *et al*, 2011):

> Two sisters argue over an orange. They each want all of it but finally agree to cut it in half. One of the sisters squeezes her half, drinks the juice and throws the peel away. The other sister makes candied orange peel from her half and throws away the rest.
>
> What might have happened if they had understood each other's real interests?

Here are a number of ideas designed to help identify interests:

- Pre-meeting preparations:
  - review previous meetings;
  - read the press;
  - research the other party's motives;
  - role play.

- During the meeting:
  - ask them (and listen to the answers!);
  - need to plan meaningful questions;
  - invite open, overview discussions;
  - listen and act on feedback.

Making the effort to understand the interests of the other side is time well spent. Significant work has gone into developing techniques to facilitate this. A particular method called 'walk in the woods' is described in detail by Marcus *et al* (2012). This method focuses on not just identifying the interests of all parties but also in aligning them.

The importance of empathy

Great negotiators distinguish themselves by having empathy for the interests, motivations and actions of their counterparts. It is important to be clear about the difference between empathy and sympathy. Empathy means that a negotiator is able to understand the other side and their actions. This does not mean that the negotiator is supportive, ie sympathetic to the other side's interests, objectives and activities.

Other factors that help negotiation performance

One of the most important contributing factors to negotiation success is the degree of confidence a negotiator has in his or her skills to make the best of a situation. This is partly a function of personality and partly driven by these factors:

- *Understanding value delivered:* as discussed in Chapters 2 and 3, understanding one's contribution to a client and their success is essential to understanding where value lies and how to get a fair share. Many professionals are far too timid in this area for no reason, after all, clients want success and the more you understand what that means the more likely that you can contribute in the right way.

- *Preparation:* probably one of the single biggest contributing factors for negotiation success. This topic is covered extensively in this chapter and Chapter 8.

- *Training and practice:* can make a big difference but will not be easily available in many cases. Practising outside the office, eg in private purchases, can materially help.

- *Fitness:* negotiations can be extremely stressful and require 100 per cent attention. Being fit and healthy helps. Consider postponing a negotiation if you are ill or have been unwell or have not had enough sleep, etc.

- *Listening:* the ability to listen and hear what the other side says and means cannot be overrated. This is a recurring theme in the book – and for good reason.

- *Open mindedness/flexibility:* it is rare that a negotiation proceeds exactly as planned. This can present opportunities and risks. Being open and flexible will help avoid missing unexpected opportunities. Creating alternative scenarios and thinking through their relative advantages and disadvantages will increase flexibility and creativity.

- *Time:* allow as much time as possible for preparations and for the nego-tiation. Deadlines reduce the scope for creativity and add to negotiation pressures. Rushed negotiations seldom produce good results and usually need to be revisited.

Assumptions and inner saboteurs

Why professionals don't like to negotiate fees and how to respond

Many professionals negotiate regularly and effectively on behalf of their clients (they may not negotiate well but at least they engage in the process), but find negotiating their own fees with those clients both stressful and diffi-cult. The reason I hear most often is that professionals worry that a robust fee discussion will offend the client and risk losing the deal and possibly even the client. One of my colleagues calls this the 'love vs money' dilemma, ie the assumption is that you can either have the relationship (love) or the fees (money) but not both. So rather than having to decide which to go for they prefer to stick their heads in the sand and hope the problem will go away. As a result, professionals avoid preparing for the negotiation and lack commitment to their position. This behaviour creates a vicious circle as the lack of success feeds further reluctance to engage constructively. The outcome is that the professional moves even further away from a positive attitude towards fee negotiation. I am of the strong view that this is a false dilemma: you can go for both love and money but you need to know how to do it. A badly handled negotiation will destroy a relationship whereas a well-handled one may in fact strengthen it.

My colleagues and I often hear that clients take a view on how well a professional is likely to be able to look after their interests based on how well he or she looks after their own during the fee negotiation. In addition, a well-crafted fee agreement, in which the professional has defined in detail the fees and any variations and dependencies, avoids surprises. In my view surprises are poison for relationships and should be avoided. Even a tough negotiation, if well handled, is therefore likely to strengthen rather than weaken a relationship.

Understanding the reasons why professionals don't like to negotiate on their own behalf helps to break this vicious circle. When discussing these issues with attendees of our fee negotiation master class we get the following responses, which we have grouped into three common assumptions.

Assumption 1: it's going to be difficult and embarrassing

Many professionals overestimate the difficulty and embarrassment inherent in a typical fee negotiation situation. They tend to assume that a negotiation is not appropriate, or not acceptable. Sometimes there does not seem to be any opportunity for negotiation. Likewise they tend to underestimate the value of and need for fee negotiations, particularly during an assignment when the scope has changed or some other unforeseen circumstances have occurred.

One of the main reasons for the 'it is difficult/embarrassing' assumption is the mismatch between the two sides' views of the purpose of the fee arrangement. Professionals assume or hope that the quality of their work or their reputation will be sufficient to:

- speak for itself, and the client will understand and appreciate the value of the work and be willing to pay for this;

- not require explanation/be self-evident: the client will find it easy to tell the difference between quality of work delivered by the practitioner or team and that delivered by others;

- generate an 'appropriate' and 'fair' fee, and that clients are both willing and able to pay for value received;

Professionals also tend to assume that clients will always understand the need for the amount and quality of work required, and will always accept that the value of the work is greater than its cost. A consequence of these views is that many professionals see the negotiation process as a source of potential or latent criticism, or at least a lack of appreciation of the value of their work or expertise. This is reinforced in some cultures where talking about money is in some way considered vulgar, and that fee negotiations belong more to the bazaar than the boardroom.

This ignores the fact that clients have alternative perspectives, operate in different environments and work to their own objectives, not to those of the professional. The growing use by clients of procurement specialists, with very different views of the world in the negotiation of PSF fees, increases this potential mismatch and so there is even greater need for practitioners at all levels to understand the importance of the negotiating process. This problem is addressed in more detail below.

Assumption 2: there is no opportunity to negotiate

This assumption misses a key point. Negotiation is a means of resolving disputes when neither side can (or does not wish to) force their will on the other, and neither side wishes to (or is unable to) accept third-party resolution (eg the courts). So unless the other side can actually force you to do what they want (rare in the commercial world) the opportunity to negotiate, rather than just give in, is there *if we are prepared to engage*. 'This is not negotiable' is in fact one of the most common opening positions beloved of all 'tough guy' negotiators and may or may not be true. It is up to us to find out by testing them.

An alternative situation is one in which there is no time to negotiate or the client does not make the time available. If the latter is the case just think why. More often than not the client realizes that the service provider has a case for a fee increase and the client is trying to avoid raising the issue until after the work, in which case the balance of power reverts to the client (see below re timing).

Often professionals will claim that they do not have the time. The fact is that just about any professional can find an extra two or three hours in the week to accommodate extra work, so why not make that time available to generate extra income rather than extra work or cost?

Assumption 3: the client has all the power

Studies of negotiators' behaviour in a wide range of environments (Diekmann *et al*, 2003; Larrick and Wu, 2007; Rubin and Brown, 1975) consistently show that a majority of negotiators underestimate their own power and overestimate that of their opponent. This stems from an imbalance of information and from a natural human tendency to expect the worst. Two psychological phenomena are at work here: 'availability bias', ie the propensity to overweight what we have easy access to (our negotiation position and problems) and underweight what we don't have direct and easy access to (their negotiation position and problems); and 'risk aversion', ie our propensity to avoid the downside. Hence we overestimate our problems or weaknesses and underestimate theirs.

A less common objection

Another (minority) group of practitioners state a different objection (usually with deeply felt pride): 'I don't need to negotiate because my clients always agree to my fee proposal.' This of course is very comforting at one level but just about every economist on the planet would observe that the complete absence of price resistance indicates chronic under-pricing. There might be special circumstances when that is appropriate, but all the time?

Inner saboteurs

In addition to the assumptions listed above I also regularly encounter a series of self-limiting beliefs. These are collectively referred to as 'inner saboteurs', a useful concept taken from executive coaching. For an overview of 'inner' or 'self' saboteurs you can read an article by Bourg Carter (2011). The concept describes how certain beliefs held by an individual can undermine that individual and reduce his or her confidence and hence performance. The best way to deal with inner saboteurs is to name them and bring them out into the open. Once this is done individuals realize that none of these beliefs has a leg to stand on. A few of the most common inner saboteurs we come across routinely are shown in Table 7.5. There is a certain overlap between the inner saboteurs and the assumptions listed above. Nevertheless it is helpful to look at these in detail so as to be able to counter their pernicious effects.

Sources and balance of power

As discussed above, most people tend to underestimate their negotiating power and overestimate that of their counterparts. This holds particularly true in the early stages of a negotiation. Power, however, is mostly a matter of perception and projection, ie it is in the head. You have power if the other side thinks you do. Likewise, even if you have power, it will be no good unless the other side sees and recognizes it.

Fundamentally, the side that has the lesser need to reach an agreement holds the most relative negotiation power, as it can assert its veto (more on this in Chapter 8). It is rare, however, for one side to hold all the power. Overplaying the use of power could lead to a bust deal and lost opportunity so this is rarely a one-way street.

Good negotiators work at changing the perception of relative power in their favour during the course of a negotiation and especially early on. There are many ways to 'have' or 'project' power (Dobrijevic *et al*, 2011). Some of the more 'acceptable' ones for a relationship negotiation are shown in Table 7.6.

Another way of looking at the issue of power is to consider the long-term impact the negotiation will have on a relationship. Clients are aware of this and therefore frequently overtly or covertly threaten 'dire consequences' to the relationship if the professional does not yield. While there may be some truth to this, in theory it always pays to consider what benefit the client gets from the long-term relationship and to remind the client that a loss or reduction of that relationship will also reduce these benefits – and any value they stand to get.

Table 7.5 Commonly found inner saboteurs regarding negotiating fees

Issue	Inner saboteur	Counter-argument
Limited benefit	• Too little in it	• Is the deal worth doing at all? • We might be able to find additional fees/margins
Too lazy	• This is the best deal available in the market (and we believe their price tag)	• It may be the best deal in the market but why not try to improve on it, even if only marginally (anyway are you sure?)
Too difficult/not worth it	• It's not worth the time and effort (anyway they told us it's not negotiable)	• How much time/effort is needed? What could be the benefits? What signals are you sending out? Do we have to believe them when they say it's not negotiable?
Personal embarrassment	• I hate having to ask for money/show how good I am/my team are	• There are subtle ways of demonstrating value • Clients often need to be told the value contributed
Risk to relationship	• They think we are too expensive/ overcharging them already. Any more and we risk losing the work or the client	• They may think this already, but maybe not! If they don't they are unlikely to tell you! May as well get them to equate the fees with contribution to their business success
Set price (and I believe it)	• There is a market price for this kind of work • Asking for more will risk the client going elsewhere	• This may hold for truly commoditized work. As soon as some customization or service elements are involved there will be scope for differentiation
Authority	• I am/they are not authorized to agree terms	• Get the authority • Get to speak with those who have it
Negotiation is not possible, or so they say	• We are not allowed to speak to anyone prior to submitting a proposal (auction) • They refuse to negotiate/will only accept their proposal	• It might be too late to speak to someone but normally some 'clarifications' are possible • Is this worth pursuing? How hard have we tried?

Table 7.6 Sources of negotiation power

Sources of negotiation power	Example	Comment
Competition, availability of alternatives	• We have another quote that is 10% better • We can do it another way/ we have an alternative	• Very effective if credible • Need to be prepared if bluff is called. Standard counter is some form of product differentiation
Self-reliance, inertia, courage, commitment	• You need us more than we need you • We don't care if we have to do it the alternative way • We will do it with or without you	• Need to be expressed carefully so as not to project a negative image or damage the relationship
Superior performance, expertise, information	• Our systems can handle 20% more • We work faster than the competition • Partner X has just returned from a secondment to institution ABC. Nobody knows as much as he does about how they think about this topic	• Good if true but features need to answer needs of other side, ie the *benefits* must be 'important'
Deadlines	• You need this deal by x. We don't	• Need to be careful not to sound uninterested
Patience	• We can wait – you should think of the costs delays will cause you	• Very effective if we really can afford to wait, but watch for the counter 'Ok we will come back next month'
Preparation	• Having all relevant facts at your fingertips • Having analysed potential trade-offs	• Relatively little preparation can get you a long way

(*Continued*)

Table 7.6 *(Continued)*

Sources of negotiation power	Example	Comment
Size, status, importance	• Bringing in a big team or senior/older executives • Sorry to have kept you waiting but I just had the Chairman/CEO on the phone	• Focus on the key decision makers and the issues. Often very senior people don't have the detailed understanding needed
Control of negotiation environment, timing, process	• We go home tonight, you go back to your low-budget hotel and try to deal with the jet lag • Shape of negotiation table, room, refreshments, etc	• It's a tough life on the road!

This point is beautifully illustrated when people negotiate with their children (or other close relatives). Why do children never hesitate to reopen an issue (such as going to bed early) when it suits them, or why will they display amazing amounts of intransigence when in other areas they almost obsessively insist on a word being kept? It is because they instinctively know that their parents do not have a choice and therefore no veto – parents can't just exchange them for other kids. And how often do parents terminate these negotiations by asserting their power of authority or by threatening dire consequences (or offering some reward)?

When to negotiate

Another critical issue to consider as part of preparing for a fee negotiation is when to negotiate. Timing can have a major impact on negotiation success in two distinct ways. The first is that good negotiators will often negotiate over several 'sessions'. Some of these sessions may not even be negotiations in the simple sense, but may be occasions in which either information is exchanged or gathered or in which they seek to influence the other party.

A classic non-PSF example of this would be the strikes or the releases of studies or surveys highlighting the economic outlook just before or at the start of a collective wage negotiation.

It is important for negotiators to consider the 'battle ground' ahead of a negotiation and to seek ways of influencing or selecting the terrain most favourable to one's position. (This theme is developed in greater depth by Lax and Sebenius, 2003, 2012.) On a more tactical but equally important basis, it is also important for a fee negotiator to understand the pros and cons of available timing options. Essentially there are three points in time to consider in relation to a typical PSF assignment:

1 Just before or at the start.

2 Close to the end or after the work is delivered.

3 During the assignment, ie while work is ongoing.

A service provider will be relatively weak at the start or the end of an instruction. This is because at the start a client will have a choice or will pretend to have a choice: they can claim to have received a competitive and attractive offer or not to need the work – a very effective tactic to put a chill down the back of all but the most seasoned (or genuinley disinterested) negotiators.

Service providers are often in a relatively weak position at the end of the instructions or when the work has been completed – the problem has been solved and the client is no longer beholden to the adviser. One of the writers on negotiation (Kennedy, 1987) refers to this issue as 'the hooker's dilemma', ie the fact that many clients value a service less once they have received it (and are no longer in need of it). My colleagues and I prefer to refer to this issue as the 'plumber's dilemma': we are more likely to agree an outrageous price for unblocking a clogged drain or toilet while we face the immediate prospect of water damage to our irreplaceable wooden floors, than on the day after when all is working normally again. Incidentally, that is one of the reasons locksmiths will always demand payment or agree their fee before they pick a lock when we have left our house keys inside.

The best moment for a service provider to negotiate fees is during the course of a project or assignment when a) switching service provider is not a feasible or economic option and b) the client still requires the work (see Figure 7.1). This needs to be done with some care and attention if one does not wish to gain a reputation for being a cut-throat (see Chapter 16).

There is an exception to this rule of thumb – if at the conclusion of the assignment the client is so happy with the outcome that they are likely to be more generous. If handled well, approaching clients for a 'bonus' at that

Figure 7.1   When to negotiate

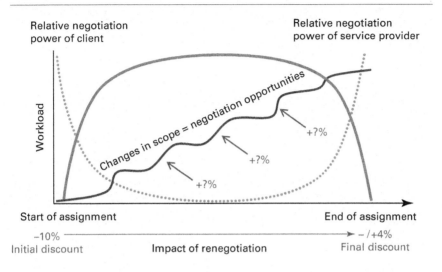

Relative negotiation
power of client

Relative negotiation
power of service provider

Workload

Changes in scope = negotiation opportunities

+?%

+?%

+?%

Start of assignment

End of assignment

−10%

− / +4%

Initial discount

Impact of renegotiation

Final discount

© Møller PSFG Cambridge 2017 – Ori Wiener

stage of euphoria may well yield valuable additional fees. This needs to be handled with a great degree of tact, however, as some clients may become antagonized by a reopening of the fee at this point.

My basic recommendation is to agree a scope and fees based on a clearly defined scope up-front. Should the client change the scope, the service provider can take a view if this change is substantial and if so should approach the client to discuss the requested change in scope and the implications for the fees (see Chapter 5 for further details). This issue has become more important as there are an increasing number of clients looking to renegotiate a fee, especially when the final fee has come in at a premium or even multiple of the original quote or estimate. Although some of these renegotiations may be entirely appropriate, it helps to reduce any additional discounts or rebates when the service provider has been careful to manage scope creep actively.

Deadlines and time pressure

It is worth emphasizing that time pressure rarely contributes to creative or value-adding solutions for either side. Imposing artificial time pressure is aggressive and does not facilitate integrative ('win-win') negotiations (De Dreu, 2003); try to avoid this. (Creative negotiations are covered in greater detail in Chapter 12.)

Table 7.7 Timing options for a fee negotiation

	Advantages	Disadvantages
During 'pitching'	Avoid being excluded from pitch due to pricing Can manage expectations, confirm scope of mandate	Can lose on basis of competitor pricing Clients have maximum negotiation leverage
At time of instruction	Less pressure from competitors' pricing Agreement sets expectations	Client may have expectations Client may not want to be distracted Client may want to defer
At start of project	Less sensitivity on pricing	Client may have expectations Client may consider this 'strong-arming' Client may not feel comfortable defining scope
During project	Fewer alternatives open to client Mission creep may blow 'assumptions'	Client may not want to 'haggle' over every small change
Close to end of project	Can point to quality and quantum of work Take advantage of pre-closing euphoria/ pressures	Client may want to focus on the work in hand May antagonize client if handled tactlessly or poorly positioned
After project has closed	Can point to quality and quantum of work Take advantage of sense of achievement, success, euphoria	Client may have different perspective on quality and effort needed 'Plumber's dilemma'

Media alternatives (personal, telephone, e-mail)

I am frequently asked about the relative benefits of using the telephone, e-mails and/or meetings for fee negotiations. In general I would always prefer a personal meeting to negotiate fees as this will afford the greatest opportunity for information exchange, building rapport and trust (Morris *et al*, 2002) and will facilitate the interpretation of non-verbal signals (Curhan *et al*, 2004). It is also one of the reasons why so many procurement processes try to minimize or avoid personal contact. Even as far back as 1597 Francis Bacon commented that 'it was better to deal by speech than by letter' (Bacon, 1597). Bacon goes on to list the reasons why personal negotiation was better than written (there were no telephones then). He includes the ability to build trust, additional information from body language and the ability to go back on his word or change a stated position.

Many professionals may not have a choice and have to deliver their fee quote in writing (via e-mail, etc). In this case I recommend trying to arrange a meeting before the submission or to provide a quote in such a way that the buyer will want to speak to you to clarify issues or redefine options. A typical way of achieving this would be to provide two or three alternative fee quotes, each addressing or including different issues or services. Clients will naturally want to get the optimal solution and will be incentivized to seek personal contact.

Although e-mail can be very convenient and has the advantage of providing a written record there are drawbacks to negotiation by this medium. The biggest are the loss of interpersonal interactions and social influence. Negotiating by e-mail also entails a loss of control over the timing and flow of information. The pros and cons of e-mail negotiation are discussed in further detail by Bhappu and Barsness (2006).

The mode of negotiation I least recommend, when there is a choice, is by phone. Pamela Meyer has shown in her 2010 book *Lie Spotting* that people are most likely to tell a lie when a) they don't see their counterpart and b) there is no record of the conversation, as is the case with most phone calls. While having frequent contact, including by phone, on the whole is positive as it builds trust and the relationship, I would caution against relying on telephone negotiation, especially if you are dealing with a new client who might turn out to be a shark or someone who does not have an incentive to build a long-term relationship.

The one situation where I would consider using the phone is with a domineering or bullying counterpart. Although personal interactions are best in terms of managing and moving a negotiation forward, there are times, particularly when one is not feeling at one's best, when using the phone to blunt the other person's impact makes sense. This should not lead to a habit of copping out – personal interactions are needed to generate the best interactions. Good negotiators have a well-developed level of self-awareness and will know when to use the phone (tactically) and when to take on the tough counterpart in person.

Having looked at preparation issues relevant for raising negotiation competence in general we now need to look at preparations and planning actions required ahead of a specific negotiation. The following two chapters are probably two of the three most critical chapters in the entire book, the other being Chapter 16, on project management.

Critical first steps: planning

08

Every battle is won or lost before it is ever fought.

If you know your enemies and know yourself, you can win a hundred battles without a single loss.

If you only know yourself, but not your opponent, you may win or may lose.

If you know neither yourself nor your enemy, you will always endanger yourself. (SUN TZU, THE ART OF WAR, SIXTH CENTURY BC)

As is the case in most other aspects of life, the more one prepares and plans for a major activity, the more likely there will be a positive outcome. This is one of the most consistent observations made by all authorities in this field (Guth, 2008; Raiffa, 1982). Sarah Fenwick, a sports psychologist, multiple record holder and international paragliding champion, refers to the 5ps of performance: 'perfect planning prevents poor performance', ie good planning may not guarantee success but it will go a long way to raise performance. Why should fee negotiation be any different? The importance and benefits of good and thorough planning cannot be overstated. (Note: I want to reiterate that I recommend avoiding a competitive mindset as explained in Chapter 7. The quote above is intended to illustrate the importance of planning and information.)

Exceptional negotiators spend at least as much time preparing as interacting with the other side (Ury, 1993). I believe really good negotiators may at times spend *more* time planning and preparing than 'negotiating' with the other side. Such preparations include:

- understanding all relevant issues and influencing factors in connection with the negotiation;
- determining potential negotiation items;
- determining potential pre-negotiation activities or influencing tactics;

- seeking all available information and setting an information strategy;
- setting a veto and possibly several depending on various scenarios or conditions;
- setting targets for each of the negotiation items;
- setting a concession strategy or strategies;
- determining alternative perspectives or other possible ideas to generate creative strategies.

Practitioners' rigorous academic and professional training ought to prepare them better than most other counterparts for an analytical and thorough approach to planning fee negotiations, including the necessary data gathering. Alas, this critical phase of a negotiation is often either completely ignored or only performed perfunctorily. I have witnessed far too many situations where considerations for an upcoming fee negotiation were discussed on the way to the client meeting, usually in a taxi. (This is probably one explanation why so many taxi drivers could out-negotiate most professionals!)

Understanding all relevant issues and influencing factors

Successful negotiators will attempt to find out in advance as much as possible about a negotiation, including:

- underlying reasons for the negotiation – in the case of fee negotiation the conditions and circumstances underlying the provision of the professional services under consideration;
- potential scope and any options regarding the scope of services;
- who the counterpart(s) is/are and what is known about them and their decision making or negotiation style;
- criteria for accepting the proposal/doing the work;
- benefits other than fees such as any contribution to the firm's know-how, reputation, etc (see Chapter 2 on criteria for accepting work).

It is essential that a negotiator not just consider the positions and interests of their own side, but also of their negotiating counterparts. This is the underlying point of the quotation at the start of this chapter. So for example, a negotiator should not only be clear under what circumstances they would accept or reject a potential client instruction – they should also have a clear understanding of what criteria the client will apply to decide whether or not to put the work out to external service providers (clients may decide not to bother or to instruct someone internal to do the work) and how the client is likely to choose between competing service providers. In Chapter 7 I already highlighted the importance of empathy for negotiators.

It may or may not be possible to get full or accurate answers to all of the issues raised above, especially from the counterpart's perspective, but this should not inhibit the efforts to answer these questions. Often the process of addressing these issues alone will throw up invaluable insights for the planning and preparations.

Determining potential negotiation items – clarifying what can be negotiated

Too many untrained negotiators take too narrow a view on the items that are up for negotiation or that could potentially be included in a negotiation. As a result they either miss opportunities for creative negotiation (see Chapter 12 for more on creativity in negotiations) or are caught unprepared when the other side starts to raise these issues. Typical fee negotiation items include but are not limited to:

- scope of work in terms of content, level of detail, level of research, etc;
- fee structure, eg hourly/day rate, fixed fee, capped fee, performance elements;
- fee levels;
- team composition and structure/leverage, involvement of specific individuals;
- timetable, delivery milestones;
- interim reporting or updating mechanisms;
- contributions by third parties or the client;
- warranties, guarantees;
- confidentiality/publicity rules;
- success/abort fees;
- expenses;
- payment terms;
- early cancellation/abort terms.

Depending on the specific negotiation and projects there may well be other issues that are material and that should be anticipated. Readers are recommended to review the 20 most recent fee negotiations or project contracts to identify all negotiation issues and to create a checklist of these for future use. This list should be reviewed at the end of every negotiation and project to ensure that all relevant or potential topics have been captured.

The hallmark of outstanding negotiators is to have an understanding of as many negotiation issues (aka negotiation chips) as possible and to understand their relative value, ie what trade-offs would be acceptable, eg payment terms vs discounts. In addition, experienced negotiators will understand how combining some or all of these will create further value or benefits.

Pre-negotiation activities

Too many professionals only consider formal negotiations as opportunities to negotiate. By doing so they fail to take advantage of opportunities to influence their counterparts and, arguably worse, don't take into consideration the potential influencing they are subjected to by savvy counterparts (Lax and Sebenius, 2003). An example of this could be a message relayed via a 'reliable contact' to the client that the CFO has demanded that no firm be hired that will not give at least a 10 per cent discount on last year's rates.

Another classic example of a pre-negotiation influencing tactic is the request for proposals, a beauty parade or 'bake off'. The service provider is signalled in no uncertain terms that the client has lots of choice and intends to take advantage of this if they don't like the proposal. Sometimes, particularly when the client thinks that several providers can deliver equally well, the competition is real. If this is the case then you are actually dealing with a pricing issue, not a negotiation challenge. Refer to Chapter 2 and the golden triangle if you are not sure why this is the case.

Often however, and more often than most practitioners think (unless they are working in a truly commoditized part of the market), clients have a clear preference or have even made up their mind to hire a particular service provider ahead of any formal selection process. They will nevertheless go through the motions of a competitive selection process to intimidate or influence the service provider from the outset – often to great effect!

Information gathering and information strategy

As the quote at the start of this chapter highlights, information is king in a negotiation. The more we know about the other side and their issues the better. Most professionals underestimate the amount of information available in relation to a negotiation or the counterpart.

Such information can either be from public sources (search engines, websites, industry databases) or, especially if dealing with an established client of the firm, from internal sources such as colleagues. My Møller colleagues and I often encounter situations in which individuals within PSFs (including partners) don't know who within their organization has knowledge of a particular client or has worked with that client. One of the greatest benefits of dedicated client teams or appointing relationship managers is the ability to access this information more easily.

Unfortunately, too many professionals still consider it almost a point of professional honour or pride not to seek support or help from other colleagues. There are many reasons for such reticence including the fear that they may have to share their fees, be forced to let someone else do all or part of the work or even not be allowed to do the work for conflict or other reasons. Although many of these fears turn out to be unwarranted, firms and their leadership should consider if any of these factors apply in their organizations and if so, how to help partners resolve this dilemma. Malhotra and Bazerman (2007) describe the risks associated with insufficient information gathering prior to a negotiation in detail. It is interesting to note that those PSFs that have introduced some form of pricing department or function include the building of reliable databases of past deals as one of their first priorities.

Perspective taking is one of the most powerful techniques that outstanding negotiators employ as part of their preparations. This involves 'putting themselves in the other side's shoes' and trying to see the negotiation and all related issues from the perspective of their counterpart. Research has shown that perspective-takers achieve significantly higher outcomes than negotiators who only focus on their own position (Epley *et al*, 2006; Trötschel *et al*, 2011). Other research (Galinsky *et al*, 2008) showed that perspective-takers consistently achieved better economic results. The research also demonstrated the difference between 'taking the other side's perspective' and being 'empathetic'. There is also evidence that effective negotiators spend more time finding 'common ground' at the start of a negotiation than average negotiators. This helps build a positive relationship between the negotiating parties (Reilly, 1994).

It is worth remembering that questions can be used for more than just information gathering. Babitsky and Mangraviti (2011) have written a fascinating book, *Never Lose Again: Become a top negotiator by asking the right questions*, which outlines how to conduct effective negotiations through the power of asking questions. This includes projecting power and effective trading.

Ask

Often the best source of information on the counterpart is the counterpart him- or herself. Many professionals become uncharacteristically shy when considering what to ask their clients or potential clients. This is rarely warranted. Often clients are all too happy to provide meaningful answers – most people find it flattering to have someone take a deep interest in their business. In fact, clients often report that they will be more likely to select a service provider who has asked lots of questions and who has demonstrated an interest in fully understanding the needs of the client. For reasons we address below and in Chapter 9, good negotiators prepare lists of questions to ask of the other side, including questions about:

- how important the work is to the client and what would happen if the work was not carried out and the potential consequences of success or failure for the client institution or the individual;
- how much experience they have of such work or projects, who will be involved;
- which features of the work or the firm's offering the client really values and which are valued less;
- who else the client is considering (and why) and what they particularly value about them or their offer;
- what the key decision-making criteria are for selection;
- what other needs or limitations the client may have, etc.

Although one always has to be careful to interpret any answers given and to beware the shark giving misinformation, it is possible to take a view if the answers conform to a pattern or confirm information gathered from other sources, or just confirm one's best estimates.

Particularly helpful are questions that provide information on potential weaknesses of the other side's negotiation position, particularly any needs, even above and beyond the immediate project (more below). The intention here is to find out as much as possible about the other side and in particular what power levers will work best in the negotiation.

Given the importance of asking questions it is surprising how little has been written about how to develop an effective strategy for asking questions. One source (Miles, 2013) suggest that there are four key determinants for an effective questioning strategy. These include:

- the purpose and type of negotiation (distributive vs integrative);
- the contextual/relative power of the negotiators;
- the need to allow the respondent to 'save face'; and
- the desire for the questioner to 'save face'.

To this I would also add issues such as the personal styles of the negotiators and relevant contextual issues such as culture, gender and the complexity of the negotiation.

Tell

Just as good negotiators prepare lists of questions to ask either ahead or during a negotiation, they also prepare lists of information they wish the other side to know. The purpose of this information is to strengthen one's own negotiation position or to start managing the other side's expectations. Typical information to share with the client includes statements that:

- highlight or remind the client how ambitious or complex the project is (with the subtle sub-message that few if any other providers can deliver as well as we can);
- demonstrate how tight or difficult the proposed timetable is (with similar subtext as above);
- that your firm has the relevant expertise (and few others have it) and why it matters; and
- that you are or your firm are busy or in demand and that you have choices (see below re the importance of alternatives).

Again it is important to take a balanced view of one's objectives. Provide too little information and a valuable opportunity to influence the other side is lost. Provide too much and the other side either struggles to understand the key messages or starts to become suspicious of the flow of information.

Keep

Good negotiators will always prepare for the worst, irrespective of whether their counterpart has prepared or not. They will hence be trying to anticipate questions that would reveal their own negotiation weaknesses. This is important, as most people will, when asked a direct question, be prone to want to answer the question, often giving away valuable and critical information.

The power of flattery, raised under 'Ask' above, should not be underestimated. Good negotiators understand how to capitalize on the propensity of most people to want to talk about themselves or their business. On the other hand, good negotiators also prepare themselves and their teams in advance so as not to answer inadvertently.

Furthermore, most of us, when asked a question that we know we should not answer, start to stutter or display other behaviours that indicate that an important question has been asked. Trained negotiators will look out for such stress indicators and will pursue these topics further, either to get to the information in another way or to just put the other side under even more pressure. It is essential therefore to prepare responses to questions that should not be answered (at least at this stage) to avoid sounding defensive, come under psychological pressure or give signals to the other side that they have hit on an issue well worth exploring further.

Figure 8.1 provides a summary of the key information exchange topics. In Chapter 9, I will show how this model should be used as part of the information exchange during the opening phases of a negotiation.

Information trading strategy

Having assembled as much information as possible ahead of the negotiation, and put together their lists of questions and information they want the other side to have and information to keep back, good negotiators will determine how best to communicate with the other side. Sometimes this is done in pre-meetings, phone calls, etc. Sometimes it is best done at the meeting, particularly in the early phases (see Chapter 9 for more on this, as well as Chapter 14 for potential cultural factors that could influence this decision).

Good negotiators also monitor carefully how much information the other side is asking for and giving, so as to avoid an imbalance between the two. The flow and relative balance between information shared and sought can be a useful indicator or confirmation of whether one is dealing with a dolphin (roughly balanced and open to providing information), a shark

Figure 8.1   Information exchange model

Tell

- Opening position
- Power statement
- Interests
- Concessions willing to make
- Options worth exploring

Ask (one at a time)	Keep
- Their interests and key objectives - Concessions willing to make - Alternatives - Constraints and instructions given - Importance of deal - Key drivers	- Sources of weakness - Importance to you - Potential alternatives to them - Internal differences

© Møller PSFG Cambridge 2017 – Ori Wiener

(lots of asking, little sharing, someone well prepared), someone with whom answers and questions come promptly or easily, or a negotiation amateur – not prepared, inconsistent, etc.

We are now reaching one of the most critical elements in the planning phase of a negotiation – setting vetoes and targets. The time and effort invested in these activities probably generate the highest returns of all PSF activities. The rest of this chapter will provide a conceptual framework on how to set effective vetoes and targets. Chapter 17 will provide the statistical evidence for just how important veto and target setting is for PSFs.

Veto setting

Having gathered as much information as possible, trained negotiators will then ask themselves one of the most important questions in connection with their preparations: 'What will happen if we fail to reach agreement?' The reason for this is that every negotiator needs to know when to say 'Yes' or 'No' to a proposed deal. There is only one answer to both: a negotiator should only accept a deal when this is the best alternative available (at that time) and should reject a deal when there are better alternatives available (at that time), taking into consideration all relevant issues including preferences.

This may sound obvious but it is one of the most common failings of untrained negotiators. When, as part of our fee negotiation programme, my colleagues and I put the question to professionals, 'On what basis do you accept or reject a fee proposal?' the most frequent answers we get include:

- if it is loss making;
- if the team is busy;
- if the counterpart is an established client;
- if the counterpart is a potential client;
- if the counterpart is a highly reputable or desirable client.

In other words, we rarely get responses demonstrating that the ultimate decision depends on available alternatives. All of the responses cited above may be important and have a part to play, as we will see below, but the fundamental decision is still one that requires negotiators to consider their alternatives and to figure out what their next best alternatives are. These may not be pleasant ones but they are still the alternatives that would offer themselves if agreement were not reached. These alternatives may either be instructions for other clients or could even be to do nothing and spend the time on other things like marketing, researching, building technical know-how or other databases, or going on vacation.

William Ury, co-author of *Getting to Yes* (2011) wrote an entire book on this topic. In *Getting Past NO* (1993) and *The Power of a Positive NO* (2007) he demonstrated both the need to develop one's alternatives and several means of positioning them in as constructive a way as possible. In fact, the author believes that some of the biggest negotiation problems do not arise from an inability of either side to reach an agreement or because of particularly strong resistance from one side, but rather from the fact that many negotiators go into a negotiation without a clear understanding of their alternatives. He advocates building strong alternatives as one of the best ways to both overcome a counterpart's resistance and to generate a 'better' outcome for oneself. I fully agree with this advice.

There are plenty of acronyms in use to describe these alternatives. To keep life simple, and to make the point about alternatives I will refer to them as the NBT (the 'Next Best Thing'). There has to be at least one if not several differences between the NBT and the deal we want to reach, otherwise the NBT would be the best thing and we should take that rather than negotiate the deal before us. Establishing what these differences are (or could be) is no easy task and putting values to them is even more difficult because we are often not given any indication by our own organizations as to how greatly these are valued.

Combining these two issues we get a very simple relationship between a negotiator's veto and their adjusted NBT:

$$\text{Veto} = \text{NBT} \pm x.$$

where NBT = Next Best Thing and

x = factors that differentiate between the value of the deal to be negotiated and the NBT.

Let me illustrate this. Say an established, medium-sized, privately owned client is willing to instruct our firm for a particular piece of work for which we know we can charge 100,000. We have been invited by a potentially new top-100, internationally listed client to do the same work. What should be our veto? We will for simplicity's sake assume that the work is virtually identical and that we can only do one of the two.

Our NBT is 100,000, given that we are highly confident our established client will give us the work for that fee quote. There may be some risk in this assumption and negotiators always need to take a view on how realistic their NBTs are. However, we believe that a) there is value to our firm from having an additional client (diversification and growing our client base), b) there is a track record benefit from working for a top-100 client (future work/reputation), and c) there is value from working for a listed company (marketing/reputation). You may conclude that a) is worth 5 per cent, b) is worth 15 per cent and c) is worth 10 per cent of the fees.

In all, considering these benefits it would still be worth getting the deal with the internationally listed client at a price of 100,000 – (5% + 15% + 10%), ie with a 30 per cent discount, setting your veto at 70,000. Please note this is not the level that you want to agree, it is the level at which it would still make economic sense to say yes to the new client, rather than doing the work for the existing client (our NBT), even if it was with clenched teeth and your back to the wall.

Another way to illustrate this is to take a client's perspective. A client has offers from two service providers (let's assume they are equally good in all other respects, to keep things simple). One is offering to do the job for 100,000 and the other is offering to do the same job with a number of additional features (eg extend the work to another product line or geography) that the client thinks are worth an extra 15 per cent. In that case it would make sense to select the second provider for just under 115,000. The client may also place additional value on working with a firm considered more reputable, or value other features to make it rational to take a higher offer because, on an adjusted basis, it is the better offer. This is not to say that the client will want to pay this amount but, if given no other choice, it would still be economically rational to do so. Incidentally, this is where many procurement individuals or selection processes can go horribly wrong as they focus too much on a single criterion (such as fees) and ignore other, potentially important value-contributing issues.

The approach to veto setting can be made more sophisticated. For example, you may conclude that in our first example the work for the new client will involve more effort or risk. This could be due to the fact that you are working for a larger company and that more work needs to be done. Alternatively, the client might be more demanding, or there may be other uncertainties associated with working for this client. This can be incorporated into the x factor to say, give a revised x of 20 per cent or 25 per cent in the example above (compared to the original 30 per cent).

Before we move onto target setting it is critical to reemphasize the importance of having a clearly established veto before entering into a negotiation. Fail to have a clear veto (or framework for adjusting the veto in case new information is uncovered in the preparations or the course of a negotiation) and you will not know what to agree to or reject. And if you did not manage to set your veto/basis for your veto before a negotiation, you are going to be even more unlikely to set a realistic and rational one in the course of a negotiation (heat of battle) when psychological and other pressures are high.

For reasons explained in Chapter 12, no fee negotiation should only be about a single issue as this will entail additional risks and challenges to finding an agreement that both sides will be happy with (Mnookin *et al*, 2000). It is therefore important to set oneself clear vetoes on each of the issues to be negotiated. In practice, some issues will be more important than others and, as shown in Chapter 10, negotiators can choose to trade off a concession on one issue against receiving a concession on another. Nevertheless, the well-prepared negotiator will know his or her vetoes on each of the issues to be negotiated.

Target setting

Having set a veto (something that even inexperienced or untrained negotiators do in some form or other – whether correctly or not), ie what you will say no to, the question becomes what should you ask for: what should be your target? This is the preparatory step that people get wrong the most. Setting targets has a major impact on the eventual outcome of the negotiation and getting this right can be critical in improving a professional's fee negotiation capabilities and success.

The traditional advice given for target setting is to 'ask for more than you want' (Dawson, 1999). Others talk about being aspirational (Thompson, 2008, 2009). Instead I advocate a methodology in which targets are set as ambitiously as possible (as will be shown below). This approach is recommended by just about all modern negotiation authorities. Chapter 17 provides statistical evidence to demonstrate the benefits of effective target setting.

We regularly see in our negotiation programmes that participants get this wrong, and dramatically so. They will sometimes set their targets too high and risk either blowing the negotiation before it has started or having to find a way of coming down dramatically, without losing their credibility (really tough). Alternatively (and this is usually the case 85 per cent of the time) they set their targets too low. This means that they may get the deal but they have left money (and often considerable amounts) on the table (see Chapter 17 for further details). When this is combined with poor preparations and weak trading (see Chapter 10) the result can often be significant amounts of money lost. Given that for established clients fees are based on the previous deal agreed, the compounding effects of getting this wrong can be extremely expensive.

So, how to set a good target? Several factors influence this:

- the other side's veto;
- the quality of information available;
- one's own level of ambition (and confidence);
- one's experience and skill.

The advantage of having a strong NBT/veto has been shown to be particularly influential in determining the outcome of negotiations in situations where the difference between the two sides is relatively small and there is little to trade (Kim and Fragale, 2005).

Other side's veto

Setting the right targets is probably one of the biggest insights that attendees at our negotiation programme gain. Most people tend to set their targets in relation to their own veto. There are many reasons for this but essentially the combination of two powerful and well-documented psychological biases combine to conspire against the uninitiated and untrained: availability and risk aversion.

The first is the tendency for people to over-value information they can access easily; the second is a deeply ingrained tendency to avoid loss. When professionals analyse their negotiation position they typically tend to over-judge their negotiation weaknesses (risk aversion) compared to those of their counterpart (availability bias), if they think of the other side at all. If they don't they will still over-value their weaknesses compared to their strengths (risk aversion again). We see this effect particularly magnified with legal and accounting professionals who tend to be even more risk averse than other professionals and executives.

Rather than set a target in relation to their own vetoes, good negotiators will seek to analyse their counterpart's negotiation position (Mnookin et al, 2000) and to estimate (it is very rare when one can know it for sure) their opponent's veto. Focusing on the other side's veto(s) (remember there may be factors that could yield different answers) brings the following benefits:

- better understanding of the other side and their potential alternatives;
- better understanding of own side's relative negotiation position;
- greater chance for identifying creative alternatives or concession opportunities;
- increased confidence or realism;
- increased likelihood of a higher (better) target;
- increased likelihood of a realistic target.

Taking the other side's perspective should also extend to understanding the relationship between the other side's negotiator and their stakeholders or constituencies. Outstanding negotiators know this and will be on the lookout for opportunities to help their counterpart 'justify' themselves to their own side. Sebenius (2013) calls this 'behind the table' challenges and describes how this can be used to great effect.

Importance of ambition

Research has shown that performance in a very broad range of human activities, including negotiation, is likely to be maximized and definitely improved when a target is both ambitious and realistic (Chapter 17 provides PSF-specific data). What can be more ambitious than to set one's own target at or close to the veto level of the negotiation counterparty? There is no

Table 8.1 Four steps for setting an ambitious and realistic target and opening bid

1	Ask 'What will we do if we don't get this piece of work?', ie identify your next best thing (NBT). Your veto is your NBT adjusted for differences in preferences (NBT ± x where x is an estimate of how this opportunity is worth more or less than the NBT)
2	Estimate the other side's NBT and veto
3	Set a target close to their NBT/veto
4	Add something to the target to set an opening bid

guarantee that one will get it, but at least it is a good start and still realistic, as anything short of the veto (assuming it has been estimated reasonably well) is realistic. This approach is well established and described in great detail by Alan Schoonmaker in *Negotiate to Win* (1989). Richard Shell (2006) talks about being optimistic and feasible.

At this stage the inevitable objection is raised: 'You can never know the other side's veto unless they are that stupid that they tell you.' I fully agree: one can never tell for sure but good negotiators spend incredible amounts of time and effort collecting information to estimate precisely that. In addition, as mentioned above, there are usually many sources of information that can help address this question, especially when we are talking about existing clients of the firm.

The work that business development or marketing departments do, or the time spent by executives or professionals in marketing or business development will yield invaluable market intelligence about the alternatives clients are likely to have. In addition, and as we will see below, clients themselves will often be a highly useful source of information that can be used to estimate their vetoes or confirm our estimates. Once we have estimated our counterpart's NBTs and their adjustments we effectively have a range of possible outcomes (aka 'area of likely settlement' – ALS) defined by our (professional service provider, ie seller) veto at the lower end and that of the client or buyer at the upper end.

I now need to take a view on where we want to put our 'opening position'. Given that we expect to have to negotiate and that we want to end up at our target we clearly need to start with an opening position that is higher (as seller) than our target. So where should we set targets and opening positions?

Figure 8.2   Four steps to setting vetoes, targets and opening bids

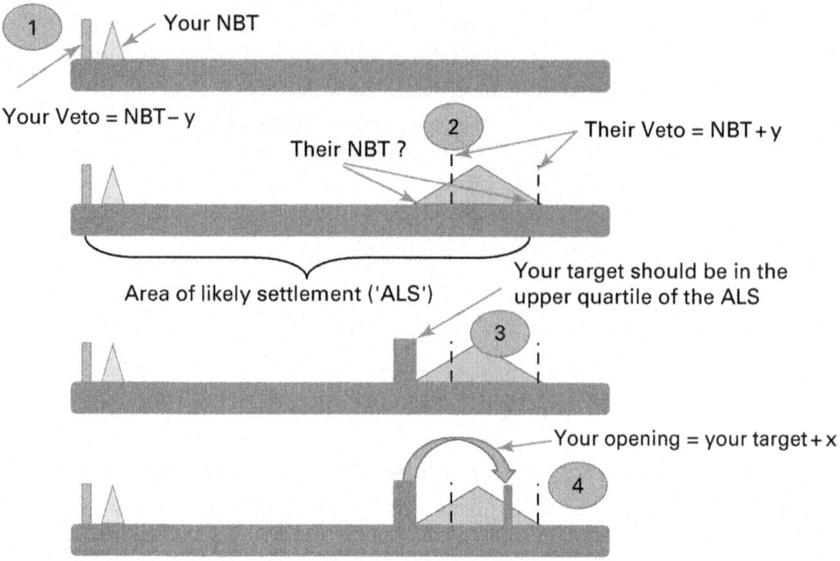

Your NBT

Your Veto = NBT − y

Their NBT ?

Their Veto = NBT + y

Area of likely settlement ('ALS')

Your target should be in the upper quartile of the ALS

Your opening = your target + x

© Møller PSFG Cambridge 2017 – Ori Wiener

This will be partly a function of how confident we are of the accuracy of our estimate of their veto and how confident we are of our own negotiation capabilities.

We recommend setting a target in the favourable quartile of the area of likely settlement. The opening position will have to be set in relation to how high/confident we set our target. For example, if we thought we had accurate information on our competitors and that we had a good fix on their veto we could set our target very close to their veto and set the opening position only a little higher, as we don't want to overshoot their veto. It's ok to overshoot by a small margin, but if we overshoot by a large margin we may have blown it (see above). On the other hand, if we were vaguer about their veto and set a lower target we might add a higher opening position. This takes experience, and practice and self-confidence will make a big difference. We find that even those using this planning framework for the first time significantly improve their abilities to set higher targets and consequently improve their negotiation outcomes dramatically.

Just as it is important to set a veto for every issue to be negotiated it is important to set an ambitious and realistic target for each of these issues. Good negotiators understand that more value can sometimes be generated by clever negotiation on 'side' issues rather than holding tough on the 'big' or main issue. This is particularly useful when dealing with a negotiation counterparty that is playing 'tough'. Often such toughness is due to factors not directly related to the negotiation – internal politics, an overly focused attention to a headline number, etc. In such cases it is often easier to allow the other side to get its headline number on the condition that they yield on several other issues.

There is ample evidence (Larrick and Wu, 2007) that negotiators consistently underestimate the ALS. The implication of this is that unless you have spent considerable time estimating your counterpart's veto you are likely to undershoot in most situations, needlessly leaving money on the table. There is also evidence (Haselhuhn, 2014) to suggest that when negotiators 'unpack' positive alternatives and aspirations, ie give likelihoods of success for different levels of targets, they become more optimistic and achieve better negotiation outcomes.

As set out in this chapter, preparing thoroughly for a negotiation is one of the most effective means of raising one's game and improving the outcome of a negotiation. Chapter 17 provides PSF-specific quantitative evidence of the impact of effective veto and target setting. However, the best preparations in the world are meaningless if you fail to initiate the actual negotiation and dialogue with the other side. Chapter 9 will cover how best to engage with your counterpart at one of the most crucial junctures of a negotiation – the opening.

How to raise your negotiation success: deliver a credible opening

09

I keep six honest serving men
(they taught me all I knew);
Their names are What and Why and When
and How and Where and Who.
(RUDYARD KIPLING, 'THE ELEPHANT'S CHILD', FROM *JUST SO STORIES*)

This chapter deals with how to manage the physical interaction between the professional as fee negotiator and their client in the negotiation process.

Structure of a negotiation

Before diving into the details of what to do and when, it will help to provide an overall structure by breaking down a typical negotiation into a number of phases or acts (Figure 9.1). Each of these involve different activities and require a different focus. I am not suggesting that all negotiations will strictly follow the structure outlined here but the vast majority do, whether conducted in person, by phone or via e-mail, albeit with variations.

Figure 9.1 Structure of a negotiation

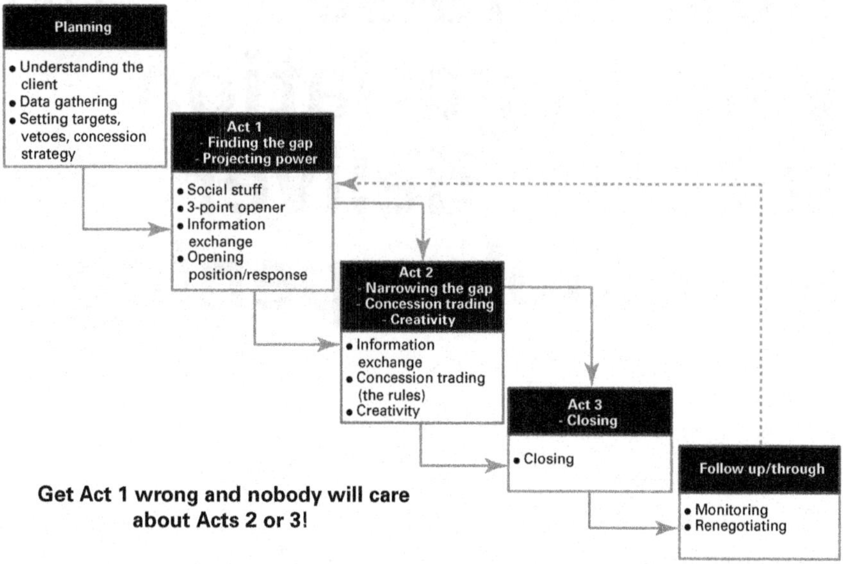

Get Act 1 wrong and nobody will care about Acts 2 or 3!

© Møller PSFG Cambridge 2017 – Ori Wiener

Preparations/planning

The preceding chapter covers the essential preparations that a negotiator should undertake prior to 'sitting down at the table' or otherwise meeting with a counterparty. If you haven't looked at that chapter and taken on its key messages go back before reading more. There is little point starting a negotiation and expecting a significant improvement if you are not properly prepared.

Act 1. The parties meet (in person or otherwise) and exchange respective positions, ie they table their proposals. This is the phase which many negotiation texts refer to as 'establishing the gap'. Even when only one side tables its proposal, the other side's reaction (acceptance or refusal) effectively indicates where they are. The phase may be protracted but one cannot or should not proceed to the next phase until each side's starting position is known. This chapter will focus on Act 1 activities.

Act 2. In this phase, having seen how wide the gap is, the parties either break off, if one or both considers the gap unbridgeable or proceed to engage in activities intended to 'narrow the gap'. This narrowing can take many forms: at best it is done via the introduction of creative ideas or solutions; usually it is done by exchanging concessions. In some cases one side might try to impose its wishes through using power or threats such as going elsewhere. This is where weak negotiators' resolve collapses and they give in. Hardened negotiators will not allow themselves to become fazed by such tactics but will respond in such a way as to move the dialogue forward to a more constructive trading of concessions. In a few cases an experienced negotiator may decide to break off the negotiation having reached the view that the other side cannot be trusted to act rationally or reasonably or to honour the agreement once reached. Chapter 10 covers these activities in greater detail.

Act 3. This is the phase in which agreement is reached (the gap is closed). I cover this in Chapter 11.

As noted above these acts should be preceded by extensive planning. In the case of fee negotiation there will also be follow-up (see Chapter 2, the golden triangle) as part of the value management. It is rare for negotiations to follow this structure in a smooth, linear manner. It is not unusual for reiteration to take place as, for example, when in the middle of a narrowing discussion both sides discover that there are additional issues that need to be discussed (cost of shipping, warranties, etc) or that could be brought in to generate a better outcome for both sides. This would be an instance of creative negotiation and is covered in Chapter 12. Likewise, one of the parties may be under the impression that agreement has been reached and, in asking for agreement, discovers that the other side has not yet agreed to a particular proposal or element of a proposal. Remember, each of the acts serves a different purpose and there are different objectives and activities associated with each.

Act 1: finding the gap

The early stages of a negotiation are particularly important as they have a disproportionate influence on the outcome of the negotiation. *If you don't get Act 1 right nobody will care about Acts 2 or 3!* Because of its importance we divide Act 1 into further segments, discussed below.

The social warm up

The first objective of a negotiator within Act 1 is to gain a feeling for his or her counterpart. Is he or she nervous, relaxed, detail-oriented, open to dialogue or just out to take a bite (in the case of a shark)? Likewise, the early moments of the meeting will be the time when the counterpart is analysing you to see who he or she is dealing with. Are you looking stressed, relaxed, confident and in control of your brief? First impressions can last for a long time and we never get a second chance to make a good first impression, so let's work at this. The early moments of the meeting, especially when counterparts first meet, are critical in creating trust and in calibrating to each other.

As will become clear further on, many of the skills of a good negotiator are about sending signals and receiving and interpreting signals from the other side. Kahneman describes in his book *Thinking, Fast and Slow* (2012) how 'priming' and the 'halo effect' can significantly influence the way people and their actions are judged, depending on the sequence and timing of impressions. The key lesson is that early impressions count and matter. Former US ambassador to the United Nations and experienced negotiator Bill Richardson considers setting mood an important early gambit in high-stakes negotiations (Richardson, 2013) as it helps frame the conversation.

Although it is almost universal that counterparties meet and greet each other at the start of a meeting, the length of time this is given can vary enormously depending on culture and personality. Many people feel that the social chit-chat at the beginning of a meeting is unimportant. It's not. You can blow a negotiation in the first few minutes! Check on the cultural norms in the place you are in (don't be late in Frankfurt or Oslo or get angry if the meeting in Rome starts an hour late). Getting down to business will take longer in Tokyo than in New York. Take the clues from your host. If the client comes from a northern European or North American background the 'social phase' is likely to last a few minutes. The further south we go the longer it tends to take. In Asia the norm can also be quite different depending on country and region. Cultural differences and their impact on a negotiation are covered in greater detail in Chapter 14.

Collins (2009) describes this phase as a 'ritual conversation'. As the phrase suggests, the conversation at this stage may follow a set choreography but it is nevertheless important. I believe that the social warm-up phase is far more important than Collins suggests. As I will demonstrate below, one may well get a better deal from actively engaging and managing this phase. Ignoring it or cutting it short may well derail the negotiation before it has started or create a less than optimal starting point.

There is evidence that negotiators can achieve faster and better outcomes if they had contact prior to the actual negotiation with their counterparts (Rubin and Brown, 1975). One particular piece of research (Curhan and Pentland, 2007) was able to predict 30 per cent of the variance in the outcomes of negotiations based on an analysis of the first five minutes of the interaction between two negotiators. So remember: *get the social stuff right!*

Information exchange

Having spent time on the social chit-chat and having had a chance to send and receive early signals about each other, good negotiators then proceed to exchange information with their counterparts. One of the few points of universal agreement in the research literature on negotiation is the importance of information for effective and successful negotiations and for the negotiator.

The information exchange serves a number of purposes including:

- confirming the basis of the negotiation;
- confirming any assumptions regarding scope or desired fee structures;
- understanding what is of primary or secondary importance to the other side;
- exploring any constraints or limits applicable to either side.

This is also an opportunity to ask questions to confirm any assumptions or estimates made during the preparation phase. Naturally some questions will need to be phrased and timed carefully.

This is the phase of a negotiation in which the negotiators also have to pay particular attention to the dilemmas of 'trust' and 'honesty and openness' (Rubin and Brown, 1975). These in essence force a negotiator to evaluate both how open and truthful his or her counterpart is and how open and honest they will be themselves during the negotiation.

I strongly advise against lying or misrepresenting facts (besides the obvious reason that this might be judged fraudulent). On the other hand a sensible approach to managing the flow of information is also needed. It has been demonstrated that 'straightforwardness' can be harmful to a negotiator under certain circumstances (DeRue *et al*, 2009). This is a particularly important issue to get right as creative negotiation requires extensive sharing of information, as described in detail in Chapter 11. There can be significant cultural differences in the acceptable approach to information exchange and sharing (Adair *et al*, 2004). Culture is covered in greater detail in Chapter 14 of this book. Professionals have to be on the lookout for potential complications arising from cultural differences, which may even be regional, functional or organizational rather than national or ethnic.

The key technique here (and elsewhere during a negotiation) is to trade information (Dawson, 1999; Diamond, 2010). This way the flow of information is roughly balanced and both sides can build trust incrementally. Use the model described in Chapter 8 and illustrated in Figure 8.1 to plan and structure your questions and statements and to prepare for questions you shouldn't answer.

One of the reasons why many experienced negotiators engage in information exchange early on is that the majority of people often only switch into negotiation mode, and become defensive about information, the moment a number or proposal is put forward. Until then, especially if time and effort have been spent getting the social phase right, they are still in social mode and are more likely to answer well-phrased questions. This can be invaluable if a critical piece of information on their alternatives can be elucidated from them. But – this needs to be done skilfully and requires patience (Sinaceur *et al,* 2013b).

A lot of information needs to be exchanged before a proposition is put forward. This is why good negotiators invest so much time and effort in planning their information strategy (as described in Chapter 8). Good negotiators stick to their plan but revise it in light of information discovered at this stage. A major distinguishing feature of outstanding negotiators is that they do not rush to the proposition until they are sure that they have told the other side all the things they want to tell them, and have asked about the things they want to know. Furthermore, good negotiators will have made extraordinary efforts to listen to their counterparts and typically ask far more questions than make statements.

As mentioned above, it is best to trade information rather than just asking or telling. This helps build trust and avoids the pitfalls of just giving information (Schoonmaker, 1989). Oliver (2011) describes the importance of and techniques for controlling the flow of information.

Great negotiators know how to ask good questions and to listen. Asking questions is a real skill in terms of timing and formulation. A technique for asking open-ended questions used by journalists (a breed of professionals who make their living from asking questions), police and researchers is known as the 'five Ws and one H' technique, also known as the Kipling method in honour of the poem cited at the start of this chapter. Be careful what you ask for: collecting or receiving information that is irrelevant to a negotiation can impair a negotiator's effectiveness (Wiltermuth and Neale, 2011).

Three-point opener

A particular effective technique used by many outstanding negotiators is the 'three button statement'. Oddly enough it is not particularly well known, even though it was identified as early as the 1950s (Deutsch, 1958; Loomis, 1959). This statement is usually made early but not at the very start of the information exchange phase. It is used to signal to the other side that the balance of power is far more in your favour than they may have thought and is structured along the following lines:

first: a general statement about the proposal and the relationship between the parties, eg 'this relationship matters to us' – *the relationship button,* followed by;

second: an indication the speaker has more power, eg 'we do have a number of alternative possibilities' – *the power button,* followed by;

third: an indication that agreement is possible, eg 'we feel that a good agreement for both of us is achievable' – *the agreement button.*

The underlying message is that we are good people to do business with, and the balance of power rests with us, but we are going to make sure it all works out all right (and you might as well recognize that right now). This is a very easy to learn and apply 'one-man' version of the 'good cop–bad cop' technique made famous in innumerable detective thriller films. The problem with the normal good cop-bad cop technique is that you need at least two to deliver it and it takes months to learn. If it is used badly, it lacks authenticity and will only serve to reduce or lose the negotiators' credibility. The three-button statement, however, allows the negotiator to deliver something with similar effect and at a lower risk.

An example that stood out during one of the fee negotiation courses delivered went something like this:

> I am so pleased that we have another chance to work together. I can still remember the thank you dinner at which the chairman thanked us for what a great job we had done and how we had saved the firm X million *(relationship button).*

> The situation we are now talking about is even more complex if anything, but fortunately we have a unique advantage having learnt many critical issues from the last instruction *(power button with an implicit threat that there are no substitutes and that this will cost).*

> This will allow us to quote highly competitive fees as we can offset the inherent challenges of this instruction with the insights we gained from the first instruction, so I am sure we will reach a fair agreement *(agreement button in which we promise to be better value than others but it will still cost).*

To achieve maximum impact it is important that each of the buttons is adjusted to reflect the situation:

- *Relationship button:* state if the two parties have worked well in the past. If this is a new relationship emphasize the desire to get it going. If there have been problems in the past acknowledge them and state that you are here to fix them.

- *Power button:* clients will often cite competition or other alternatives as their power button. The professional service provider has to consider which aspects of the assignment can be used to their advantage. This may include complexity and the need for expertise or experience, an ambitious timetable and the need for the right resources being available immediately; there may be special issues or processes that require special know-how or resources. Once professionals start thinking about this, they inevitably find at least one if not several good points. The reason why this technique can be so effective is that making an implicit (rather than explicit) threat during the early stages of a negotiation can generate an average 10 per cent greater willingness by recipients to make additional concessions – in the context of most fee negotiation it can give a highly valuable edge to the negotiator able to use this technique (Sinaceur and Neale, 2005).

- *Agreement button:* this is usually relatively easy to define, but again it always helps to make it as specific to the negotiation as possible.

One of the reasons good negotiators don't begin the information exchange with this three-button statement is so they can check beforehand which of the possible power buttons would hit home best. No point going on about a tight timetable when the client has actually already decided to double the time available to complete.

The three-button statement should happen relatively early once basic information has been exchanged, as many of the power arguments are likely to be repeated during Act 2. These arguments will carry more weight, ie appear less tactical if they have already been introduced earlier in the discussions.

Going first vs going second

Eventually someone has to put forward a proposal. Most people will, if asked, state a preference for going second. One piece of research (Wheeler, 2016) found that 28 per cent of *Harvard Business Review* readers prefer to go first, 59 per cent prefer to go second and 13 per cent don't think it makes a difference. When asked why, they will inevitably make some comments about the benefits of receiving additional information if the other side goes first. When this line of reasoning is explored further almost all will confess that deep down their desire for additional information is connected with a hope that the first number or demand made by the other side will be more favourable than their own first number would have been. In other words – most people hope to get lucky. Here is a question professionals should ask themselves: how high is the likelihood of positive surprises in their working lives? I rarely get answers above 10 per cent when we pose the question. This would suggest that going second is not likely to have the desired effect in more than 10 per cent of negotiations. Is it worth relying on this?

This is probably the area in negotiation literature where there has been the greatest change over time. Traditional advice used to be to let the other side go first (ie go second) so that the negotiator could then respond by saying 'not good enough' (Dawson, 1999). This is a form of flinching (see below) and can be very effective. Together with most modern commentators, I do not normally advocate going second, as it is rather passive and as it allows the other side to take advantage of a highly effective technique known as 'anchoring' or 'signposting'. The reason why anchoring works is that most people will relate the progress of a negotiation and the eventual outcome to the number or proposal that was first mentioned, ie the anchor. Psychologically it is easier for a service provider to start high and allow themselves to be 'negotiated' down than for a client to go first and be pushed 'up'. Anchoring is an extremely well-researched phenomenon (Galinsky and Mussweiler, 2001) and most experts consider it will work in just about all cases even when one is up against experienced negotiators (Malhotra and Bazerman, 2007). Only the most self-disciplined can ignore a well-positioned anchor. One research study (Englich, et al, 2006), for example, found that judges were swayed in their sentencing by the throw of dice.

There are some additional points to consider about going first vs going second. If you have done your planning correctly and have set an ambitious and realistic target, you are unlikely to be much below what the other side would have offered. Also, if the other side have prepared properly they are much more likely to open with a barely acceptable number or proposal: why let them anchor you?

There are two exceptions to the general principle of going first with a high anchor. The first applies in the rare circumstance that you are quoting in a totally new environment or service and simply have no data on where a price should be. In this case there is a high risk that going first will result in either a number that is beyond their veto and you blow the negotiation or your own credibility, or that it is way too cheap and that you will be stuck with an unsatisfactorily low price (and also blow your credibility). My advice under such circumstances would be to delay the negotiation and engage in further research, information exchange or other preparation. Going in blind is poor negotiation.

The second exception is to go in first but with a low number. This can make sense when a deliberate low starting number is expected to generate interest or initiate a dialogue. The aim is of course to have a higher number by the end. A classic example of such a strategy is a competitive auction where the seller sets a very low reservation price. The intention there is to generate bidders' interest which will lead to a bidding frenzy. Some work has been done to establish that similar effects can operate under some negotiation conditions (Ku *et al*, 2006).

This discussion may strike some as rather moot given that more often than not clients expect their service provider to 'give them a number'. My experience is that many service providers do go first but rather defensively, thinking that the other side has the advantage. However, if the service provider has properly planned and gone for an ambitious and realistic target, being invited to go first is a definite advantage and should be grasped with both hands (along with anything else that helps to keep the advantage).

Professionals should be on the lookout for clients wanting to apply the anchor effect in their favour by starting this part of the negotiation with a statement such as: 'We have been offered this service by a competitor of yours for x. If you are able to offer us a y per cent discount on x we can give you the instruction' – tough not to shrink at such an opener! The best way to respond to this would be to first flinch and then to ask lots of detailed and probing questions to establish a) if this alternative is real, and b) how comparable it is to your offer. Often the offer either does not exist or is simply not comparable as it may for example not be as extensive in scope.

Delivering the opening position

This is probably one of the most critical phases of a fee negotiation – get it right and things become easier (not easy, just easier); get this wrong and the rest of the negotiation will be about damage limitation, not profit optimization. This is one of the reasons why our fee negotiation programme attempts to give attendees as much practice of this stage of a negotiation as possible. It never ceases to amaze our participants how practising this two or three times in one day can deliver such massive improvements.

Once information has been exchanged and the decision has been made to deliver an opening position it is essential to remember that it's virtually impossible to get anything better than the first thing asked for, so it is critical to *be bold but believable*.

At this stage three things need to be got right: the content, the delivery and the theatre. Any one of these done poorly will damage the effectiveness of the rest.

1. Content

This is what should have been subject of the preceding discussions and information exchange. It is essential to include (and plan for) all elements that are required to describe the fee arrangement. This should include not just the fee and fee structure but items such as payment terms, warranties, other service provisions, penalties, bonuses, etc.

2. Delivery

Do not just blurt out how much the fee is going to be. If you do, the other side is likely to be thinking about the fee and will not be listening to other essential elements of the proposal and any conditionalities. Rather, use this moment of the negotiation, when the other side will be paying you maximum attention, to describe the scope of the assignment, any conditionalities or caveats and to spell out in detail what either side will be contributing. Make sure you tell them what is going to be done or delivered and what the value to the client is from this work. Then tell them who is going to do the work, how long you expect it to take, anything else that is important or relevant, and then and only then tell them how much it is going to cost, ie 'On that basis the fees will be x.'

Then shut up. Anything said after that will either sound like an apology (no need, it's a sane number) or an explanation (no need, we should have done that already). Also at this stage you need to *observe carefully* the other side's reaction. What are they doing? Are they nodding their head or flinching at the number? Unless the other side has undergone negotiation training, their first and immediate reaction will be a valuable indicator of whether the number is roughly right, and only minor concessions need to be offered for it to be acceptable, or if the number really is unacceptable and needs significant revision.

When delivering the number think about framing it in the most favourable way, ie when the number is a cost try to pitch it at the smallest possible unit to make the number sound small. If you are delivering a service or want to describe the amount of time, effort or resource being deployed try to find a way to make the number sound as big as possible.

Be careful when delivering numbers as percentages. Nobody can work out in their head the value of a 12½ per cent discount on 375,000 (46,875).

One side will inevitably refer to the number but wrongly, thus setting up later problems or disagreement. If you want to deliver the proposal to include a percentage give the numbers as well as in: 'On this basis we are able to offer a 12½ per cent discount on our standard fee of 375,000, that is to say a discount of 46,875 making the fee 328,125.'

3. Theatre

When we deliver our opening number (or when we reopen as part of the subsequent concession trading) we need to sound and look as if we mean what we say. We have to demonstrate that we are committed to our proposal, ie that our number is sensible and that we mean it. If we fail to signal at this stage that we are fully committed to our proposal a trained negotiator on the other side will know that we can be moved from it – and will set out to do so. How to signal commitment to our number or proposal? Here are some of the key things to consider.

Use firm language, ie avoid floppy language (Schoonmaker, 1989). Examples of such 'floppies' include phrases such as:

- 'We were sort of hoping you might go to something like 500,000 or so. I know it sounds like a lot.'
- 'Would 500,000 be acceptable?' – what do you think they will answer?
- 'How about 500,000?' – they may well respond 'How about 250,000?'
- 'Under normal circumstances our fee would be 500,000' or variations on this – it suggests that the current situation is different.

Avoid ranges. If you open with: 'x will cost you between 450 and 550' the other side will, a) only hear the lower end of the range, and b) know that this is a moving feast. If the fee depends on a number of factors you need to spell it out as in: 'In scenario A the fee will be 450,000 and in scenario B the fee will be 550,000.'

When delivering the number you also need to watch your own body language. There is plenty of evidence that demonstrates that people gain more information from visual and non-verbal cues than from the content of our words. Our body language and tone of voice are critical in supporting our words. You need therefore to avoid any body language or changes in pitch or voice that suggest that you are not committed to the proposal. These include:

- raised eyebrows;
- cocked head (means a question not a statement);

- avoiding eye contact when delivering the number – looking down, up, at a colleague, etc;
- mumbling;
- shuffling in your seat (the famous bum shuffle);
- putting a hand to your mouth or nose while delivering the proposal.

You also need to avoid:

- raising your inflection at the end of the sentence (makes the sentence a question rather than a statement);
- clearing your throat repeatedly;
- stammering;
- suddenly increasing the speed (you want to get it over and done with);
- increasing the pitch of your voice (stress indicator).

Our response – 'the flinch'

The second most critical point in a fee negotiation is the moment when the proposal has been delivered or when the other side have delivered theirs. Just as vital clues are generated from non-verbal signals, it is important to signal as soon as possible after the number has been heard that the number is not acceptable.

Most people will naturally 'flinch' when hearing a number they consider 'unattractive'. The reason for this has now been well established by cognitive scientists. As one of the world's foremost authorities on this, Daniel Kahneman, Nobel Prize Laureate in Economics, writes: 'cognition is embodied; ie we think with our bodies, not only with our brains' (Kahneman, 2012). As a result, a strong adverse reaction to a number or offer will cause some form of physical response in all but the most self-controlled. Brilliant negotiators have, ever since mankind started to engage in serious negotiations, ie from the early dawn of civilization, been careful to look out for such body language clues.

The absence of such a flinch is therefore usually a good indicator that the number is not that bad really. The presence of a flinch on the other hand does not necessarily indicate that the number is unacceptable, as trained negotiators will always flinch at a number or proposal presented to them. Be careful with advice that suggests that you should always assume that a flinch is genuine, ie 'Blink test' (Kind, 2007). If a number is unacceptable the other side will let you know in no uncertain terms. If, on the other hand, the number was already acceptable, ie good, why not try to make it into a better number? Flinching is therefore appropriate (and good) in all cases and comes highly recommended by a wide range of authors in this field (Dawson, 1999; Schoonmaker, 1989). More recent research (Fassina and Whyte, 2003, 2005) showed that negotiators that flinch (they called it 'demurring') immediately in response to an opening offer claimed significantly more value without affecting the impasse rate or the value created.

It is probably one of the oldest negotiation techniques used and still remains very effective, especially on the unwary and untrained. This is one of the most important reasons why the poker school of negotiation – ie no signalling to the other side – is not as effective in reaching a good outcome. When interpreting a flinch, a negotiator should try to assess who flinched and how. If the counterpart had until then not shown any signs of being a trained negotiator or has not applied any of the techniques outlined so far, then the flinch may be genuine. If, on the other hand, the negotiator on the other side has been applying most or all of the techniques described in this book, then there is a good chance that their flinch is just another display of their competence and the professional nature in which they are pursuing their objectives and treating the negotiation.

To maintain credibility, avoid amateur dramatics when flinching. The ideal flinch should match the flincher's personality and general mannerism. This is one of the key reasons why good negotiators make time for the social chit-chat: they can calibrate their counterpart to be in a better position to judge if a subsequent flinch is genuine or staged.

Flinches come in an amazing (sometimes amusing) variety. Flinches can express surprise or disappointment. A good variant is also to convey painful sorrow, eg 'I really don't think those sort of numbers are going to work for our people.' For a flinch to be effective it needs to have both verbal and non-verbal components. It should also be prompt. *Remember – a flinch delayed is a flinch devalued.*

The reason why the flinch needs to have a verbal component, eg 'Not possible', 'How much?', 'Oh dear' is that often the person delivering the number will not be looking at the recipient. The non-verbal components that help amplify the message will therefore be lost. Also, some non-verbal components that are frequently used by the more restrained type of negotiators, such as raising an eyebrow are easily lost on anyone but the keenest observer.

Avoid flinches that could be interpreted as challenges or even insults, eg 'You must be joking', 'Have you gone mad?' or similar. Even flinches such as 'outrageous' or 'preposterous' can be overkill and should only be used judiciously. One of my former banking colleagues for example would make a point of looking behind him when it came to flinching. Inevitably he was asked why. To which he responded: 'I am looking behind myself in case there was someone there naive enough to believe this number.' I should add that this colleague only used this when he thought he could get away with it.

Flinching is worth practising and it is worth developing two or three variants. This helps in being able to adjust the flinch to the situation and to avoid being predictable when dealing with a regular counterpart or during an extended negotiation. One other thing: many people have a tendency to write down 'the number' when they hear it. Try to avoid this as it will delay the flinch and could be taken as a sign of acceptance or acceptability, ie 'I will think about the number.' Why let the other side even start thinking that their number could work?

If you have put forward a number or proposal it is critical that you find out what the other side's number or proposal is, otherwise you will not know how big the gap is between the two sides. One (shark) tactic is to respond to any proposal with a flinch such as 'Too much' or 'You'll have to do better than that' without saying how much better. The unwitting or untrained will be prompted to make one or several concessions without the counterparty having to declare where they stand. This tactic has been referred to as the 'Noah's ark' tactic (Kennedy, 2004) – so old that Noah had to let two of them onto the ark. The best counter to this tactic is to respond along the following lines: 'Well, I have told you my number/proposal. What's yours?'

Having successfully put forward a credible opening position, having found out what theirs is and having provided every sign to the other side that their opening position won't do, we have established the gap separating the two sides. We are now faced with the challenge of closing this gap as effectively as possible. This is done by trading concessions and is described in the following chapter.

Act 2: managing the flow of concessions to capture value

10

Effective negotiators look for opportunities to create value by making trades across multiple issues. (DEEPAK MALHOTRA AND MAX BAZERMANN IN NEGOTIATION GENIUS)

Once we have established the gap, ie once both sides have stated their opening positions, we have to find a way of closing the gap to reach agreement. Just about everyone will have learnt (the hard way) that restatements of the original proposition are unlikely to work. If the other side didn't agree the first time to our demands or proposal why should they the second, third or fifth time? In fact, the more a demand or proposal is reiterated the more likely that resistance against it will build up, no matter how slowly (or loudly) the demand is repeated. The only sustainable way to close the gap is to 'trade' concessions. Interestingly, in many languages such as German or Spanish the verb 'negotiate' (*verhandeln/negociar*) is a derivative of the word for 'trade' (*handel/negocios*) and there are no alternatives compared to English, where trading can be used as an alternative to negotiation and the word 'trade' can be used as an alternative to 'business' in some cases.

This phase of a negotiation – Act 2 in our structure – is probably the area where the most tactical mistakes are made during a negotiation but, in some sense, they are easiest to fix. Although I believe most value is given away due to poor planning and unambitious target setting, I also believe that good concession trading can generate significant extra value. Good trading can make a real difference in situations where the overall level of fees may be determined by a 'going' rate and ambitious targeting may not be possible. In this case good concession trading can not only make the difference between breakeven and profitability but could also be the key to competitive differentiation. The skills and techniques covered in this chapter are also highly relevant when combined with fee management of ongoing instructions (see Chapter 16). Handling scope creep constructively is very much a question of managing the flow of concessions, as is shown in that chapter.

The essential concept for Act 2 is concession trading, *not* concession giving. If neither side is prepared to make any concessions there will be no progress and we will have reached stalemate. It probably also means that at least one if not both sides had little or no interest in reaching a 'fair' or reasonable deal. This does not mean both sides have to make equal numbers of concessions or equally big ones, but if there is no intention to budge then it is likely that at least one side believes that it can or wants to do better elsewhere. We often find such situations in competitive tender situations where the buyer has identified a number of service providers and where they will be happy to take the firm that will yield on all points – usually in the belief that all bidders are good enough.

The key issue at this stage of the negotiation is to manage the flow of concessions. There are a number of 'trading rules' that will help with this. Before reading on it is important to remember that a demand withdrawn is the same as a concession made.

The rules

1. Never make or give unilateral concessions (no presents)

The cardinal sin in any negotiation (even more so than not preparing or going in too cheap) is to yield to a demand of the other side without demanding and receiving something in return. This deceptively simple rule lies at the core of negotiation and its universal importance has long been recognized. One of the earliest modern texts on negotiation, *Discours sur l'art de negocier*, written in 1737 (Pequet, 1737/2007) describes this in detail. Just about every text on negotiation endorses the principle that *concessions must be traded or exchanged, never given.*

There are two reasons for this. The first is that we want to improve our negotiation outcome, but how can we if we get nothing in return for a concession? The second reason is actually even more fundamental and important to understand. If you yield to a demand from the other side without making the other side give you something in return you are training them to keep making demands: if there is no cost to them for asking why stop? By making a counter-demand, even if it is for something symbolic, you are showing the other side that they cannot make a demand of you without it costing them something. This will reduce their propensity to keep asking and will also raise their understanding that an agreement will require movement from both sides.

This concept can even be applied to the final stages of a negotiation when the other side is demanding to get one last concession. In this case the trained negotiator will link such a final concession (assuming they have one to give) to the condition of agreeing the deal, ie they have extracted from the other side the counter-concession of 'agreement'. Just by focusing on this rule alone professionals will generate significant improvements in fee negotiation outcomes for themselves and their firms. Remember: *the first unilateral concession is the start of a slippery slope to capitulation.*

2. Monitor the flow of concessions

Ideally, of course, we want to make the fewest concessions possible and get the other side to make as many as possible. To do so it is important that all concessions made and received are tracked and given a value. Some readers may argue that not everything subject to negotiation can be given a value. I agree that some items may be more difficult to value than others but it is a feature of all negotiations, particularly fee negotiations, that if either side is asking for something, they do so because they ascribe value to these items. Otherwise why would they bother? Good negotiators will have an idea of what these values might be, both from their own and the counterparty's perspective. For reasons we discuss below (see 'Variable values'), they will also discuss these views with their counterparts. Sophisticated negotiators track all concessions made or received during a negotiation to generate important information including the ratio of movement.

The ratio of movement (ROM). This is the sum of the value of concessions received divided by the sum of the value of concessions made:

$$\text{ROM} = \sum_1^n \text{CP concessions} \ / \ \sum_1^n \text{S concessions}$$

where CP concessions = value of counterparty's concessions; and S concessions = value of own concessions.

Top negotiators will monitor this ratio constantly and will try to ensure that it does not fall below 1.

3. Ask using 'if you – then...'

It is amazing to observe some of the most seasoned professionals failing to ask for even the most obvious counter-concessions. It becomes even more amazing to see their reactions when observing their performance on video and realizing how obvious and easy it would have been to slip in that extra demand or two. This is why I believe that good negotiators really make an effort to plan what they will ask for, irrespective of what the other side does. They will of course modify timing and method to the flow of the negotiation, but will have clear objectives pre-planned. Good negotiators are not afraid of asking for concessions.

One of the most common mistakes, which can be fatal if dealing with sharks, occurs when one side in a negotiation makes a demand and the other side concedes with the intention of following that concession with a counter-demand. Often the side making the first demand will grab the concession received and move on without letting the other side put its counter-demand forward. A magic tool to prevent this is the use of the syntax: 'If you do X, we can do Y'.

To illustrate this, imagine a fee negotiation in which a client wants an additional discount (say 10 per cent) and the service provider would be happy to give this discount in return for more work (say 15 per cent) over the course of a year. The negotiation would probably sound something like this:

Client: 'We want an additional 10 per cent discount.'

Professional: 'We could do that. I would in return...'.

Client interrupts: 'Fantastic, let me just clarify – the 10 per cent discount will apply to your standard rates for all team members irrespective of seniority? I also expect this to apply to any other support staff that you are using on the team. By the way – how many support staff will you be using, I really don't want to have to deal with too many new faces.'

Before we know it the discussion moves on to the issue of permanent team members vs temporary support and the professional will find it difficult to return to the issue of discount vs volume. The client has 'bagged and moved on' the concession, ie taken it and moved on to the next issue to be discussed.

Here is the same discussion using the magic syntax:

Client: 'We want an additional 10 per cent discount.'

Professional: 'I see. Well, if you will agree to give us 15 per cent more work this year we can give you the 10 per cent discount you want.'

The client may or may not agree to this counter-demand but whatever happens the issue of discount is firmly linked to the issue of additional work and raising one will allow the other side to discuss the other. Incidentally, when confronted with this technique sharks will try to obtain a hard concession against giving a vague promise, ie 'If you give us a 10 per cent discount, we will think about some additional opportunities for working with you' – don't let them. Firm demands and firm counter-concessions or vague concessions and vague counter-concessions. They will soon understand this principle and stop trying to get the better of you.

Generally speaking, any concessions given or accepted should be recorded. This is particularly important when negotiating with sharks, who will otherwise find ways of 'forgetting' what is convenient for their side. If concessions are properly documented, it will help prevent either side from unilaterally backing out from commitments made or concessions given.

4. Emphasize progress/thank them

It is one of the distinguishing features of PSF fee negotiations that these take place within the context of either an existing or potential long-term relationship. No matter how well a negotiation is being conducted, it never hurts to emphasize progress made. This can be done in a variety of ways but one of the easiest and most commonly used is to thank the other side when they have made a concession that is helping to narrow or bridge a gap.

From a psychological perspective, thanking the other side appropriately and authentically is another means in which we help ourselves as we are rewarding the other side for making progress. All but the most cynical negotiators like to be seen by the other side as being constructive and like having their efforts appreciated.

Furthermore, paying complements and being friendly and polite will put a counterpart at their ease. Neurologically, this means that the counterpart will be less anxious and more likely to contribute (Hazeldine, 2014).

This is another argument against 'poker face' negotiation. We strongly believe that active signalling (positively and negatively) really helps both the negotiation and the relationship. This is a way of allowing a negotiator to be warm on the people while being tough on the issues.

5. Plan your concession strategy

Planning is everything, especially when it comes to concession trading. As mentioned elsewhere in the book, the best negotiators spend over half of their total negotiation time and efforts on planning. A considerable proportion of this planning time is dedicated to planning a concession strategy. Just as I recommend carefully planning the information exchange (Chapter 8) I strongly recommend planning the concession strategy, ie the concessions you can give, the concessions you want to ask for, concessions that are unacceptable (deal breakers) as well as the timing and sequence of concessions. The model in Figure 10.1 summarizes what to focus on.

Figure 10.1   Concession planning tool

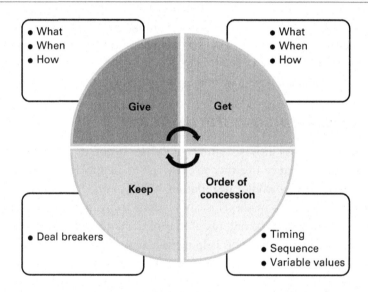

Timing of concessions

The basic rule of concession management is to make the other side 'work' for their concessions. This way they will value the concessions more. It has been shown that the timing of concessions influences the value attributed by the other side and the credibility of the negotiator (Kwon and Weingart, 2004); making gradual concessions also raises the level of satisfaction with the outcome. Subsequent research (Kwon and Weingart, 2005) showed that concession timing does not have an impact when negotiation partners are believed to be cooperative or acting in the best interest of the relationship, suggesting that fee negotiations for established and trusted service providers can proceed faster than in new relationships.

Generally speaking, negotiators have to be as vigilant at the end of a negotiation as at the start. Some commentators believe that 80 per cent of concessions are made in the last 20 per cent of time (Dawson, 1999). I have seen some of the biggest gains or losses in terms of value made at the very end of a negotiation, almost as an afterthought. Beware the nibble! This is when a negotiator will ask for an apparently tiny concession right at the very end, when you may no longer be focused as the deal is as good as in the bag. Sometimes these requests actually carry significant value. Some negotiators have perfected the art of 'nibbling' to a high skill.

Size and sequence of concessions

One of the biggest issues during Act 2 is that the flow of concessions will be scrutinized for clues to the other side's ability/willingness to make additional concessions, in terms of magnitude, sequence and timing. Figure 10.2 illustrates the four possible patterns that are seen in negotiations. They are:

a big concession given early (A);

small concessions followed by bigger ones (B);

a random order of concessions (C); and

a small concession given relatively late, followed by a smaller concession even later (D).

The importance of looking at the impact of these four patterns can be explained as follows: all negotiators, even the untrained, tend to track the relative value of concessions received, some explicitly, the untrained more by instinct. Generally speaking they feel encouraged to demand additional concessions when a relatively important concession has been received early on in the negotiation (Pattern A) – if things are off to a good start why not try to get an even better outcome? When the value of subsequent concessions received remains roughly the same or even increases (Pattern B) most negotiators, but particularly those trained to look out for these signals, will dig even harder for additional concessions, prolonging and therefore increasing the pressure on their counterpart. This becomes a real issue when the other side has nothing left to give, as disappointment sets in or the side is suspected of holding out unreasonably. In which case the disappointed side

Figure 10.2 Concession sequencing

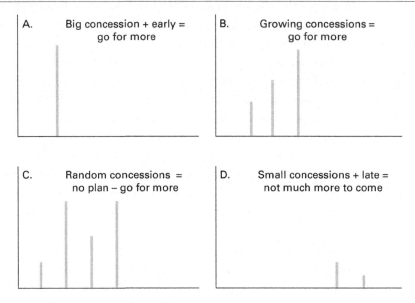

© Møller PSFG Cambridge 2017 – Ori Wiener

will look for opportunities to claw back more concessions either later in the negotiation or during the project – not the best way to sustain or support an ongoing relationship.

An apparently random pattern of concessions (C) also tends to encourage negotiators to dig in and look for more – if there is no pattern, who is to say that the next concession will not be a big(ger) one? Random patterns are encountered more frequently than thought. They typically occur when the details of fee agreements are negotiated in the order in which they are listed in the draft contract ('page turn').

Most negotiators tend to give up digging when the only concession they get is a little one, relatively late in the course of a concession, followed by an even smaller one later (Pattern D). This is why many top negotiators always try to delay giving concessions and when they do, they try to break these into smaller pieces. One of our clients told us that in one particular negotiation the only 'concession' that their client was interested in was a rebate of around 10 per cent. Our client decided to hang tough and then to only offer a 5½ per cent rebate. His client promptly asked for a greater discount. Our client eventually conceded another 2 per cent, but at a higher volume of business. The client asked for one more increase and they eventually settled for another 1 per cent but at an even higher volume of business. By doing so our client managed to almost double the volume of business to be sent his way and to reduce a nominal 10 per cent discount to 8½ per cent, with the average being considerably less. This negotiation alone was estimated to have generated incremental profits of around £200,000 a year. Not bad for 15 minutes' work.

I would always recommend focusing on the big issues first then moving to smaller ones, signalling to the other side that there is less and less to go for. Sometimes, however, I will seek to reach agreement on a small issue first, to generate trust and goodwill. Another reason for starting with the big issues – why fight over lots of small issues if the big ones can't be resolved? This view is shared by most negotiation authorities. A second, more traditional school of thought (Rubin and Brown, 1975) advocates starting with small concessions to build goodwill and trust. However, advocates of this approach point to the danger of not having small concessions available to help resolve the bigger issues if they have already been 'traded away'.

As is often the case, there is no definitive right or wrong. Good negotiators will flex their approach depending on the circumstances. They know that the appropriate framing of demands and concessions can make a difference to how easily the other side will accept a proposal or counter offer. They therefore spend part of their concession strategy planning time on formulating reasons and arguments as to why their proposals are constructive and will help the other side reach their objectives. The principle is very clear: the easier we make it for the other side to come towards us the less likely we have to move towards them.

Another reason for planning the sequence of concessions is highlighted by Cialdini (2007) who described the framing effects of size and sequence. He points out that it is better to negotiate a big concession first: that way a subsequent concession demanded will look relatively small. This is why experienced salespeople will first focus on the main item and proceed to smaller extras at a later stage. Often these extras generate the greatest margins.

6. Look for variable value

One of the most fascinating features that defines exceptional negotiators is their ability to capitalize on differences between the two sides rather than allowing them to get in the way of an agreement (we will return to this in greater detail in Chapter 12). There is an opportunity to add value to both sides by looking for negotiation items that have 'variable value'.

A negotiation item is said to have variable value when each side ascribes different value to it. This could be because each side puts a different priority on an item or simply because they assign different value. Ideally we would like to make concessions to the other side that don't cost us much but which they value highly, and vice versa. An example of this could be the timing of a deadline. Whereas a service provider may be flexible on the timing of delivery of a piece of work (if slower they can work on a number of projects in parallel, if faster they can start another project sooner), the client may need certain work delivered to a fixed deadline. These differences can create value for both sides. The demand that the work be delivered with 100 per cent certainty by a particular date could allow both sides to agree to a higher fee (the fee is not as important to the clients as the potential impact of not having the work completed on time). Shorter payment terms would have little impact on the cash flow of most clients, particularly in a low interest rate environment, but are highly valued by many PSFs given the amount of WIP (work in progress) and capital most of them have tied up.

It is important to remember that what matters is not what a concession costs you, but how important it is to the other side. People tend to give things away if they do not value them, without even thinking how valuable they might be to the other side, when of course they should be thinking, 'What is this worth to the other side?' Table 10.1 shows some examples of variable value concessions that may be valued by a client and could be offered by a service provider at relatively little cost.

Variable values can be a source of real value-added in the course of a negotiation and can help to resolve many impasses. However, variable values also carry some risk. Imagine the situation in which one side has been careful to give concessions (with appropriate counter-concessions) in a declining pattern. That side believes it has been signalling declining room for manoeuvre. However, due to the variable value effect the other side has been receiving concessions of increasing or randomly changing values. What was conceived as a signal of declining values is being received as a series of increasing or random signals and will very likely cause misunderstandings and drag out the negotiation.

To overcome this it is critical that both sides exchange views on the value of potential concessions and understand their variable values. Dolphin negotiators will be happy to make life easier for the other side if it does not cost them anything or very little, and vice versa. This exchange of views should also take place during the information exchange phase but is likely to take place during Act 2 as clarity about the range of possible concessions is reached. This is one of the reasons why many negotiations tend to iterate

Table 10.1 Perspectives on variable value concessions

Item	PSF perspective	Client perspective
Use of meeting rooms	Part of fixed overhead	We don't have offices in x city. It would cost us y to rent serviced offices
Seminars/ training	Being conducted anyway for internal purposes	External courses very expensive
	Keeps in-house team up to date	Value-added
	Relationship builder, sets precedents	
Access to know-how system	Minor IT costs to provide access	Limited legal budgets makes extensive access to know-how prohibitive
Relationship review	Can be invaluable to understand future opportunities and meet key decision makers	Client would spend time anyway to ensure quality of provider
Response times	Easy to ensure someone can respond relatively quickly	Managers may need fast answers when responding to board or authorities
Pro bono	Builds relationships, deepens understanding of key contacts	Contribution to CSR agenda PR value
Dedicated hotlines	Likely to get enquiry that will lead to additional business	Ability to react rapidly to unforeseen event

between Acts 1 and 2 or Acts 2 and 3 as both sides invariably discover additional ways to skin the cat and want to explore them.

Another complication to take into account when trading concessions is that many negotiators will attach a higher value to a concession they offer than to a concession they receive. This phenomenon has been termed 'reactive devaluation' (Malhotra and Ginges, 2005). Smart negotiators therefore look to find ways for the other side to 'ask' for the concessions they had intended to offer them anyway.

7. Take adjournments

There will be times during the course of a negotiation when it becomes necessary to take a break. This may often be due to the fact that so much additional information has been unearthed during the course of the negotiation that the negotiator wants to reflect on it. Alternatively the other side may have made proposals that need to be reflected on and maybe even discussed with colleagues back at the office. In some cases it may also be that the other side is putting on the pressure in an attempt to browbeat a service provider into agreeing to something that, when reflected on coolly, they would not agree to. Most fee negotiations (with some notable exceptions during formal tender or selection processes) don't have to meet a fixed deadline, so taking an adjournment can be a valuable tool for taking the time to reflect on the new information, the radically different than expected proposal, or to escape undue pressure. I recommend taking such an adjournment – if the negotiator (or any member of the team) feels the need for a break, then it is likely to be worthwhile.

Award-winning Harvard Business School professor Michael Wheeler (Wheeler, 2013), discusses the pros and cons of adjourning versus taking action. In his view, taking a break can make sense when:

- all options remain open;
- time is on your side and options may improve;
- learning more will help make a better decision; and
- thinking it over may help one or both sides become more comfortable with the decision(s).

If these factors don't apply, Wheeler would advocate continuing with the negotiation. I think he would also add fatigue and psychological pressures as good reasons for considering an adjournment.

There is an art to taking an adjournment. It should be done along the following lines:

- Tell the other side that they have given you additional and important information and that you need to reflect/consult with colleagues/recalculate, etc.
- Tell them how long it will take (half an hour, two days).
- Gather your belongings and leave politely. Don't allow them to keep you back and ensnare you with attempts to continue the negotiation.
- If you need longer let them know.

- When you get back, thank them, reiterate the importance of the new information and then proceed to tell them what new proposal you have for them on the basis of that new information.

Adjournments are likely to mean that when meeting again there will be a short reiteration of the social chit-chat and information exchange phases. This is to be encouraged – something may have changed on their side as well.

A summary of trading rules is given in Table 10.2. Good concession trading requires preparation, practice and patience: preparation to know which concessions to offer and demand, practice to do so in a manner that will

Table 10.2 Summary of trading rules

Do	What	Why
Plan	Consider: what can we give, ask for and what are we going to stick on?	Give yourself space to move, and to respond to other side
Ask	Don't be afraid to ask for things	It's usually true that if you don't ask you don't get
Use 'If'	Gets you into 'trading' mode	The most powerful phrase in the negotiators' handbook: 'If you do x, then we can do y'
Thank them	When they make concessions (they will appreciate it)	But pursue more: 'This is very helpful, many thanks, but we still need more… to reach agreement'
Think	About the order in which you introduce *concessions*	If you offer up a big concession early the other side will most likely get greedy. The sharks smell blood! If your concessions get bigger as time goes on they smell more blood!
Look for different views of value	Things that are easy/ cheap for us but valuable to them and the other way round	This is vastly under-used and can materially increase the total pie
Adjourn	Nothing wrong in taking time out to think, review, reconsider	Good negotiators make strategic use of adjournments

yield optimal results and patience because there are occasions when it will take time for one side or the other (or both) to be able to make the concessions needed to bring the negotiation to a successful conclusion.

Experienced negotiators know when to stop digging for more and when to move to the closing. Chapter 11 covers the most important closing techniques for PSFs.

Act 3: locking in gains through effective closing

11

When dealing with people, remember you are not dealing with creatures of logic, but creatures of emotion. (DALE CARNEGIE, US COMMUNICATIONS AND MOTIVATION TRAINER, 1888–1955)

Men keep agreements when it is to the advantage of neither to break them. (SOLON, ATHENIAN STATESMAN AND POET, 630–560 BC)

It is not uncommon for firms in some industry sectors to spend considerable time and effort training their sales forces in the art of closing. Whole industries and careers have been built on teaching such techniques. For PSFs, however, I believe that there will be little value gained in focusing on these techniques for a number of reasons:

- They take considerable time and effort to learn and practise before they can be applied. Most professionals will not invest the necessary time required and in this case, applying a little knowledge can indeed be a dangerous thing.

- Many of these closing techniques are most relevant in the context of a one-off relationship or at least a non-continuing relationship – think of the proverbial car salesperson. The best are able to generate repeat business from their clients but have relatively little contact between individual sales opportunities. Inevitably there will be a very small percentage of car salespeople for whom this will not apply, eg those working with fleet buyers. These salespeople will not be using many of the classic closing techniques precisely because the nature of the relationships are radically different to the typical car salesperson to individual retail buyer relationship.

- To work well, most closing techniques also require that the recipient is not aware of their use. As many legal services are either bought by individuals in firms who have received sales training, or by procurement specialists, it is likely that these individuals will recognize such closing techniques, particularly if applied by someone who will only have had limited time to learn and practise these.

There are, however, a few techniques that may be helpful at the closing stage of a negotiation; these are discussed below. (As most professionals are good at documenting agreements or decisions, we will not dwell on that aspect of the closing phase of a negotiation.)

Techniques

Basic closing

Although I generally don't advocate trying to apply advanced closing techniques, professionals do need to know how to bring a negotiation to its conclusion when agreement has been reached or seems to be very close. Unfortunately many service providers and professionals are tempted to rush to the closing far too early in their efforts to 'clinch the deal'. In so doing they expose themselves to unnecessary risk and let slip some important items of value. To illustrate what I mean imagine the following dialogue:

> Service provider: 'I am glad we have agreed – so the fee will be £100,000.'
>
> Client: 'Yes, I am delighted we have agreed £100,000. Let's shake on it.' As they do so the client adds the following: 'Oh and just to be clear – you guys will cover the costs of documentation and training.'

The problem with this example (which we keep on hearing about) is that the service provider did not check if there were any other outstanding items the client wanted to agree. Sharks love to lie in wait and spring this trap on the unsuspecting or maybe even worn-out counterpart. This can either be a big issue or just a few small issues – also known as 'salami slicing'. A better and safer way of closing would follow this structure:

> Service provider: 'I think we seem to have reached an agreement. Are there any other issues that you think we need to cover?' Looks at the client.
>
> Client: 'No, I think that covers it.'

Service provider: 'In that case, I believe we have agreed... on the basis of... (proceeds to outline all relevant items) with training and documentation to be provided at cost (or whatever else was agreed), etc... ' the fees are £100,000.

Alternatively the client has a few more issues to raise, in which case we are back to Act 2 and need to understand where the remaining gaps are.

Where there are other members on either negotiation team, good closers will ask everyone on their or the other side's team if there are any outstanding issues before proceeding with the summary of the final agreement. By going through this structure and process the service provider will minimize their exposure to nibbles and salami tactics.

Split the difference

There are times when final agreement is held up by differences on one outstanding item. If the difference is small then it may be appropriate to apply the following technique (first check that this is the only item outstanding and confirm the difference between the two sides):

Service provider: 'On the basis that this is the only item standing between us and an agreement and on my understanding that you are at £90,000 and we are at £110,000 (check this is correct), if you agree to the deal, let's split the difference.'

Notice the use of the 'If you... then we' syntax. If they agree you have the deal; if not you are back in Act 2 but you have not moved without a counter-concession.

Please note that making regular use of a 'split the difference' approach can be highly dangerous (Dawson, 1999; Thompson, 2008). If the service provider is known to have a preference for splitting the difference they are likely to fall prey to the simple tactic of their counterpart moving their own demands at the start of the discussion. By so doing the shark will have moved the outcome, ie the midpoint, in their favour without much effort and will even come across as accommodating!

Splitting the difference/meeting in the middle works so effectively because of the combination of two phenomena: the reciprocity bias and the fairness bias. Most people have a strong desire to reciprocate a concession and what could be fairer than both concessions being (apparently) of equal size? The reciprocity bias is also the basis for another technique we will discuss in Chapter 12 (advanced tactics).

Concession clause

As mentioned in Chapter 10, there may be a time when the service provider is willing to make a final concession in order to close. In a change to the 'split the difference' example above one can make the concession but should make it conditional on acceptance of the rest of the proposal. This would sound something like this:

> Service provider: 'On the basis that this is the only item standing between us and an agreement and on my understanding that you are at £90,000 and we are at £100,000 (check this is correct), if you agree to the deal, I will be happy to agree to £90,000.'

Once again the use of the 'If you... then we' syntax protects you from yielding £20,000 without anything to show for it.

This technique should also only be used if there is clarity that there are no other issues outstanding; otherwise we are back to Act 2.

Warm puppy close

This is a classic closing technique and in far greater use with PSFs than most professionals realize. The technique relies on the fact that once someone has become familiar with a service or individuals, he or she will be reluctant to change in mid-course. The technique gets its name from the classic pet shop situation where the pet shop employee (having been trained to do so) will place the warm and fluffy puppy in the arms of the child rather than the alarmed parent. Once the puppy has licked the child's face (natural instinct) the child has fallen in love with the puppy and which parent has the heart to refuse their child such pleasure?

We see similar situations in the PSF world. Investment banks or consultants for example will frequently work with clients, informally and unpaid, on the feasibility of a major project. By the time a management or board decide to go ahead with the project they are either so deeply in discussions with the bankers or consultants that they could not stomach the prospect of changing adviser (especially if the timetable is tight), or they run a selection process but with a definite front-runner.

Law firms will engage in similar tactics and will also second some of their best lawyers to clients. Generating strong personal relationships and deep understanding of the internal processes of a client are two of many benefits that a secondment generates for the law firm – both are part of a warm puppy close.

General approach

Within the context of relationship-based PSF fee negotiations I believe that trying to apply clever closing techniques in order to hoodwink your counterpart to agreeing to something they will likely regret later is not advisable. I much prefer to apply the basic closing technique outlined above, ie check for any outstanding issues before moving to the close, summarize all points that have been agreed and offer to send a written draft of the agreement so that all sides can check that their understanding of the agreement is correct.

Inexperienced negotiators will try to close too early when in fact differences still remain. In addition, many agreements do not reach the optimal outcome possible because they did not consider other potential solutions and options. Experienced and well-trained negotiators will apply creative negotiation techniques to both, resolve outstanding issues and create additional value for all parties. The next chapter will describe how they do this.

General approach

Creativity: 12
the ultimate
negotiation skill

Good negotiators do two things: They create value and they claim value.
(DAVID LAX AND JIM SEBENIUS)

There will be times when no matter how well Act 2 has been conducted there still remains a significant gap between the two sides and no amount of concession trading will close the gap. Good negotiators will attempt to apply creativity long before reaching this impasse. In addition there are often opportunities to create an even better deal for both sides using a creative negotiation approach. Creative negotiation can arise from one of three sources:

1 differences between the parties, usually their preferences, interests, restrictions or fears;
2 reframing objectives, perceptions or changing the shape of the deal;
3 processes intended to uncover opportunities for the first two.

Benefits of using creativity

Creativity can have a positive impact on the outcome of negotiations, especially when the aim of both parties is to look for real 'win-win' situations. To set this in the right context we need to understand what is meant by this.

In the case where there is only one item to be negotiated, say the fixed-price fee for an instruction or project, the gains made by one side, ie higher (if service provider) or lower (if client) fee are offset by an equal loss on the other side – we are talking about a zero-sum or win-lose situation. This is known as 'distributive negotiation' as in effect the available value is distributed between the two parties. Not surprisingly this is usually competitive (my gain vs your loss) and does not help to build or strengthen relationships. Such situations are typical in one-off negotiations where we don't care about the relationship. It is also the type of negotiation we are most familiar with and it is not surprising that many professionals worry about negotiating with clients when they associate it with such distributive, competitive processes.

Another way to visualize this situation is to use the fixed pie analogy – we only have a fixed amount of value to split amongst us (the pie) so we are in effect fighting about the size of the slice of pie. As long as we only have one item to discuss we can only engage in distributive, ie competitive negotiation. Imagine, however, both parties working together not only to decide how to divide the pie between them but also how to make the pie bigger. If they succeed in creating a bigger pie, then more value can be shared between the two of them. An example of this could be a discussion in which one side is willing to offer additional work in return for a discount on the current project. A creative fee negotiation could include the following elements:

- fee size/discount;
- volume or likelihood of future work;
- payment terms;
- opportunities to cite the work or client as a reference;
- training;
- secondments;
- referrals;
- access to professionals or other resources;
- service-level guarantees;
- other forms of guarantees or liability cover such as indemnities.

Each of these should be discussed in detail during the information exchange phase. The sooner a negotiation can move from a simple 'trading' of concessions as described in Act 2 to a more creative style in which both sides work with each other to create a bigger pie, the more likely we will end up with a good deal for both sides. This is the true meaning of win-win, ie where both sides will be better off than the alternative. The term used for such negotiation is 'integrative' as both sides have to work with each other to find additional layers to the pie to make it better. Some commentators believe that there are several levels of 'integrative' negotiation (Thompson, 2009), so there are few limits to being creative other than the limits of our imagination. Furthermore, training in creative thinking has been shown to help individuals reach more and better integrative solutions (Ogilvie and Simms, 2009).

The biggest challenge to integrative negotiation is that most untrained negotiators tend to operate under a zero-sum or 'fixed pie' perception. This means that they worry that any gains the other side make will be at their expense, so they avoid engaging with the other side, leaving value untapped. It is important to draw them out of this one-dimensional perspective, preferably early on during the information exchange when most are still more open-minded and thinking less tactically. There are other ways to address this, for example accountability: having to explain to others why you could not find a creative solution has been shown to be effective and particularly relevant to professionals (De Dreu *et al*, 2000b).

However, even though in integrative negotiation both sides cooperate to increase the pie, at some stage the two sides will have to consider how to split the bigger pie. The challenge, and it is a major challenge, is that we have to be integrative/cooperative and distributive/competitive at the same time. The literature also refers to this duality as the value creating vs value claiming tension. This is extremely difficult but *effective negotiators do both!* Competitive and cooperative behaviours have been shown to wax and wane across the various stages of a negotiation (Adair and Brett, 2005). Effective negotiators know how to attenuate either behaviour, depending on what they are looking to accomplish at that stage of the negotiation.

There is also a secondary complication involved in this. Having established that the negotiation includes not just the headline item but several others (the more the better) there is a decision to be made on whether these items should be negotiated one by one in sequence or if they should be bundled as packages. Different negotiators will have different preferences, but as a general rule of thumb it is likely that a one-by-one approach will favour the side with the power to go for the other side's veto position. Likewise, the negotiator with the 'weaker' position is likely to be able to get a better deal by packaging and including items where the balance of power may be more in their favour. Finally, there is nothing to stop the negotiator dealing with some items on a one-by-one basis and with others as a package or several packages.

No matter where the balance of power lies or whether items are negotiated as a package or sequentially, the key objective of integrative negotiation is to generate a 'bigger pie' so that even if one had to concede a greater share of the total pie, one would still be left with a greater piece, as illustrated in Figure 12.1.

Figure 12.1   Creative negotiation

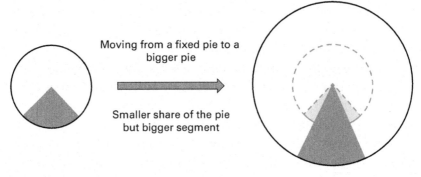

© Møller PSFG Cambridge 2017 – Ori Wiener

It is very difficult to be prescriptive on how to be creative, but there are a number of factors that are known to inhibit or promote creative negotiations. I have listed some of the more important ones below.

Barriers to creative negotiation

Fixed-pie thinking is not the only barrier to creative negotiation. It has been shown that mindset can make an important difference (Sribna, 2005). Those negotiators who have a positive mindset, thinking 'What can I gain' tend to outperform those with a negative mindset, thinking 'What is my cost' (Bazerman *et al*, 1983). Other commonly cited barriers to creative or integrative negotiation include (Thompson, 2009):

- *Preference for precedent over innovation:* this is typical when one of the negotiators is either very inexperienced or does not have authority to go beyond their brief. It can also happen with a negotiator who has been dealing with a situation for years and sees little reason for changing. The latter is likely to be less common given the general intellectual competencies of professionals, but when more experienced professionals cite precedence it may suggest that they are unfamiliar with alternative approaches and may fear the change. Exploration of potential benefits and risks will be crucial in helping these professionals jump over their own shadows in dealing with these risky ideas.

- *Adversarial vs collaborative mindset:* often found with relatively young and inexperienced or highly ambitious negotiators who see the negotiation as either a competitive sport or as an opportunity to impress colleagues with their zest, zeal or just naked aggression. Here, looking for mutual benefits and helping the other side see how a better deal would help them show their peers or managers how hot they are at bringing extra bacon home is likely to work best. The temptation in such situations is to go head to head (headbanging) with the aggressive negotiator. There may be times when it will be important to show the other side that you will not let them throw their weight around to gain their respect, but as soon as that message has been received it is important to move onto the constructive track to point at the potential benefits they can brag about back in the office.

- *Risk aversion:* this is a variant of the precedent problem, above. Here the other side is not so much worried about keeping to precedent as it is about taking positive decisions that could lead them into trouble later. Again, exploration of their fears and worries, and patient discussions on how these risks could best be managed, are likely to lead to the best outcome.

- *Tight time pressures:* many of the approaches above require time to be implemented. Artificial or real tight deadlines tend not to help creative thinking, which is often about working with fragments of ideas or thoughts, bringing these out in full and then discussing alternatives for dealing with them in a cooperative atmosphere. Even when there are no tight deadlines, it is likely that a negotiation will have to meet some sort of timeline; good negotiators know this and therefore try not to get stuck in parts of a negotiation that take up time but do not contribute to a better understanding of a situation or the client's needs and interests. There is a fine balance to be struck between having a focused negotiation and exploring diverse needs, restrictions and ideas.

Although it is difficult to tell people how to be creative it is often helpful to remind them what to be creative about. The ultimate aim of a fee negotiation is to have agreement on specific elements and it is worth remembering that getting there might mean being creative.

Sources of creativity

As outlined elsewhere, good negotiators find opportunities in many different situations. Some of the more common ones include the following.

Exploiting differences

For example, exploiting differences in:

- valuations of assets, liabilities, services or other negotiation issues: this is the classic basis for variable values;
- expectations regarding uncertain events: here is where conditional arrangements can work well;
- risk attitude: again an area where conditional arrangements work well;
- time preferences;
- capabilities.

Creative negotiators frequently report seeing differences as opportunities rather than as barriers.

Reformulating or unlinking

This means finding ways to redefine or split one issue into a number of components that can be traded off against others. This helps add more layers to the pie. For example, getting paid a certain amount can be split into sub-issues such as:

- depending on outcome (success, failure);
- depending on reaching milestones;
- a number of fixed and variable components;
- timing (terms of payment);
- dependent on completion of certain types of work;
- location and currency, etc.

Research has started to identify some of the key ingredients that will promote creativity in negotiations (De Dreu and Carnevale, 2003; De Dreu *et al*, 2000a, 2006). Ideally both sides will:

- have an optimistic, collaborative, risk-tolerant mindset;
- avoid taking setbacks personally;
- be aware of and seek the benefits of creativity;
- undertake extensive planning and preparation, understanding the issues and interests of all sides;
- seek to exploit differences rather than avoid or minimize them;

- exchange information, seeking to understand interests, asking questions;
- be able to communicate ideas effectively, focusing on benefits for each side;
- be willing to invest in personal relationships, build trust;
- constantly seek opportunities to improve the outcome; and
- take a long-term optimization rather than short-term maximization approach.

Anything that can be done ahead or during the negotiation to instil or strengthen these attributes will not only help build a solid and robust relationship but is also likely to result in a more constructive negotiation and better outcome. If you find that the other side is not willing or able to adopt most of the attributes listed above it will be far more difficult to be creative. You may also find yourself dealing with a shark rather than a dolphin.

Methods and techniques to facilitate creativity

There is a broad range of strategies available to support creative negotiations (Thompson, 2009). I have outlined some of the more relevant or applicable methods and techniques for PSFs below. Each may be of use at one or several points of a negotiation, depending on the dynamics of each negotiation:

- *Planning.* It cannot be overstated how great a contribution planning will make to a positive negotiation outcome. This is especially important in the early phases of the negotiation to ensure all options are considered and potential surprises are avoided.

- *Brainstorming.* This form of collective idea generation is particularly good in demonstrating that both sides are working together to achieve a common goal. Remember not to engage in evaluation during the idea generation stage so as not to discourage truly 'out of the box' thinking. Start with the concept that all ideas are good initially, in fact the more the better! Filtering and ranking should only be done at the second stage. This technique can be applied more than once but needs to be time managed carefully.

- *Reshaping a deal.* It is often illustrative to consider the impact and implications of the deal under negotiation being made bigger or smaller.

Likewise are there any ways to make it look different? What are the key assumptions that are brought to the table? Can they be changed? What are the sources of the problems, what could avoid this situation from recurring, what could make it even more profitable?

- *Rephrasing.* Glass is half full not half empty – how fixed are certain perspectives or assumptions? What is particularly good or bad about the current situation? What could be really different?

- *Unlinking, reformulating.* Often certain issues are linked or brought to the table as a package. Can these links be unravelled? Does data gathering have to be linked to analysis? Does due diligence or document review have to be conducted by the same adviser providing structuring advice?

- *Using variable value.* Exploit differences in value of an issue to each side (see Chapter 10).

- *Take it upstairs.* Can more senior management provide new perspectives? This can be very tricky to get agreed as it could be seen to undermine the negotiation position of the lead negotiator. Sometimes, however, a fee negotiation may well be better positioned as part of an overall relationship or strategic resourcing discussion with a department head or the board.

- *Take it downstairs.* Set up a joint working committee or consult with those at the cutting edge as to how the issues could best be tackled.

- *Wise counsel.* Bring someone from outside, respected by both.

- *Asking 'what if' or 'open' questions (Kipling method).* Explore options, ideas without making them appear as demands. Explore their reasons for likes and dislikes with 'What are the reasons for...', 'What do you like/dislike about...', 'When would you...', etc. Avoid 'why' as this can put a defensive spin on the question (see Chapter 9).

- *Sleeping on it.* Avoid rushing into a final decision. Sometimes having some extra time to mull things over can produce valuable ideas.

- *Taking the other side's perspective.* This technique is particularly valuable as it is surprisingly effective in generating insights and potential ideas for a creative and integrative approach (Diamond, 2010; Thompson, 2009). It is my personal favourite.

One of the most creative fee management processes I have witnessed was in relation to a major privatization. The selection of the privatization adviser was being conducted under a rigorous procurement-led process. The request for proposals stipulated in great detail the information required, which essentially asked competing banks to provide their track record, an indication of the privatization process proposed and their fee. In addition, any questions raised by one of the shortlisted bidders would, together with the answers, be circulated to all other bidders. The submissions would be graded according to a pre-set and transparent scoring system that was notified to the bidders in advance.

At first sight it appeared as if the process would be determined purely on price as all the competing banks were roughly equally well experienced and as the process for a privatization was generally well known. At the time the perceived wisdom was that this privatization would most likely be achieved through a number of trade sales. It was thought that the banks would be bidding a percentage of the sale value and that this would be in the region of several million US dollars.

One of the banks, however, having spent considerable time analysing the process, the scoring system and the broader objectives of the government sponsoring the privatization, came up with a different conclusion. It thought (correctly as it turned out) that the selection process would generate bids that were similarly scored for track record and proposed process. The bank felt that the government in question would be equally open to alternative privatization methods such as stock listings as this would also promote the country's emerging stock market.

The bank therefore took the decision to bid on the basis of the privatization mandate being purely an advisory one, ie there would be no transaction. Having checked that winning the advisory mandate would not rule out the bank from winning any subsequent transactions such as the lead role in an initial public offer (IPO), the bank bid on the basis of a low, monthly fee (as permitted by the rules of the tender).

As a result the bank won the initial mandate, which ended up generating several million US dollars as the advisory project took over 24 months to complete. The advisory mandate furthermore allowed the bank to gain such knowledge of the privatization process and the privatized assets that it also won the subsequent disposal mandates. This ended up netting the bank significantly higher fees than were originally thought to be available in the privatization. In the process the privatizing government ended up with a better privatization process, greater political acceptance of the privatization (public stock ownership) and the benefits accruing to the local stock market from greater investment from international institutions.

The creative approach here was to reframe the apparent transaction being put up for bid, to break the privatization into several pieces and to accept certain risks such as the possibility of the privatization being cancelled or the rules being changed to prevent the government adviser competing for the lead follow on roles. These risks were either accepted or managed during the life of the project.

This was also an example of a 'fee negotiation' process taking place over several stages, preliminary information gathering, understanding the interests of the client, and going for the follow-up transactions. Although there was relatively little fee negotiation in the conventional sense of bargaining going on during the initial RFP, the whole privatization was an example of a highly sophisticated approach to fee management.

Creative fee negotiation is in my view the ultimate fee negotiation skill and requires a long-term mindset and seeking to create value for both sides. The ability by some negotiators to apply more creativity in a negotiation is in part determined by the personal styles of the negotiating parties. The next chapter will explore the impact of individual styles and how differences in style can best be applied in a negotiation.

Negotiating with style

13

Negotiation, regardless of the context or issues involved, is fundamentally about human interaction. (DEEPAK MALHOTRA)

As Malhotra (2016) observes, all negotiations are influenced by the behaviour of the people conducting the negotiation. Personal characteristics such as preferences, dislikes, experiences and personalities all influence these behaviours. People in general tend to display consistent patterns of behaviours (even inconsistency is a form of consistency in this case) which are referred to as styles.

The interaction between the styles of those involved in a negotiation shape the process and outcomes of these negotiations. As every individual is different, the nature of the interaction between two or more negotiators will be unique. This is why the outcome of most negotiations cannot be predicted on the basis of quantitative variables such as vetoes, targets and available concessions alone. This point was raised by one of the earliest modern works on negotiation, *A Behavioural Theory of Labour Negotiations: An analysis of a social interaction system* (Walton and McKersie, 1965). The authors showed how influencing, or 'Attitudinal Structuring' as the authors referred to this, is central to the negotiation process. It is the interplay between 'objective negotiation issues' and 'subjective individual variables' and the resulting myriad of possible outcomes that make negotiations so fascinating to observe and so challenging for most professionals to conduct.

Experienced negotiators understand how individuals and their different negotiation styles affect behaviours and negotiation outcomes. Good negotiators are aware of their own negotiating style and can identify the styles of their counterparts. Outstanding negotiators know how to capitalize on the strengths and how to mitigate the weaknesses associated with their personal style and that of their team members. Just as importantly, they can also adapt their approach or select tactics in light of their counterpart's style and associated strengths, weaknesses or preferences.

There are three reasons why 'negotiating with style' is part of a high-performing negotiator's repertoire. The first is that if a negotiator is comfortable with and understands the strengths and weaknesses of their personal style, they are more likely to be confident in what they are doing and are more likely to project authority and credibility.

The second is that familiarity with the styles and associated character-istics of their counterpart will allow a negotiator to identify approaches or techniques that are best suited to work with that individual or group of individuals. This of course does presuppose that a negotiator has sufficient 'flex' to be able to adapt to the style of their counterpart.

The third reason why an understanding of and ability to utilize negotia-tion style is important is that negotiators are often part of a negotiating team. Understanding the styles of team members and how best to capitalize on different strengths, compensate for weaknesses and deal with different preferences will determine the difference between effective or ineffective negotiation teams.

To fully understand the impact of style one has to understand the impor-tance of process on a negotiation.

The importance of process

The outcome of just about every negotiation is significantly influenced by the overall process of the negotiation. This in turn is made up of a number of key sub-processes. As highlighted in Chapters 7 and 8, the depth and quality of preparation has a significant impact on subsequent negotiation performance. Key processes therefore do not just start at 'the table' but way before, and they matter throughout the negotiation. The way in which social warm up and information exchange (Chapter 9) are driven will have a direct bearing on outcome, as will the manner in which an opening posi-tion is delivered, 'flinched at' or the way in which concessions are exchanged (Chapter 10). All of these processes are strongly influenced by the behav-ioural styles of the individuals involved on both sides.

The sequence, advocated in Chapter 9, of social warm up, followed by information exchange and only then delivery of an opening position, is an example of how process influences outcome. In a negotiation conducted along this sequence, most negotiators will find the information exchange easier and more productive. The social warm up helps to settle down both parties and to build rapport between them. During this step of the process, style differences need to be recognized and accounted for in terms of the time and approach taken to the social warm up. Trust is built further when both sides are open and freely exchange relevant information regarding their objectives, interests, constraints or any other relevant information. By the time an opening position is delivered and responded to, both sides feel comfortable with the gap and can proceed to look for trades, exchanging concessions to reach agreement.

If, on the other hand, a negotiation is opened immediately after the most minimal and token form of social interaction (the social warm up is rarely practised well under these circumstances), with a strong opening position and then followed by information exchange, the negotiation will proceed along a very different route. Such negotiations tend to be characterized by greater degrees of posturing and distrust. Experienced negotiators know that once an opening position has been tabled, both parties become more tactical and defensive and that this influences the flow of the negotiation.

Another example of how process influences outcome is the way in which the information exchange stage proceeds. When both sides exchange information in a relatively even and reciprocal manner there is typically a building of trust. This is not to say that each side has to disclose everything or to answer all questions. Rather, each side is seen to be willing to contribute to a 'good' and 'fair' outcome by actively engaging in a two-way flow of information.

Compare this to a situation in which one or both parties do not share information or in which the information has to be dragged out of them. Such behaviour inevitably reduces the amount of trust between the parties as well as limiting information that may help create a more value generating agreement. Even if one party is forthcoming with information – it will soon limit this, if sufficiently experienced, so as not to give away too much, without getting anything in return. Such posturing is either the result of one or both sides wanting to play 'hard ball' or one or both negotiators not understanding the potential value from a trusted relationship and integrative negotiation – which can only be conducted when information is made available.

Process, however, can work both ways. If one of the negotiation parties is defensive and acting tactically, it may become more constructive when the other side establishes clear criteria for responding to information requests, ie makes it clear that an agreement will only be possible when both sides contribute to the information exchange. In so doing the parties establish mutual respect, which may not be the same as trust, but at least helps to get to a more constructive outcome.

Broadly speaking, most negotiators respond positively if they feel that a negotiation is proceeding in a fair, constructive and appropriate manner. What negotiators consider fair, constructive and appropriate is determined to a large part by their negotiating style, their behavioural style and their cultural norms. See Chapter 14 for more on the impact of culture.

Style, personality and behaviour

One of the biggest challenges for a negotiator is to predict the most likely behaviour of their counterparties during the negotiation. In theory, the better the predictive skills of a negotiator, the more likely that negotiator will be able to apply approaches or tactics that will obtain a better deal.

Many factors influence an individual's behaviour. The most important are thought to be their personality, personal circumstances and the past and present social and physical environment. Whereas we may be able to determine objectively some of these factors such as environment, personality is actually something that is very difficult to determine, even by experts.

Personality is thought to be determined by upbringing, genetics, experience and several other factors and there are many different methodologies and diagnostic tools to determine a person's 'personality'. Some of the most commonly known tools include Rorschach Inkblot test, Minnesota Multiphasic Personality Inventory (MMPI), Myers–Briggs Type Indicator (MBTI), DiSC, NEOPersonality Inventory and many others. The Five Factor Model (FFM) of personality is the most well established and is determined using five dimensions: Openness, Conscientiousness, Extroversion, Agreeableness and Neuroticism. On the other hand, MBTI, one of the most commonly used personality profile tools in the workplace, only uses a type model of personality that has four dimensions.

The biggest challenge with all of these personality assessment tools is that it takes extensive testing or responding to detailed surveys to be able to reach a reasonably accurate conclusion. Also, those interpreting the results of these tests or questionnaires need to be qualified in the use of psychological diagnostic tools.

Although negotiators may be willing to undergo psychological tests of this nature to reach a better understanding of their own personality, they will almost never have access to an accurate psychological profile of their negotiation counterparties.

Personality predicts behaviour, so a more pragmatic approach to predicting likely behaviour is to review the behaviours seen to date. It turns out that people tend to display consistent patterns of behaviours, also referred to as style. There are many models that have categorized these. The great advantage of using style models is that, by definition, the focus is on something observable – behaviours. The other great advantage is that behavioural questionnaires tend to be easier to administer and can be applied to the behaviours of third parties. You simply have to observe someone to be able to start to draw some conclusions about their likely style. Naturally, the longer and more varied the observation, the more likely it will be accurate.

An analogy I have found helpful in distinguishing between personality, style and behaviour is to draw a comparison to a pie or cake. We can only see the external features of the cake (the equivalent of style) and can draw certain conclusions as to what type of cake it is. The personality equivalent would be the ingredients of the cake, which we could only determine if we were to cut it open. The behaviour equivalent would be the taste and texture when we are eating the piece of cake or pie (and our taste buds are interacting with the cake).

A number of style-based frameworks are available in connection with negotiation behaviours; I have found the ones below most helpful.

The origin of style models

A large number of personal styles models have been formulated over the years. Rubin and Brown (1975) were among the first in the negotiation area to develop such a framework in the early 1970s. They identified two variables as determinants of personality on negotiations. The first was interpersonal orientation (IO), ie how socially adept/aware a negotiator is. A negotiator with a high interpersonal orientation would be influenced by the nature of the relationship with their counterpart; a low interpersonal orientation would mean that a negotiator would not be influenced by a relationship with their counterparts. The second variant was motivational orientation (MO), ie how competitive or co-operative a negotiator is.

As a result, they identified four styles: Competitor, Avoider, Accommodator and Collaborator. They also observed that none of these styles was better than any other but simply different and that the success or failure of a negotiation style was dependent on the specific negotiation situation.

The work presented by Rubin and Brown also reviewed the link between a propensity to be high or low in terms of IO or MO and a broad range of social background factors such as gender, culture, intelligence or even parental occupation.

Thomas Kilmann Conflict Mode Instrument

Two years after Rubin and Brown's publication, Thomas and Kilmann published a similar framework in 1977. This framework (often referred to as the TK model) was designed to help individuals identify how the importance of the relationship and the importance of the negotiation substance interact and how this influenced the actions taken by the negotiating parties. They reached a similar insight to Rubin and Brown, ie that relationships impact on decision making and hence behaviours.

This framework's two variables were labelled cooperation and assertiveness and postulated five types of behaviours: Collaboration (when both variables are high), Compete (high assertiveness, low co-operation), Avoid (both low), Accommodate (low assertiveness, high co-operation), and Compromise (both variables intermediate). The model provides a helpful perspective on the likely behaviour of negotiators, once their propensity (or instructions) for each of the two variables is known.

Although the model is helpful in understanding the likely behaviour of unsophisticated negotiators it does not provide any insights as to how to encourage the other side to become more co-operative. Experienced or trained negotiators may also use a range of approaches depending on the particular issue being negotiated or on the phase of the negotiation.

The model also breaks down when one or both parties of the negotiation are hostile, ie when the behaviours seen include blocking, sabotage or exclusion. These negotiation situations tend to occur when relationships have broken down or when things are taken 'personally'. This has led to an 'extended TK model' known as the BT Extension to the TK model, developed by Baumoel and Trippe in 2015.

Table 13.1   Thomas Kilmann Conflict Modes

		Assertiveness	
		High	Low
Cooperativeness	High	Collaboration	Accommodate
		Compromise	
	Low	Compete	Avoid

BT Extension to TK Model

This model substitutes the TK variables of assertiveness vs cooperativeness with substance vs relationship (something done by other researchers (Savage, *et al*, 1989)) and considers the situation when the relationship (cooperation) is negative. Compete, Collaboration, Avoidance, Accommodation and Compromise are distributed as in the TK model, eg High Relationship/High Substance = Collaboration; Low Relationship/ Low Substance = Delay (Avoid).

Where the relationship has gone into negative territory, Baumoel and Trippe postulate the following:

High Substance/High Adversarial Relationship = Sabotage, ie actively undermining;

Low Substance/High Adversarial Relationship = Blocking, ie actively avoiding;

Medium Substance/Medium Adversarial Relationship = Excluding, ie actively trying to keep the other party out of a decision-making process.

Although this extension is useful in some circumstances it still suffers from the shortfalls of the TK model in that it does not help identify actions that can be taken to mitigate the behaviours of one or both of the negotiating parties. It also tends to be of limited value for fee negotiations that presuppose a relationship.

Qualitative Style Model

A typical qualitative negotiation style model is the one developed by Professor Andrew Gottschalk of London Business School, working with experienced business negotiators in the late 1960s and early 1970s. His model included four negotiation styles: Warm, Tough, Numbers and Dealers (Gottschalk, 2008).

The four styles are also described in terms of 'habit' and 'managed' zones. Habit zones are difficult to change and require long-term effort. Managed zones can be adapted faster through practice and training. In practice I find that most professionals do not have the time or motivation to change their styles but can flex at the edges.

The framework is helpful in that, through a few observations, it is possible to determine the likely style of one's counterpart. With this it is possible to adapt approaches more suitable for the counterpart. Warms emphasize

Table 13.2 Negotiation styles

Style	Potential strengths	Potential weaknesses
Warm	Friendly, good at personal relations, interested in the other side's point of view, constructive, informative	Soft touch, avoids conflict or disagreement, gullible, can't say no
Tough	Determined, decisive, competitive, clear grasp of their own position, hard working	Aggressive, domineering, impulsive, impatient
Numbers	Logical, analytical, well prepared, confident in own skills	Uncomfortable with people, feelings and emotions, bogged down in the detail
Dealers	Creative, flexible, charming, fluent, quick thinking	Maybe tricky, 'too clever by half', believes one thing today, another tomorrow, and 'the rules' don't apply

relationships – hence trust building will work with them better than, say, exchanging facts and figures but, as a warm negotiator is likely to use personal arguments ('you've got to help me with this problem') it is probably better to keep a certain distance to a warm counterpart. Taking them out to drinks may well help a negotiation.

Negotiating with a numbers style on the other hand may be best supported by providing details and maybe even a spreadsheet. They are more likely to respond to factual arguments and data than to a glass of beer or wine after hours or during a working lunch.

Most individuals we work with fear a tough, inflexible negotiator as they are worried about being steamrollered into an agreement not to their liking. The best approach to dealing with a tough is to show them the 'value' they would lose if they did not want to consider alternatives to their proposal.

Using a four style model such as the one illustrated above (Table 13.2) can be very helpful. Professionals working with me find these easy to identify for themselves and their counterparties. This helps to spot potential weaknesses in one's own negotiation approaches as well as to anticipate the actions of the other side.

It has to be remembered, however, that these styles are only summary descriptions for a series of complex behaviours and that most negotiators will display a mixture of the behaviours described, depending on the circumstances. Trained negotiators will also have a broader repertoire of behaviours and will be able to deploy them flexibly.

The other drawback of frameworks with 'memorable' tags is that often the tags are associative. Many professionals, for example, describe themselves as 'warm' when in fact they are not. This is because they want to think of themselves as warm people (which they may well be). There is a confusion between personality or type and negotiation style and it is difficult to remember this. We also find that when others' style is described, women tend to be categorized disproportionally as either warm or tough. Although we are not sure about the reasons for this, there is a suspicion that those doing the assessment are influenced by gender and that women are judged to be 'tough' when the same behaviours by men would be judged to be numbers or dealer (see Chapter 14 for a discussion on the impact of gender and role congruity).

Alternative style models

The seminal work by Rubin and Brown was, for a long time, the source for most negotiation style models. A new inspiration for style models has come from advances in neurosciences. In large part due to the development of sophisticated magnetic resonance imaging technology, researchers have formulated new behavioural models. One example is the **four colour model** by Hazeldine (2014). This model is based on the interactions between a person's neural networks and neurotransmitters. Based on a person's genetic make-up and personal development, each person will display different behavioural preferences.

TRACOM SOCIAL STYLE® Model

A useful styles model is the social style and versatility model published by the TRACOM Group. This model has its origins in work conducted in the 1960s, which looked at the accuracy by which people could describe the behaviour of others. The work identified two, independent dimensions of behaviour: 'Assertiveness' and 'Responsiveness'.

Assertiveness described behaviour ranging from 'asking' to 'telling' and indicated how forcefully an individual presented themselves when interacting with others. Those on the 'ask' side of the spectrum behaved differently to those on the 'tell' side and the typical behaviours for either could be identified easily (see Figure 13.1 and Table 13.3).

Responsiveness behaviour ranged from 'controlling' to 'emoting' in terms of how much an individual displayed their emotions. Again, each end of the spectrum is associated with different, easily identifiable behaviours.

The research established that the two dimensions are independent of each other, ie there is no correlation between the two. On the basis of these two dimensions a framework was formulated identifying four social styles: Analytical, Driving, Expressive and Amiable. Each is associated with typical behaviours, orientations and associated weaknesses. Based on these, recommendations can be made on how to compensate for these weaknesses and how to engage with someone depending on their style. As in the work by Rubin and Brown, there is no 'best' style. Success is distributed across all styles and is more the result of how a person chooses to use their style rather than their style itself.

As with several other frameworks, style can be identified relatively easily and accurately by individuals with no special training in the use of psychological diagnostic tools. All that is needed is a relatively simple (but highly sophisticated) questionnaire. Once a personal style or the style of a negotiation counterparty has been identified it becomes easier to anticipate which approaches will be more or less likely to have the desired outcomes and how best to engage with someone. When the counterparty's social style is determined, it gives insight into how that person prefers to be approached, use their time and make their decisions. Knowing these elements enhances the likelihood of being able to engage in a productive negotiation.

Of particular relevance to negotiation is further work by Merrill and Reid (1984) who were able to identify a fifth dimension, 'Versatility', as the link between the four styles and success, defined as interpersonal effectiveness. This is directly relevant for negotiators as the most effective negotiators display a high degree of personal flexibility. They are able to adapt their approach and behaviour to their counterpart, looking for the most effective ways of getting the best deal agreed.

Merrill and Reid were able to demonstrate that Versatility was driven by four key contributors:

- **Image**: which includes attention to appearance and is particularly important early in a relationship.

- **Presentation**: defined as effective communication. This includes how well ideas are organized and the use of appropriate language.

- **Competence**: defined not as technical know-how, IQ and education but by the extent to which others see individuals deliver on promises. Key components are: Perseverance, Creativity, Flexibility, Timeliness, Optimism and Conscientiousness.

Figure 13.1 SOCIAL STYLE® Model

Verbal and non-verbal behaviour anchors

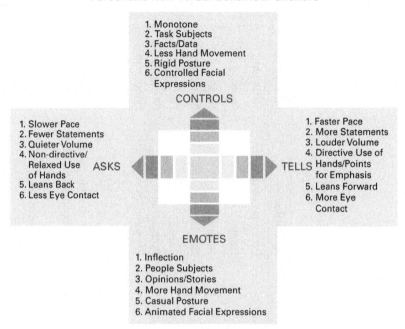

CONTROLS

1. Monotone
2. Task Subjects
3. Facts/Data
4. Less Hand Movement
5. Rigid Posture
6. Controlled Facial Expressions

ASKS

1. Slower Pace
2. Fewer Statements
3. Quieter Volume
4. Non-directive/Relaxed Use of Hands
5. Leans Back
6. Less Eye Contact

TELLS

1. Faster Pace
2. More Statements
3. Louder Volume
4. Directive Use of Hands/Points for Emphasis
5. Leans Forward
6. More Eye Contact

EMOTES

1. Inflection
2. People Subjects
3. Opinions/Stories
4. More Hand Movement
5. Casual Posture
6. Animated Facial Expressions

Typical descriptors of each style position

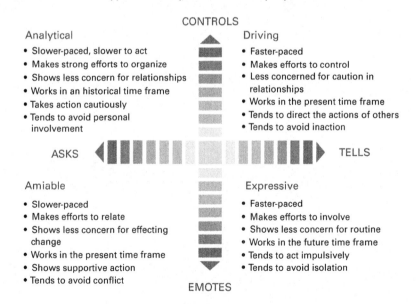

CONTROLS

Analytical
- Slower-paced, slower to act
- Makes strong efforts to organize
- Shows less concern for relationships
- Works in an historical time frame
- Takes action cautiously
- Tends to avoid personal involvement

Driving
- Faster-paced
- Makes efforts to control
- Less concerned for caution in relationships
- Works in the present time frame
- Tends to direct the actions of others
- Tends to avoid inaction

ASKS   TELLS

Amiable
- Slower-paced
- Makes efforts to relate
- Shows less concern for effecting change
- Works in the present time frame
- Shows supportive action
- Tends to avoid conflict

Expressive
- Faster-paced
- Makes efforts to involve
- Shows less concern for routine
- Works in the future time frame
- Tends to act impulsively
- Tends to avoid isolation

EMOTES

NOTE SOCIAL STYLE® is a registered trademark and the SOCIAL STYLE Model™ is a trademark of the TRACOM Group; they are used with permission.

Table 13.3 Outline summary of TRACOM SOCIAL STYLES®

	Driving	Expressive	Amiable	Analytical
Needs	Results	Personal approval	Personal security	To be right
Orientation	Action	Spontaneity	Relationships	Thinking
Potential weakness (overuse)	Autocratic	Attack	Acquiesce (appear to give in)	Avoid (Withdraw)
General appearance	Focused Bold Controlling	Energetic Attention seeking Creative	Casual Approachable Conforming	Formal Conservative Structured
Pace	Brisk Impatient, quick to decide Disciplined use of time Risk taking	Fast paced Talkative Impatient, quick to decide Undisciplined use of time Risk taking	Unhurried Pleasant Casual, slow to decide Undisciplined use of time Minimizes risk	Reserved Cautious Distant at times Slow to decide Disciplined use of time Minimizes risk

Gestures	Hand movements to emphasize Pointed gestures Facially controlled	Sweeping, expansive movements Facially expressive	Limited gesticulation Avoids large, sweeping movements	Little gesticulation Minimal facial expression Keeps distance
Communication style	Outspoken Direct Confrontational Blunt	Engaging Persuasive Emotional Easily shifts focus	Open Accommodating Polite Pliable	Imposes standards Detail focused Formal Impersonal or detached
Listening style	Interrupts Focused on highlights Examines critical details Impatient Sometimes superficial	Overly talkative Seeks dialogue, exchange of views Focused on big picture, readily changes topic Impatient	Considerate Patient Needs time to process Empathetic Focused on people Avoids disagreements	Listens for data and logic Focused Perfectionist Displays little emotion

SOURCE Based on Mulqueen and Collins (2014)

- **Feedback**: the ability to give clear and accurate verbal and non-verbal feedback to promote mutual understanding and to build mutually productive relationships. It is measured by active listening, empathy and interpersonal effectiveness.

Competence and Feedback were shown to be the two most important variables, but that image had the fastest impact in the short run. The reason for this is that most individuals make very quick, early judgements, based on what they see. In the medium to long run, however, their judgement will be impacted by the quality of work they see, the manner it is delivered and by the way in which understanding of the other side is reflected and acted upon.

I personally like working with the TRACOM model because of its emphasis on Versatility as a key factor for negotiation success. Another bonus of the TRACOM model is that the company has questionnaires and databases that reflect national as well as functional differences. This can help when having to negotiate across geographic or functional cultures.

For further details, see www.tracomcorp.com.

Other benefits of using style models

As already alluded to above, although the primary benefits of considering style arise from a better understanding of one's personal strengths and weaknesses as well as those of one's counterpart, an important secondary benefit is the ability to assemble teams with complementary styles.

I have often noticed that teams composed of two or more negotiators with the same style tend to become more extreme in their collective style, ie the team members tend to reinforce each other in their behaviours. Although this can make for more harmonious co-operation there is a significant danger in this. Such teams can easily fail to engage with their counterparts and are likely to miss out on the best deals. This is similar to, but not the same as, the phenomenon known as 'group think', in which a group that is very close may start to see the world in a very specific way and will lose touch with 'reality'.

Where possible, it is almost always better to assemble teams in which members, or at least the most senior members, have different styles. This will allow team members to complement each other, rather than potentiate, as in the single-style team. On the assumption that these team members will collaborate – an assumption that may not always hold true – such heterogeneous teams will very likely outperform their more homogeneous counterparts. This is an important reason why good negotiation training programmes include elements that focus on style and the benefits of versatility.

As mentioned in Chapter 15 on tactics, paying attention to styles and their application to potential tactics is no substitute to good preparation and information gathering. Outstanding negotiators know this and will include collecting information on their counterpart's style in their preparations. They will also consistently double check their assessment regarding style and will look for signs of flexibility.

The role of emotions in negotiation

In *Getting To Yes* (Fisher *et al*, 2011) two key approaches were proposed as part of 'Principled Negotiations': to separate the people from the issues and to establish objective criteria on which a negotiation should be based. The aim is to reach 'fair and wise' outcomes, ie outcomes that can objectively be judged as 'good'. Many interpret this to mean that emotions have no part to play in well-conducted negotiations.

This could not be further from the truth. In *Getting To Yes*, the authors highlight the potential impact of emotions on a negotiation and the negotiators. They observe that 'feelings may be more important than talk'. A large body or research now supports this empirically (Fulmer and Barry, 2004; Barry *et al*, 2006).

It has long been known that decisions are affected by emotions. Who has not regretted a decision taken in anger or when overly euphoric? The quality of preparation can be significantly affected by a negotiator's emotional state. Many of the inner saboteurs listed in Chapter 7, for example, are based on emotions.

Research has shown that not only is decision making affected by emotions but emotions are in fact essential to the decision-making process. Early evidence for this came from work with brain-damaged patients where the damage was located only in those parts of the brain involved with emotions. Many of these patients were incapable of taking decisions despite retaining their full analytical faculties. Some of these patients simply could not decide what to do or what was better, when given simple choices. It turns out that even basic concepts such as 'good/bad' or 'better/worse' had an emotional component. After all – everyone likes 'good' and dislikes 'bad'.

Experienced negotiators know that if they help their counterparts feel 'good' about an agreement or concessions to be traded they are more likely to achieve better outcomes. Alternatively, if the other party does not feel good about an agreement they will often look for an excuse or reason to renege or cheat on the agreement. Experienced negotiators know that a negotiated agreement is only any good if both sides keep to their part of the bargain (assuming nothing material has changed). So they need to understand and work with the emotions of the other side.

Negotiators need to develop an awareness of their own emotional state during the preparations and the conduct of a negotiation to handle the stress associated with difficult negotiations. One of the symptoms and causes of certain mental illnesses is an inability to acknowledge or experience emotions. Negotiators intending to retain their sanity cannot ignore their emotions, especially any that emerge during the course of a negotiation. The tougher or more important the negotiation, the higher the likelihood for stress and hence for strong emotional pressure to emerge. These emotions must not be allowed to run their course unchecked. Research (Pulido-Martos *et al*, 2013) has shown that raised levels of emotional regulation (also referred to as emotional repair) will contribute to higher effectiveness in negotiations. Experienced negotiators recognize their emotional states and know how to avoid decisions and the negotiation process becoming unduly influenced by these.

Emotions, used appropriately, can be a powerful influencing or even manipulative tool. My colleagues and I regularly observe that some negotiators are extremely good at extracting amazing concessions from their counterparts by working at the emotional level. These negotiators know exactly when to get personal. They know exactly when to cajole, plead or use 'guilt'. Often their counterparts do not even realize how much emotional pressure these negotiators exert on them because it is applied so skilfully. Emotional negotiators can be highly charming and appear to have nothing but warm feelings for their negotiation counterparts. Such emotional negotiators are often far more difficult opponents to manage than the archetypical 'hardball' negotiator that most of our negotiation workshop attendees tend to fear. Often they are the most dangerous to underestimate.

When good negotiators feel emotional during a negotiation or whilst preparing they will look into the causes for this. They will assess if they have been triggered to feel good or bad and if so by what. They also ask themselves how the other side can be made to feel good about the particular conces-sion under discussion. They can also apply the SOCIAL STYLE® Model to determine what underlying needs might be influencing the emotions and behaviour of their counterparts so that tension is kept in a productive range.

Experienced negotiators know how to use emotions and styles as a complementary tool for managing a negotiation. They also know that these are no substitute for rational thinking and good preparations. What is considered rational and appropriate, however, is influenced significantly by a negotiator's background, culture and gender. The next chapter will set out some of the biggest issues associated with cultural and gender differences and how to navigate around some of the more common obstacles associated with these.

The impact of culture and gender

14

Culture is the way we do things around here. (DAVID BRIGHT AND BILL PARKIN)

I failed as a negotiator because I gave up early. (JENNIFER LAWRENCE ON WHY SHE ENDED UP BEING PAID LESS THAN MALE COLLEAGUES)

In business, you don't get what you deserve; you get what you negotiate. (ANONYMOUS)

After personality and style, culture and gender are generally considered to be the next most powerful influencing drivers of behaviour. Culture is acknowledged to exert a strong influence on how people think, communicate and behave and consequently how they negotiate or respond to counterparties' negotiation behaviour. There are plenty of anecdotes where the poor outcome of a negotiation is attributed to cultural or gender differences. Yet, when reviewing many of these anecdotes it becomes clear that the problems lay not so much with the differences in cultures as much as in the negotiators' expectations and their inability to communicate appropriately with their counterparts.

Good negotiators will always seek to build a direct, personal relationship with their counterpart and will not allow personal, cultural or gender differences to get in the way of these. Understanding the impact of culture and gender, on the other hand, can, if appropriately used, help adapt to the counterparty's expectations and help avoid negative surprises, especially at the early, highly sensitive phases of a negotiation, when relationship building can easily become derailed.

When I am consulted with cross-cultural negotiation challenges, I advise my clients to try to identify their counterpart's most likely and 'relevant cultures'. Relevant culture could be geographic or ethnic, or it could be related to their specific function such as procurement or legal or finance. I refer to cultures in the plural as many individuals will have been exposed to more than one culture (ethnic, organizational or functional) during their lives. I then advise my client to use these cultures as a very crude starting point from which to draw some 'working hypotheses' as to what their counterparts might or might not be thinking, what their motivators or drivers might be and how best to engage with them. I consider the 'working hypothesis' caveat as really critical to make sure that whatever assumptions are made are thoroughly tested and verified.

How understanding culture can help

It is actually surprisingly difficult to define in simple words how culture affects people. A good definition is given by Sarkar (2010), who describes the impact of culture as '... directs the attention of the negotiator to the issues that are more important and influences the negotiators' interests and priorities. Cultural norms define the behaviours that are appropriate and inappropriate.'

Research (Adair *et al*, 2004) has shown, for example, that when working with representatives from six specific cultures, an understanding of an individual's cultural background made it possible to improve information exchange and deal with unusual power strategies. Other research (Adair and Brett, 2005) was able to demonstrate that the pattern of changes between cooperative and competitive behaviours across four distinct negotiation stages (relational positioning, identifying the problem, generating solutions, reaching agreement) differed consistently across cultures. The work showed that knowledge of cultural differences could be particularly helpful at the relational positioning and problem identification stages.

Trying to define 'culture', however, is a bit like trying to define an elephant: difficult to do but you know it when you see it. Definitions of culture are as numerous and often as vague as definitions of negotiation itself (Salacuse, 1999). There are broad differences of opinion about what culture includes or how it affects individuals. Broadly speaking it appears to be the set of values, norms, attitudes or expectations that influence judgments and determine behaviours of what is appropriate or fair. Culture can be based on a national, ethnic or even organizational or functional grouping. Culture tends to be socially transmitted rather than biologically inherited, ie culture affects 'learned behaviours'. This means that the impact of culture can be identified and that one can 'learn' to operate within a culture, usually by observing individuals and groups.

To best identify the relevant cross-cultural issues, it is helpful to look at four key elements (values, norms, attitudes, behaviours) as layers of an onion, with values at the centre, followed by norms, attitudes and at the outermost (visible) layer, behaviours. By observing a counterparty's behaviours one can draw insights into their attitudes and from there explore norms and values. When one is able to do so, one can then better engage with the other side to find common points and move to a joint problem-solving approach, which is more likely to be value creating and lead to a positive negotiation outcome.

As illustrated in other chapters of this book, to be fully effective a negotiator has to be able to understand their counterpart's perspective on the negotiation and associated issues. This understanding has to include drivers such as values, norms and attitudes. Where we share similar 'cultural' backgrounds we are likely to have a similar view on these drivers. Cultural differences, however, are likely to cause us to view such drivers differently to our counterparts. This in turn could lead to communication problems as we send or receive messages that may be understood differently by our counterparts.

These differences often start with language. I have often observed individuals speaking a foreign language to be actually speaking in their home language but using the words of the foreign language. You know this is happening when individuals get syntax wrong. When this is happening it is almost always because the person is translating a sentence being thought of in their home language into the foreign language – literally word for word.

As words and phrases are often associated with different ideas or norms in each language, this can easily lead to major misunderstandings when both sides think they are speaking the same language, whereas in fact they are using the same words but in the context of different languages. This is the major reason why the hallmark of a good translation is not how literal it is, but how much it reflects how a native speaker would have expressed the views or ideas being translated.

I encountered one of the best examples of this very early in my career. A very prestigious Continental European client of the firm, and one of the first entrusted to me, wanted to instruct my firm (a bank) on a particular innovative, cross-border financial transaction. Given the importance of the deal and the client, a conference call was arranged with my team leader and the client to confirm all relevant details. Given that my senior colleagues only spoke English, the call had to be conducted in English. This was not thought to be a problem as my client spoke fluent, albeit heavily accented English. During the call, the client repeatedly commented that he 'did not want to exchange principal'. This had near disastrous consequences, as in the context of the transaction, in English, it meant that the client would not accept the foreign exchange risk inherent in the transaction.

The conference call became more and more heated and after about 30 minutes, my senior colleagues concluded that 'the deal is off', walked out of the room and left me to deal with a highly agitated and extremely irate client. Only when I switched to speaking to my client in his native language did it transpire that the client simply did not want to transact the required foreign exchange transaction himself, but that he was willing to accept the foreign exchange risk – and had always said that he would be willing to do so. Once this was clarified the solution became relatively simple – we also undertook the foreign exchange transaction on behalf of the client (and were thus able to improve our profit margin as well).

Although this sounded like a simple 'translation' problem, it only became solvable when all parties realized that what was being said by one party was not what was being understood by the other. Only when we literally paraphrased every important step of the transaction could both parties be certain that everyone had the same understanding.

This particular financial transaction was relatively simple. We 'only' had to agree a relatively small number of clear, objective issues. Imagine how much more room for misunderstanding there will inevitably be if the issues at hand are more complex, subtle and subject to greater personal stress and risk.

Another example of important cross-cultural differences is how different cultures say 'no'. In some cultures (eg American, German), saying 'no' is relatively easily and not associated with giving offence. In other cultures, however, this is not done. Phrases such as 'this is difficult' are used as subtle, indirect alternatives to saying 'no'. When one member of a direct culture negotiates with someone from an indirect culture saying no can give offence. If, on the other hand, the other side responds with 'it's difficult', the first side may think it may still be acceptable, whereas in fact it is not. Frustration is bound to follow.

But there can be major misunderstandings even within speakers of the same language. US English has different usages to UK English. My favourite example is the usage of the word 'interesting'. Generally speaking, if someone from the UK says that an idea is 'interesting' it often means that the idea is not worth pursuing and that the person wants to be polite. Unfortunately, many Americans and other non-native English speakers with excellent English will not pick up on this subtle clue and will actually believe that their counterpart is genuinely interested in exploring this 'interesting' idea further. I have made it a personal habit that, when being told that something is 'interesting', I double check if this was an 'English interesting' or if there is genuine interest. I usually get a laugh from my counterpart and whatever the answer we tend to be clearer and happier. A good article on this is the April 2013 *Harvard Business Review* article by Andy Molinksy.

Another graphic way to highlight differences between cultures was developed by Richard Lewis (2005), who has mapped communication patterns, leadership styles and cultural identities. Lewis claims that understanding of cultural roots can provide a surprising degree of accuracy in terms of predicting the reaction of others and how they will approach others. Although he considers cultural analyses to be rife with 'inaccurate assessment', he believes that it is possible to determine 'national norms'.

For example, Lewis categorizes cultures on whether they are 'linear-active', ie task oriented and organized (many northern European countries), 'multi-active', ie people oriented and not schedule focused (many southern European countries) or 'reactive', ie introvert listeners (many Asian countries). Understanding the impact of such differences can be helpful in anticipating preferred (or accustomed) behavioural norms. If, for example, you are from a multi-active culture in which communication is relatively free flowing, expect to have to slow down and allow more time if communicating or negotiating with someone from a reactive culture who will want to spend more time thinking and reflecting on what is being said before responding.

An alternative way of working with culture is to identify key cultural factors relevant to negotiation. Salacuse (1999) lists ten cultural factors that impact negotiations. These include:

- **Goal**: is the purpose of the negotiation to get to a contract or to get to a relationship?
- **Attitudes**: are the negotiators expecting the negotiation to be distributive (win/lose) or integrative (win/win)?
- **Personal styles**: are negotiators expecting the negotiation and negotiators to act and dress formally or do they prefer a more informal approach?
- **Communications**: some cultures prefer a more direct style of communication whilst others tend to be more comfortable being indirect. This may also affect the extent to which it is acceptable in some cultures to make threats during a negotiation, how they are expressed, how seriously such threats are taken and how they are responded to.
- **Time sensitivity**: this is typically about a combination of being punctual and speed to agreement.
- **Emotionalism**: this is about how acceptable it is to show emotions during a negotiation.

- **Agreement form**: some cultures want to get to very specific agreements, spelling out how to deal with change. Other cultures prefer a more general agreement on the basis that as things change the spirit of the agreement will determine how to deal with the future.

- **Agreement building**: this describes whether agreement is driven bottom up or generated top down. This is often also described as inductive vs deductive, ie does the negotiation start from a general principle or does it start with specifics? There is also an interesting difference between some cultures in how deals are constructed. Some tend to start with presenting a maximum deal (building down) for which both sides need to agree relevant conditions. Others, on the other hand, prefer to start with a minimum deal (building up) which can be broadened as additional conditions are accepted.

- **Team organization**: there are typically differences in how teams are lead and how consensus within the team is created. In some cultures, it is expected that the most senior person takes key decisions. In other cultures, consensus is built up and the leader acts more as a facilitator for the consensus building.

- **Risk taking**: certain cultures are more risk adverse. In negotiations this can be seen in terms of how information is given, how decisions are taken and how to deal with ambiguity.

Working with negotiators from 12 different cultures it was possible to establish clear differences in default positions for each of these factors and cultures.

The importance of context

One particularly important cultural difference that I believe negotiators must be aware of is 'context'.

In a high-context culture, negotiators will pay attention to how the context agreement was reached, ie who said what to whom, what was their status, what was the background, etc. The agreement itself is of 'lesser' importance. In a low-context culture, on the other hand, the context is only marginally important, if at all, and what matters is what has been agreed between the two parties, ie the agreement or contract itself (assuming this is sufficiently clearly documented).

This is really important for negotiators to understand as a negotiator from a high-context environment will need to feel comfortable that a proposal has the appropriate backing of all relevant stakeholders and why.

Only then will an agreement be durable. Consequently, negotiators will need to pay attention to a broader range of stakeholders who may not be 'sitting at the table' and will need to engage in activities to demonstrate the appropriate backing, etc. The advantage of working within a high-context situation is that co-operation tends to be enhanced (Mintu-Wimsatt 2002).

On the other hand, 'low-context' negotiators will not be sympathetic to attempts to bring broader, external factors or issues into the negotiation and into the interpretation of the meaning of an agreement, as they will expect to reach a 'stand-alone' agreement. They would also expect all parties to abide by the letter, rather than the spirit, of an agreement, especially if the circumstances that have changed are not directly relevant to the agreement.

The danger with cultural assumptions

It is tempting to jump to conclusions regarding a person's likely behavioural norms and preferences based on their perceived cultural 'background'. Below is a table summarizing some major cultural negotiation differences. However, in an increasingly international and global business world it is becoming increasingly difficult to meet mono-cultural individuals.

What should one expect of an Asia-born individual who was raised in the United States (or Europe)? Or how should one prepare for negotiating with an Italian, French or German citizen who was educated or who worked extensively in the UK?

In fact, we all know that there can be significant cultural differences even within a particular country or even company. Anybody with experience of major corporations or professional service firms will know that different departments may well engender very different approaches to working or negotiating with outsiders (even within a firm). And from personal experience I know that people from, say, Yorkshire or the Midlands are quite different to people from Cornwall or the Home Counties. Many Germans will consider Bavarians as very different (and some Bavarians still think that Bavaria is not really part of Germany). Ask any Italian about the difference between Italians from the North and the South. One can laugh about stereotypes, but unless one really understands the subtle differences within a country or company it can be dangerous to make assumptions that there is a single culture to deal with.

Most research on cultures points to the risks associated with stereotyping. Salacuse's research quoted above, for example, echoes such concerns. He showed that, although certain values were significantly more prevalent

Table 14.1 Typical negotiation attributes by geographic culture

Cultural group	Attributes
United Kingdom	Some individuals will signal through subtle use of language. Target and opening positions are relatively close. Relative importance is signalled through different emphasis, language. Protocol is of importance but in an informal way. Punctuality relatively flexible. Some negotiators believe in the power of improvisation.
United States	Less subtle use of language than UK. Similar to UK but less formal. May be tempted to apply 'cookie cutter' methodology, ie same as last time. Splitting the difference a common example of seeming to be focused on 'fair outcome'.
Germany	Typically more formal than UK/US. Places greater value on punctuality, less humour oriented. Tend to be high in terms of stating own views, less question oriented. Importance of an issue often signalled by high opening position relative to target. High data orientation.
France	May be perceived as somewhat aggressive due to higher use of threats/warnings, interruptions, face gazing. More likely to say 'No' or 'You'. Like to focus on principles, tend to favour deductive focus.
Spain	Less self-disclosure or information sharing. Some tendency to issue commands, frequent interruptions, frequent use of 'No' and 'You'. High-context orientation.
Brazil	May be perceived as somewhat aggressive due to frequent use of 'No' and 'You', use of commands, physical contact, facial gazing. Prefer bottom up (inductive) approach.
Mexico	Very different to Brazilian or Spanish. Negotiation style closer to that of US. High-context and relationship orientation.
French-speaking Canada	Similar to French, ie higher use of threats, warnings, interruptions and eye contact.

(Continued)

Table 14.1 (*Continued*)

Cultural group	Attributes
English-speaking Canada	Relative low use of aggressive persuasion tactics such as threats or warnings. Higher use of interruptions and 'No' than US.
Russia	Lots of asking. Greater use of silence but less use of 'No' or 'You'. Less direct facial gazing. Low on information sharing. Will often keep big issues to the end of a meeting.
Japan	Least aggressive/most polite. Great importance on avoiding open conflict hence avoids saying 'No' or giving rise to disappointments during meeting. Comfortable with and requires longer period of silence in dialogue. Bottom-up consensus building. Senior person does less of the talking.
Korea	Greater use of threats, commands than Japanese. Comfortable with use of 'No' and interruptions.
Israel	Prefer to keep cards close to chest. Likely to attempt to persuade through promises and recommendations. Tactical use of competitor offers or other normative tactics. Interruptions seen as sign of engagement not disrespect.
Mediterranean	'Warm', effusive, exuberant uses of posture and gestures. Sometimes difficult to pin down to details or specific phase of a negotiation. Greater focus on relationship than contract.

in some cultures than in others, there were always exceptions to any of the factors within any culture, ie one cannot rely blindly on the typical cultural norms to predict the preferences of any one individual.

Table 14.1 lists 'typical' attributes associated with particular groups, based on personal experience and various research studies. These should be treated with extreme caution and are merely intended to illustrate potential misinterpretation of verbal or non-verbal signals.

No matter how complex and controversial cultural differences may be, these challenges are nothing compared to the issues associated with gender-based differences. Compounding the challenges of looking at the impact of gender on negotiation is the fact that gender-related issues can very easily become subject to a high degree of emotions and emoting, sexist posturing and political correctness. This risks adding confusion to uncertainties regarding cause and effect.

The impact of gender on negotiation behaviour

No wonder women don't negotiate as often as men. It's like trying to cross a minefield backward in high heels. (SHERYL SANDBERG, FACEBOOK COO)

There is a large body of research on gender differences in negotiation. A useful summary can be found in *Negotiation* by Lewickic *et al* (2010). Many of the best-known studies have focused on issues such as the gap in wages or job progressions. It is broadly accepted that there are significant differences between what women and men are paid for the same work or that men tend to get promoted faster and higher (the Glass Ceiling). Much of this is attributed to factors such as discrimination, job distributions or life/work balance preferences.

Some of the differences, however, have also been attributed to differences in the way that men and women negotiate. In essence, there are suggestions that women do not negotiate as well, or as much, or as aggressively as their male counterparts. The quote at the start of the chapter (Lawrence, 2015) is just a particular example that caught the public's attention. Recent years have seen a flood of books and articles targeting the needs of women negotiating and providing descriptions of how to remedy this (Conti, 2016; Babcock and Laschever, 2007).

Babcock, for example, quotes a study of US MBA graduates that found that on average men negotiated a 4.3 per cent increase on an initial pay offer compared to women who only negotiated an average 2.7 per cent increase. Over a career this was extrapolated to demonstrate that men would end up earning almost double the amount that women would.

The picture, however, is muddied by other social factors. For example, research (Eriksson and Sandberg, 2012) using over 200 Swedish students points to a propensity for men to be more likely to initiate a pay-related negotiation. However, the results also showed that things were a lot more complicated. It turned out that the difference between men and women, in terms of initiating the negotiation, was only large and statistically significant when the counterpart was a woman. The difference between men and women initiating was only 5 per cent (and not statistically significant) when the counterpart was a man. When the counterpart was a woman, though, the difference rose to 24 per cent. Other research (Riley Bowles and Flynn, 2010) points to differences in the degree and manner of persistence, ie willingness to continue to seek concessions from a nay-saying counterpart. The research showed that this behaviour was partially dependent on the gender of the counterpart and that women persisted more with nay-saying men than with nay-saying women. Things can also be affected by negotiation competence. The work of Riley Bowles and Flynn, for example, showed that high-performing women adjusted persistence more than low-performing women.

Whether or not men really are better negotiators than women in the population as a whole is yet to be resolved and likely to take a lot more time and evidence. The data my colleagues and I have been collecting suggests, however, that there is no significant difference in how well male or female mid- to senior-level professionals negotiate. The only difference our data has shown is that women tend to be less ambitious in setting targets above their vetoes, but this difference does not result in a significant difference in outcomes. Our data does not provide any evidence for the stereotypical assumption that men are better negotiators than women. I should emphasize that this conclusion is based on our client base, ie those attending our various negotiation programmes and the outcomes achieved in the first negotiation of the day, ie when a baseline is being established and we have not yet proceeded to provide any substantive fee negotiation training.

We think that this is in part due to the fact that, by the time our clients attend our workshops, the male and female delegates are at a similar level of skill and experience (see below for research supporting this conclusion). We also think that this is in part due to the fact that our population of delegates is almost entirely PSF based.

What my colleagues and I have observed, however, is that there are differences in how men and women negotiate.

Our views are echoed in the literature. A 2003 book written by Deborah Kolb and Judith Williams, *Everyday Negotiations*, was originally called *The Shadow Negotiation: How women can master the hidden agendas*. The first edition highlighted the different approaches taken by women negotiators, in particular their greater attention to relationships, hidden barriers to negotiation and identifying hidden opportunities for negotiation. It was only in the second edition that the name was changed, as it was thought that these approaches would also be useful for male negotiators to adopt.

A meta-analysis, looking at over 50 independent research studies (Mazei *et al*, 2015) makes the following observations:

- Research has often yielded mixed evidence on relative effectiveness due to gender. Over the studies included in the meta-analysis the overall difference favouring men was relatively small.

- Some studies indicate that gender differences favouring men can be eliminated or even reversed under certain conditions (Bowles *et al*, 2005).

- A number of theories (stereotype threat, power, evolution/biology), have been put forward to explain differences due to gender. Particularly relevant and predictive, however, are social role theories, especially 'role congruity' (Eagly and Karau, 2002) which, simply put, postulate that (at least in Western cultures) the behaviours required for effective negotiation (competitive, assertive, profit oriented) are not congruent with the behaviours ascribed to women (accommodating, concern for others, relationship focused). Women whose behaviour contradicts preconceived social norms run the risk of 'social backlash' from both men and women, which has been shown separately to be of greater concern to women than to men. Women therefore feel greater social pressure to avoid or tone down effective negotiation behaviour.

- Incongruity could explain why the women in our data set were, on average, less ambitious than their male or mixed-group counterparts. A fascinating corroboration of differences due to cultural norms comes from a research study comparing the competitiveness of men and women in patriarchal and matrilineal societies (Gneezy *et al*, 2009).

- The study showed that women were more competitive in a matrilineal society than their male counterparts.

- The incongruity between women's gender role and effective negotiation behaviour can lead to reduced expectations of personal effectiveness and greater backlash from negotiation counterparts (from men and women).

- Role incongruity explains why women are more assertive when negotiating on behalf of others than on their own behalf (less expectation of backlash).

- Gender differences in outcomes are reduced when there is more information about the bargaining range.

- Increasing negotiation experience also reduced any gender differences. This finding would explain why we do not see any difference between gender in terms of outcomes in our workshops.

- Women with higher status/title tend to be less concerned about social backlash.

The implications from this analysis are quite clear. Whatever differences there may initially be between genders, these can effectively be eliminated when women prepare well and practise. Negotiation training may therefore have a disproportional benefit for them. Women negotiators may also benefit more from attributing the gains or benefits of any negotiation to their organizations and colleagues, rather than just themselves, ie they are advocating on behalf of others.

The following quote illustrates this further:

> Women scored a salary that was 18 per cent higher when they negotiated the salary for someone else. Men pretty much negotiated the same salaries whether it was for themselves or for someone else, and the levels were pretty consistent with what the women negotiated when they represented someone else. It appears that the women executives were particularly energized when they felt a sense of responsibility to represent another person's interests. (Liu, 2014)

The data from the Mazei study furthermore comes to a highly provocative conclusion: it suggests that when women are experienced and well prepared they may in fact have an advantage compared to their male counterparts and achieve better outcomes.

One of the most obvious observable differences between men and women during negotiations is the way in which the genders communicate.

Gender differences in the use of language

One of the biggest areas of controversy in the research regarding gender differences concerns the potential difference in the use of language. Some authors believe that the kind of problems which arise in negotiations between people with different first languages described above are mirrored in negotiations between men and women who, believing they speak the same language, use and interpret the language differently. Although some authors have written about this topic (Tannen, 1994; Locke, 2011) there is still disagreement as to whether these differences are real and widely spread or whether they are more a function of cultural norms, ie country or culture specific, rather than truly gender driven.

Based on my own observations I believe that some women negotiate or make demands in a more indirect manner than their male counterparts. Then again, I have also observed male negotiators using a more indirect approach. I have also seen women negotiate every bit as directly and forcefully as men.

Much depends, in my view, on the perception of relative power and on experience. Typically, those who feel in a less powerful position will tend to be less direct in their use of language. In fact, use of direct or indirect language is usually a good indicator of where either party believes power is distributed, and a common tactic to shift the perception of the balance of power is in the use of 'direct' or 'forceful' language (eg avoiding floppy language – see Chapter 9).

In any event, few front-line negotiators seem to take such potential differences into account in either the delivery of their own positions or in their interpretations of positions declared by negotiators of different gender. It probably is worth spending some time reflecting on the potential for differences in the use of language, not just because of gender differences but also potential cultural differences.

One area in which understanding the influence of culture and gender on a negotiator will be critical is the selection of the most appropriate negotiation tactics to help expedite a negotiation or secure an optimal outcome. The next chapter will provide an overview of some of the most common tactics encountered, and show how some can be helpful and how to recognize and protect oneself from those that use tactics to further their own interests at the expense of the other negotiation party.

Having another go at squeezing the lemon: advanced techniques and approaches

15

Your goal is not to win over them, but to win them over. (WILLIAM URY IN *GETTING PAST NO*)

The basic techniques of opening with an ambitious but realistic number or proposal, trading but not giving concessions and being creative will, if applied properly, be sufficient for most professionals to generate significant gains most of the time. If given the choice, I would advocate that professionals spend their time, money and efforts honing these basics. However, there are some advanced techniques or approaches that can help in particular circumstances. Below are given the ones encountered most often or that have proved to be most useful, that illustrate an important principle. Before discussing these in greater detail let me raise the issue of using manipulative or influencing tactics.

Manipulative tactics

It is not always clear where clever techniques end and manipulative tactics begin. The risk is that untrained or semi-trained negotiators will set too much store by particular, often questionable tactics. The problems are compounded when the tactics come at the expense of applying a structured, planned approach as outlined in this book. However, the skills of a good and experienced negotiator include recognizing tactics and knowing how to counter them. Generally speaking the way to deal with tactical plays is to:

● acknowledge and counter or deflect the tactic;

● use the same tactic back;

● use questions, either reflective ('so you feel that...') or open (what, why, when, how, where and who – see Chapter 9 for more);

● openly identify the tactic; a tactic that is consciously noticed loses a lot of its power;

● alternatively, recognize but ignore the tactic.

Some counters need to be thought through carefully to avoid the risks of 'tit-for-tat' or escalations.

Please note that some tactics are constructive, eg seeking lateral solutions, inviting exchange of interests, building trust in small steps. These should be supported.

There are tactics that are definitely not recommended as they do not contribute to a long-term, sustainable relationship and may also detract from a positive short-term outcome. These include bullying, lying, bluffing, playing at being irrational, becoming abusive or threatening. There is a growing body of evidence that demonstrates that using threats or emotions will actually result in short-term but in particular long-term loss of value to the side applying such tactics. This is due to the likely reaction from the other party and losses in trust and integrative approach (Sinaceur *et al*, 2013a; Van Kleef and Côté, 2007; Van Kleef and De Dreu, 2010).

Advanced techniques

Use of conditionalities to exploit differences

Sometimes negotiations reach an impasse because each side has diametrically opposing views on the future or the likelihood of certain conditions or eventualities happening. This is an opportunity to apply some form of conditionality. Good negotiators see differences as opportunities rather than as insurmountable obstacles. The use of conditionalities is a great illustration of generating added value by using rather than minimizing differences.

This is illustrated by the following situation encountered a few years ago by one of our programme participants, which combined this and the

'If you ... then I' techniques. A partner in an international advisory firm had just transferred to the US main offices of the firm and was rather eager to sign up his first US instruction. A potential client offered him a reasonably sized instruction but asked for a major discount on the firm's previously agreed and negotiated rates. (Notice how many clients have no compunction in reopening an agreement if they think they can benefit.) On exploring this opportunity further it emerged that the client was anticipating the project being closed within six weeks as all major terms with a third party had been agreed in principle. The client was adamant that this was as good as done and that the support required was merely going to rubber-stamp the agreement.

The partner reached a different conclusion following a brief review of the project; he expected it to last 12–16 weeks. Following some consultation with us, the partner ended up proposing the following conditional arrangement: if the project closed in six weeks he would do the work at the discount the client suggested. However, if the project took longer than seven weeks, the client would agree to the firm's standard rates. In either event the client would be committed to finding additional opportunities to working together (at standard rates or close to them). The client agreed, having had no basis to back off from the previously claimed certainty of closing within six weeks. In the end the project took 18 weeks to close, the client paid and the partner was well into working with the client. (This technique is described in more detail in a *Harvard Business Review* article by Bazerman and Gillespie, 1999.)

Red herring/decoy

Experienced and advanced negotiators take advantage of two powerful psychological drivers: reciprocity bias and fairness bias, described in greater detail by Cialdini in his 2007 book, *Influence*. They start the negotiation with a very high target or include a significant demand that they do not value greatly or expect to get (the red herring). During the negotiation they then withdraw the demand. As a demand withdrawn is the same as a concession made, their counterparts feel obliged to make a counter-concession. Fairness bias will see to it that the concession offered will be about as big as the perceived value of the original demand withdrawn. Good negotiators will know how to direct this concession towards something that they value.

The effectiveness of this technique was demonstrated in an experiment when strangers were asked to accompany orphans on a half-day outing to a local attraction such as the zoo. The success rate was dramatically increased if the test subjects were first asked if they would mentor these orphans by meeting them for two hours a week for six months and on having this request rejected the subjects were asked if they would at least donate half a day to the same kids. Test subjects reported the strong urge to make a concession (the half day) in response to the tester withdrawing the mentoring idea. This is also the reason why starting with a high opening number and agreeing to come down is often considered to generate a better and more acceptable outcome than starting with a lower number and not moving much.

Russian front

A similar technique, but just as effective, can be to offer one alternative that is deeply unattractive to the other side. As the other side recoils in horror ('anything but the Russian front') (Kennedy, 2004) the opening side can then propose or offer an alternative much more to their liking and which the recipient will value greatly, compared to the first offer.

This is a take on the framing effect mentioned in Chapter 11. Some real estate agents apply a very interesting but nevertheless effective variant of this. They will often take prospective buyers or renters to see one or several poor-quality properties. Once the potential client starts to believe that there are only substandard properties out there, the agent takes them to the property or properties they had intended to show them in the first instance. The success rate of this approach is reported to be very high.

Another variant is to show a potential buyer (say of a car or a property) some items that are above the potential buyer's original budget. Once the buyer's interest has been piqued the agent will come down to the buyer's budget. Naturally the cars or apartment on offer will not quite meet the awakened interest and as a result buyers tend to increase their budget.

Trading concession on the headline rate vs gaining value on side issues

Similarly, as mentioned in Chapters 8 (preparing) and 10 (trading) good negotiators will know the relative trade-off values of various negotiation issues. Depending on the data gathered during the information exchange in Act 1, they may have figured out that their counterpart puts a greater value or priority on one or two specific items, particularly headline terms, than on several others that may on closer inspection yield more value. Clever negotiators will hold out on these headline items while working the supposed side items to their maximum. As a result the other side may feel greatly satisfied (they got what mattered to them the most) while the sophisticated negotiator will be happy (they got the financial value). The classic example in this case is when clients want to avoid any worries and risks of overrunning a project budget. Clever negotiators will work on these worries and will get the clients to agree to a higher fixed fee in exchange for a guarantee that any unforeseen issues will be dealt with within the budget.

Other examples of such trade-offs are to give on a headline rate (that may have been inflated ahead of a negotiation) and to agree faster payment terms, or to the use of more junior members of the team, each charging a lower rate but generating more hours and a greater profit margin.

Giving a choice of two or three

Clients often ask us how to overcome either 'tough' negotiators or how to indicate a willingness to negotiate without putting forward a floppy opening. One way to do this is to give the client a choice of two or three.

Tough negotiators typically like to decide – give them a choice of options that are acceptable to you. If you are trying to invite a counter offer, without showing that you are flexible on price (or whatever else is important), for example to overcome attempts to extract full and final offers without negotiations, offer two or three options that are not just successively more of the prior one. By including or excluding certain features from each of the two or three, clients will be tempted to cherry-pick the combination that suits them best or that they find most attractive. In so doing they will need to enter into a discussion and hence a negotiation of their preferred option.

The advantage of only offering two options is simplicity. The advantage of offering three is that it is often possible to position the third option as dramatically more expensive than the first two. Research has shown that buyers will often pick the lowest option if given two (they don't want to be seen to be extravagant) but will pick the middle option if given three (they don't want to be seen by their colleagues or competitors as cheapskates and after all, picking the middle option shows that the project is not being gold plated).

Silence

Highly valued by many negotiators and writers on negotiation (Raiffa, 1982) as most people will fill silence and usually give away either information or concessions. The problem with this is that most professionals, especially those in a consulting or advising role, where people pay you for speaking, find keeping silent excruciating. Ambassador Richardson (Richardson, 2013) provides a chilling account of negotiating with Saddam Hussein and being subjected to the silence treatment. They consequently either put themselves under considerable additional pressure to engage in an activity that is alien to them and does not help build a relationship, or still don't find this technique helpful. It is really tough to maintain silence. I don't recommend playing this tactic too often as it could lead to a battle of wills and in general does not support the signalling efforts that should be supporting a negotiation. However, judicious use of silence when coupled with careful listening and observing can be invaluable.

A classic example of this would be the compound flinch after a first proposal has been tabled. Imagine your reaction if, after having put forward a competitive offer, the other side, having flinched, just sits there glaring at you. Most untrained negotiators will respond to this silence by making an excuse or asking what the client thinks, opening themselves to a major onslaught.

Threatening to walk out

Under some circumstances and with some cultures one side will not think that the other side is serious until that side has walked out on a negotiation at least once. Several of my clients have reported that certain clients don't even think that a negotiation has started in earnest until one if not both sides have walked out or threatened to do so. When dealing with western European counterparts in the context of a fee negotiation this can be a very risky tactic to use and should only be contemplated when there is high certainty that the client does not have ready alternatives.

Walking out is an extreme form of flinching and just as with flinching it needs to be done authentically lest the negotiator's credibility be damaged. A great example of this would be when one side has put an offer on the table and the other, rather than responding, gets up, proclaims painful sorrow to note that the proposing side has not understood their requirements or something in that vein, and prepares to walk out rather than waste any more time. This is rare in the context of a PSF and if it happens then the professional has to quickly decide if they have made a significant error or if the other side is using strong-arm tactics. In my experience it is best to let a side walking out go – if they had an interest in reaching a reasonable outcome they would have found an alternative way of letting you know that they want you to make a concession.

Dealing with ultimatums

Closely related to the 'walking out' tactic is the 'final ultimatum' tactic. This is one of the few tactics that is best ignored. If the receiving party responds or in any other way refers to the ultimatum it will more difficult for the side that set the ultimatum to back off (Richardson, 2013). Best to ignore the ultimatum or any implications. Focus on progress being made and on the diminishing obstacles to an agreement.

As emphasized at the start of this chapter, inexperienced or misguided negotiators tend to put too much time and effort into trying to apply clever tactics in their efforts to best their counterparts and gain additional benefits during the negotiations. This can generate considerable additional risk that the negotiations will become counterproductive to the long-term relationship. Experienced professionals and good negotiators know that far more can be gained (or lost) by managing the project or assignment and monitoring progress of the work for opportunities to renegotiate (or cross-sell). These skills are covered in the next chapter.

Managing PSF project profitability

This chapter will outline the most important principles affecting project profitability and how to manage an instruction or assignment from a fee perspective. Please note that implicit in all of the discussions below is an assumption that practitioners know how to manage all relevant technical issues in connection with the work and that they can control all aspects relating to technical quality. A broader review of profitability management can be found in a report entitled *Targeting Profitability* (Roche, 2013). Another really useful resource, which provides an integrated overview of pricing and project profitability is *Smarter Pricing, Smarter Profit*, written by my former colleague Stuart Dodds. Although both focus on law firms the principles apply to just about all PSFs.

As highlighted in the Introduction to this book, fee or value management involves three distinct but interconnected areas of competence – setting, getting and keeping the fees. I have referred to this as the 'golden triangle'. Most practitioners will spend considerable time and effort thinking about what to ask for (set) and then proceed to fret about how to ask for it (get). Having won the mandate or instruction most practitioners, if left to their own devices, will then forget all about the fees, happily ploughing away at the work.

What these practitioners fail to understand, however, is that the execution phase of an instruction is typically the phase where most profits are lost, ie where the greatest profit leakage occurs. A number of my clients have data showing that they lose about twice as much profit due to poor project fee management as they do from up-front discounting, ie they lose more because of poor internal processes than they lose due to external competition or poor negotiation skills.

Figure 16.1   Example of common profit leaks

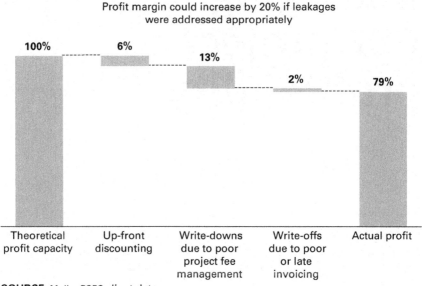

Profit margin could increase by 20% if leakages
were addressed appropriately

Theoretical profit capacity	Up-front discounting	Write-downs due to poor project fee management	Write-offs due to poor or late invoicing	Actual profit
100%	6%	13%	2%	79%

SOURCE Møller PSFG client data

© Møller PSFG Cambridge 2017 – Ori Wiener

A good illustration of this is shown in Figure 16.1, which provides actual data from one of my clients (anonymized). In this particular instance, profits lost due to poor project fee management account for more than twice the profits lost due to discounting and competition. This particular client estimated that the firm could increase its profit margin by between 15 and 25 per cent without raising its rates, if it were able to address the most common profit leaks better. This has become a major priority area for the firm. Generating double-digit profit growth by focussing on internal project management issues also carries a number of additional advantages:

- less reliance on the success of new business development and other marketing efforts which are often considered difficult, costly and uncertain;
- less exposure to short-term market fluctuations;
- an ability to minimize any damaging fee negotiation; and
- better risk management and client satisfaction.

My Møller colleagues and I find it helpful to look at project fee management as essentially three disciplines. These are managing the client, the team and the work.

Figure 16.2 Project fee management: the second golden triangle

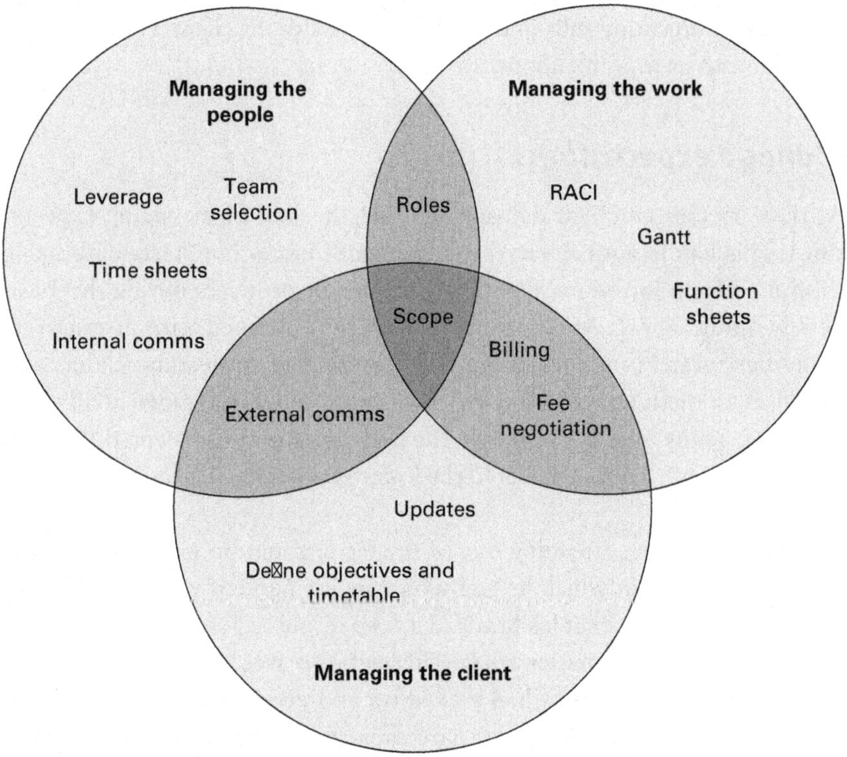

© Møller PSFG Cambridge 2017 – Ori Wiener

The second golden triangle

We have developed a second golden triangle to illustrate the interplay between these three areas of attention for effective value management. Figure 16.2 illustrates how good value management involves the careful coordination of a large number of interactive and interdependent activities. At the core of all of these, however, lies the ability to define, manage and monitor the scope of an assignment.

Manage the client

Managing clients is one of the keys to success for a professional and the chapters on fee negotiation are all about how to manage this process. It is worth highlighting some of the more important issues here, to ensure that no critical area is inadvertently left out. Much of client management is about communicating fully and appropriately with the client. Here are some of the key areas to think about.

Manage expectations

At the very core of client management lies the skill of managing expectations. This can include a very broad range of issues but starts with being careful and specific when making any claims or promises during the 'business winning' phase. Most professionals I have worked with instinctively avoid deliberately making exaggerated, wrong or misleading claims and promises (something that is highly risky and should be avoided at all cost). However, many practitioners get themselves into subsequent difficulties because they have not considered the long-term consequences of particular claims.

A senior partner, attending one of my fee negotiation programmes, told me of an instance in which he had won a major piece of work on the basis of assuring the client that his firm had a deep resource pool available to meet the client's needs, no matter what. Although this was true in principle, the problem was that business had picked up and everyone had become busy and that there was in fact little spare capacity within the relevant part of the firm. The 'deep pool of resources' claim backfired when the client, about a quarter into the project, suddenly had to accelerate the timetable and my course attendee had to increase the headcount on his team by a good 30 per cent virtually overnight.

The only way to get the extra headcount was for the team to work extremely long hours and for additional team members to be taken on from other teams with promises of major financial rewards. The final outcome was that the client noted a decline in the quality of work and service (due to the team's exhaustion) and at the same time resisted any calls for significant fee increases (other than for increased headcount) – the business had been won on the basis that the firm could easily provide extra resources. This resulted in a reasonably profitable mandate becoming a major loss maker for that firm.

The key learning point here is that there is a direct link between the actions taken and commitments made during the business-winning phase and the execution phase. Professionals and their firms must constantly bear this in mind. Other claims, for example, that can have a similar impact include:

- flexibility;
- availability;
- responsiveness;
- cost control;
- special expertise.

One of the most frequent mistakes committed by professionals is not to provide their clients with regular updates and understanding of the amount of work delivered or undertaken. As Figure 16.3 illustrates, most PSF clients do not, unless suitably informed by the service provider, fully appreciate or understand the amount of work that is being delivered. The reasons for this often include lack of expertise or knowledge concerning the work required – that is after all usually why they have awarded the instruction to a specialist to begin with.

Clients also frequently lack any understanding of the differences in effort that different project phases may involve. Keeping them fully informed is critical if the clients are to understand how their professional service provider is delivering the benefits and services they have contracted for. Really sophisticated practitioners will in fact try to manage expectations around a smooth 'average' such that clients are spared the impression of any major variability in workloads or pressures.

Figure 16.3 Managing client expectations

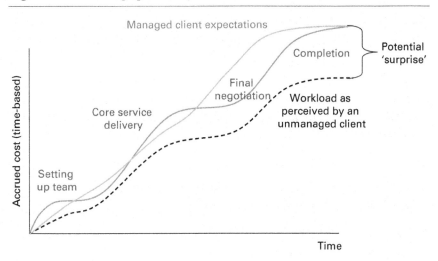

Given that most PSF projects tend to end with an intensive final phase in which either last-minute changes are incorporated or a final negotiation or similar is required, sophisticated client managers will manage perceived workload up to just prior to the final phase so as to be able to come in at a level that the client has been 'prepared for'. This approach is especially appropriate where fees are time-based and where bills are typically much higher in the final stages of a project.

Manage scope creep

Managing scope creep is probably the single most important client-related activity within fee or value management. This is why it is firmly placed at the heart of the triangle. (Scope creep is discussed in detail in Chapter 5.) The key elements that must be defined at the start of an assignment or that the professional should have considered in detail include:

- the nature and amount/extent of services provided;
- objectives of the client;
- deliverables at the end or during the assignment;
- timetable;
- resource requirements;
- dependencies.

The challenge for professionals and PSFs and the problem most frequently encountered is that clients have a tendency to ask for more during the course of an assignment. This may be due to unforeseen circumstances but is often due to the client's objectives or needs changing or discovering that they want more done than originally thought. Sometimes the change in scope can involve either extending or collapsing a timetable. It is worth reiterating this point: a change in timetable is a change in scope. This would not be an issue if clients are open to pay for any additional work and effort associated with the change in scope; many, however, are not. A number of reasons may be at work here. These include the client:

- not being aware that there has been a change in scope;
- not understanding (or choosing not to understand) that the change in scope will result in additional work;
- expecting to get extra work for free;
- accepting that the changes are in fact a change in scope but not accepting that the changes merit the extra fees.

The situation becomes particularly difficult for the service provider when an assignment has been won as a result of some form of competitive tender and the fee quoted is already at the bottom range of acceptable profitability.

In some instances clients may claim full understanding of the additional cost but will point to some other reason (set budgets, terms of the public RFP, etc) why it will not be possible to pay more for the additional work. Some of my clients have told me of instances where with hindsight it had been obvious to the client that the scope would have to change from the outset of the instructions and that the client deliberately agreed terms up-front that they had no intention of altering once the changes became obvious. At this stage most professionals would rather do the work than create a reputation for leaving work undone.

In all of these situations it is necessary to reopen a fee agreement so as to reflect the changes in scope. The procurement world has a saying: 'There is a price for a job and a job for a price. Change the job – change the price.' Unless practitioners and their firms are willing to stand by this principle they will risk being taken advantage of by clients. To be able to manage scope creep, service providers have to be willing and able to raise this issue with their clients as soon as possible after a scope change has been requested.

Renegotiating halfway through the project is something that scares most service providers (and clients). Chapter 7 outlines the workings of the inner saboteurs such as guilt or worries about risks to the relationship and how these hold professionals back from engaging with clients. In the case of reopening a fee discussion there are additional concerns that the client either starts to doubt the professional's word or integrity ('We can't rely on their estimates or forecasts') or that it is an admission of incompetence ('I got it wrong – I need more money'). Either way, professionals worry that this will harm their client relationship. Professional pride and worries therefore get in the way of sensible fee discussions. Sharks know this and will take full advantage of these worries to extract significant additional value from practitioners.

To deal with this, practitioners need to take the client's perspective and try to understand the downside to a client if a service provider is not compensated appropriately for the work delivered. In many circumstances the clients may not care for the relationship but do care about the quality of work. In other circumstances the client may feel dependent on the service provider for any follow-up work that a project may require. It is the practitioners' responsibility to understand their client's perspective and to respond accordingly.

Practitioners need to understand the risks to the client if a project or assignment is not completed on time or if the work is not done to the level required. In addition, it is always useful to understand a client's switching cost, ie the incremental costs and risks that would be incurred if the client were to switch service provider in mid-stream. This should not be seen as a licence to 'blackmail' a client in mid-assignment. Most professionals would balk at such an idea. However, as discussed in Chapter 8, by identifying the client's NBT, ie their alternatives, it becomes easier for a professional to develop a sensible negotiation position with regards to reopening a fee agreement.

If the client values a relationship then a sensible fee discussion will be possible. If the client does not, then the fee discussion may be more difficult but the downside, including in terms of potentially lost future business, is also much lower.

Focusing on the future

Another core reason why professionals don't wish to reopen a fee discussion is a desire to avoid a discussion on who is to blame for the pending overrun. Discussions typically either take the 'You should have known this and told us before we started' or the 'We told you this would happen – no you didn't – yes we did' route. Professionals rightly try to avoid this type of unproductive argument.

At this stage experienced negotiators will try to identify key issues, matching interests of both sides and focus on the future to resolve the temporary problems. The experienced negotiator will also, having assessed the other side's perspectives and particularly their vetoes and NBT, be better placed to position any additional costs in comparison to the overall value and benefit to the client of completing the project.

The difference between scope and assumptions

As mentioned above, one of the most frequent and frustrating experiences for a professional arises when clients think or hold out that the required change was something that should have been anticipated and that consequently should already have been reflected in the agreed fees. Many of our negotiation programme participants report this to be particularly the case in projects in which the service provider was awarded the work as the result of a competitive selection process in which clients stipulated or asked for a list of the underlying assumptions that went into the fee quote or proposal.

I believe that the use of assumptions to justify or explain PSF fees lies at the heart of the problems discussed here as they are often confused with the scope of assignment to be agreed. Here are my suggestions on how best to deal with this confusion:

- Clearly differentiate between the scope of the assignment, ie the work that the client wants done, and the assumptions applied by the service provider in delivering the work required. This may require extensive discussion and negotiation with the client.

- Clearly and fully document the scope and assumptions and the basis for both. This may require additional time and effort.

- If the assumptions turn out to be wrong, ie if the professional's expert view turned out to wrong, I would expect the professional to have to absorb the additional costs (or most of them). The only exception to this would be where the assumptions were based on false or faulty information provided by the client.

- If the client asks for a change in scope, ie when the client is changing what they want, the additional costs should be borne by the client – after all they are asking for the change.

- If the change in scope is due to unforeseen developments not triggered by the client then client and service provider should enter into a reasonable discussion as to how to share the additional cost in a fair and transparent manner.

- Regularly consult the scope document to determine if additional work required is in or out of scope.

This approach has been strongly endorsed by a number of professionals I have worked with over the years. Many of our negotiation programme participants are surprised to hear that successful fee negotiators within their organizations often spend more time negotiating a scope than the actual fee.

Another way to look at this is to remember that the fee or engagement letter is a commercial contract between the client and the service provider. Good contracts don't apply prices on the basis of assumptions but on the basis of conditions. When these change so does the price.

The key principle to remember is that if the professional made the wrong assumptions he or she pays, but if the client is asking for additional or different things, the client should pay. The only way to apply this principle is if attention and effort has been invested at the start to clearly establish and agree the scope of the work to be delivered. This is the same approach that any industrial or corporate client would apply to their business.

When to negotiate

Timing, as in other walks of life, can make a critical difference to success or failure. As highlighted in Chapter 7, there are strategic choices to be made about when a conversation on fees should be held. The balance of nego-tiation power between client and professional is more in the professional's favour during the project than at the start or the end. As the preceding discussion should have made clear, a well-defined scope should greatly facil-itate having the right discussions at the right time.

Many professionals are tempted to get on with the work in the hope that the client will value the 'get it done' approach and pay. Many clients may value that attitude but they will not pay, or will pay only a fraction of what the extra work has cost to provide. Although I am in sympathy with a desire to demonstrate a strong working relationship and to get on with it, it is important that not too much time is allowed to pass between the start of the extra work and a clear discussion on fees. Most reasonable clients also appreciate a prompt discussion in relation to a change in scope as they don't want to be surprised or feel they are being presented with a fait accompli.

Manage the timetable

Fundamental to most PSF projects is the management of sometimes quite complex project timetables. These may often be subject to external devel-opments, some of which are bound to be beyond the control of client and service provider. Such changes should be allowed for in a fee agreement (ie they are assumptions). There are times, however, when clients will want to either extend or compress a timetable. Where such changes are due to client demands rather than forces beyond their control they constitute scope changes and should be treated as such, ie any additional costs or benefits arising from such a change should result in a renegotiation of the fees.

Particularly in the case of time-based fees (hourly or day rates) clients are tempted to see a shortening of the timetable as a means of reducing the bill. Many professionals will follow this view. This is a major error and should be avoided for a number of reasons; these include the client getting extra value (the same work earlier) – the fees should reflect this. Compressed timetables are usually associated with substantial increases in workload and pressure – people want to be compensated for this directly or indirectly, ie personnel costs go up. Also, delivering the same work faster may lead to a higher risk of making mistakes – the firm may either have to compensate for these mistakes or the firm's indemnity insurance goes up due to negligence claims. Only in the rare case of a reduced timetable being due to reduced work requirements should a reduction in fees be considered a possibility.

Look for cross-selling

Many professionals underestimate the potential for cross-selling the services of other parts of their firm while on assignment for a client. This can be a rich source of premium work as the identification of genuine client needs as well as a good understanding of the client's internal processes should generate highly valuable insights and opportunities. A structured approach to collecting useful client information and to identifying cross-selling opportunities may well compensate for any low fees that had to be agreed to get into the client.

Many of the activities mentioned above, particularly the monitoring of scope creep and the structured approach to cross-selling require a structured approach to managing team members on an assignment.

Manage the team

Managing the delivery team within a PSF project is something that most professionals are experienced in. Nevertheless there are a number of points worth emphasizing from a fee management perspective.

Assign roles and tasks effectively/use leverage

It is vitally important that the right tasks are assigned to the appropriate members of staff both in terms of competence and experience as well as seniority. It is always tempting for professionals to assign particular tasks to the most experienced person, including themselves – this way the work gets done in the shortest time with the least amount of supervision needed, but this approach risks two things. The first is giving up on the financial benefits that leverage can generate – in particular the ability to sell junior hours at a profit. This assumes that the rates at which the juniors, work can be 'sold' to the client include a profit margin and that this is sufficient to cover all required supervisory efforts and time.

The second risk is that professionals have a tendency to hold onto the work themselves, thus delegating as little as possible. This 'sticky finger' tendency can worsen as personal utilization falls and is driven by the fact that many professionals measure their worth solely in terms of the time or amount of client work they have performed and billed. The problem with this approach is that the senior professionals get stuck in technical details (which they love dealing with) rather than looking for ways to build their practice by generating new business, creating new IP, etc – something that is typically less comfortable for professionals.

Communicate

Regular communication with all team members is one of the most effective means for team leaders to provide guidance and receive feedback on progress and the emergence of any problems. In my experience an 'all hands kick-off meeting' is one of the most effective ways of ensuring every member of the team understands the overall objectives of the project and their contributions, and provides an opportunity to resolve any open issues. It also helps create a sense of team identity and helps team members from different offices or practice areas connect with each other better, something that can be particularly helpful when contact is not frequent.

Regular team meetings and debriefings further help foster teamwork and can create an environment in which individuals can be more productive and creative. It is probably not an exaggeration to say that one can't communicate too much with the team – as long as there is something to say.

Communicating with the client is also a major challenge and responsibility for a project leader. Particularly for large and complex transactions, having a regular time slot to review a project with a client above and beyond that which is said during working meetings can prove extremely helpful. Such meetings allow a considered review of the project as well as providing an opportunity to focus on the client relationship. Too many professionals assume that client appreciation of the work and the relationship will be automatic when the service is being delivered, but it is in the interest of the professional to step away from the work at hand and to focus on the relationship, if necessary helping the client to appreciate the services received.

Here again it is essential for the professional to be well prepared and to have something meaningful to discuss with the client. There are few if any major PSF projects that don't merit discussion and review so if a practitioner does indeed think that there is nothing to discuss it should set off warning bells that something is being missed.

Monitor

Regular communication within the team and with the client will also allow the project leader to monitor progress on the project and to identify any unexpected developments in a timely fashion. Some PSF projects can become so big and complex that unless the team communicates regularly and effectively it becomes virtually impossible for the project leader to retain a timely overview and to be able to react as appropriate, particularly when team members are being asked to take on out-of-scope work.

Act on developments

Most PSF projects develop a life of their own sooner or later. This typically results in work that was not part of the original scope and fee quote having to be carried out. Often this may be due to factors beyond anyone's control. However, some clients have become very successful at extracting additional value from their service providers by deliberately negotiating a starting scope they knew would not be sufficient. Either way – practitioners need to react promptly to requests for out-of-scope work. Please note this is not about some minor bagatelle but about anything that will require additional resources or time or which may constitute some additional form of risk. Each professional needs to determine the boundaries between trifles and meaningful work but at an individual as well as a cumulative level as many smaller issues could, when summed up, have taken a meaningful amount of time to deal with.

Project leaders need to avoid clients assuming that there will be no impact on the fees or they will be surprised and possibly annoyed at an overrun for work that might not have been requested if the impact on fees had been made clear. Failure to respond to out-of-scope situations promptly will therefore either result in fee write-offs and/or additional relationship problems.

Manage yourself

Fee management is difficult, demanding, time-consuming and risky. Most professionals feel reasonably well paid and for many money is not the most important motivator. Put these two views together and need anyone wonder that there is a tendency to avoid or skim fee management responsibilities? There is no easy response to this other than for professionals to remind themselves, and for their firms to help remind them, that fee management is worth practising as it improves financial reward, personal wellbeing and client relationships.

It is important that professionals understand these issues and find ways to motivate themselves. In my experience this is best done when professionals support each other, share successes and the burden of setbacks.

Manage the process

This is the area where most professionals feel strongest – running the technical aspects of a project. It is also probably the area where each profession will have different approaches that have been designed to deal with specific issues. Nevertheless it would be remiss of me not to raise a couple of issues in this area.

Have you met Tim Woods?

A lot of interesting PSF process optimization work is coming out of industrial production research and efforts to reduce costs by eliminating waste and increasing efficiencies. Two of the best known approaches in this area are Six Sigma and Lean. A particularly useful acronym, 'TIM WOODS', summarizes the key areas of focus for PSF process improvement.

Table 16.1   TIM WOODS

Area	Issue	Improvement
Transport	Movement of documents between stakeholder for input or approval	Use of collaborative software
Inventory	Work in progress	Appropriate timing, acceleration
Motion	Searching for information or data	Better data retrieval or storage, categorization of precedents,
Waiting	Downtime waiting for input or approvals	Project management, coordination
Over production	Too much or too detailed	Clear specification of what is needed to get job done
Over processing	Excessive number of turnarounds or checking of documents.	Review of when inputs/ checking is optimal
Defects	Mistakes, use of wrong templates, Poor instructions	Better initial instructions, retrieval of appropriate templates
Skills	Insufficiently qualified Work allocations at the wrong level of seniority/expertise	Allocation of work at the lowest qualified level Appropriately qualified staff

Reviewing working processes applying these eight headings is likely to lead to significant efficiency improvements in many PSFs.

The difference between project and process management

Many professionals consider PSF projects as too complex or unpredictable to be project managed. Others, on the other hand, don't think that process management is worth applying to simple processes. Both views are deeply mistaken. The reason for this misconception is a fundamental confusion between project and process management.

Project management is about responding to changes in a project – it is literally about managing the project to reach its end – irrespective of what is happening. Consequently, the more complex or unpredictable a project the more important it is that it is project managed as best as possible to keep budgets and timetable under control as much as possible or to mitigate the impact of change.

Process management is all about optimizing a process to run as efficiently and effectively as possible. Hence the best processes to be process managed are those that occur frequently and can be standardized as much as possible.

Most PSF projects actually require both, as many complex projects include many simpler, standardized processes.

Using project management tools

Firms and professionals should consider using established project management tools or techniques. Often, the benefit is as much about the thought processes and planning that go into them at the start of a project as the actual day-to-day operation of the tool. Gantt charts are an excellent way of thinking about key steps, interdependencies, bottlenecks and timing issues. I have used a range of tools, from dedicated Gantt software to pencil and paper – they all work. Even a simple Excel spreadsheet in which the Gantt bars are drawn as rectangles can be effective.

RACI Matrix is a simple but highly effective way of defining responsibilities and tasks within a project. The acronym stands for Responsible (who is responsible for doing the work), Accountable (who has to sign off or approve the work), Consulted (any special expertise that needs to be included) and Informed (anyone who needs to know but is not directly involved in the work). I have also come across variations such as RASCI in which the additional S stands for Support allocated to those responsible. The basic approach is to break a project down into its constituent steps or phases and to assign the roles outlined above to individuals. The purpose of this is to avoid rework or confusion due to unclear objectives or specifications for output, etc.

A simple version of responsibility mapping is a Function Sheet. This summarizes key tasks, deadlines and deliverables and allocates these to individuals. I have come across a limited number of clients who use this approach. They often find that applying it helps uncover gaps and accelerates problem solving as individuals either know who to approach or, given that they are clearly named for a particular task, start anticipating potential issues.

Although most professionals would shudder at this kind of formal approach to their work the approach mirrors tacit or implicit roles found in most PSF projects. The benefit of adopting a more formal approach comes when projects become more complex and clarity of deliverables is required to ensure on-time and on-cost deliverability.

There are a lot of other process issues, many of them relatively simple, that need to be actively managed. These can range from understanding and clarifying with the client the PSF's billing procedures (the number of bills that have been unnecessarily delayed due to a missing or wrong purchase order number are legion) to more complex ones involving accurate specifications of deliverables.

Fee negotiations are something that falls both in the work process and client management categories for obvious reasons. The more professionals view this part of the project as just that – part of the normal work processes – the more they are likely to engage with it in a constructive manner.

Applying the RULES of PSF projects

A useful way to summarize all of the above is to mention RULES. This is a set of guidelines used in many PSF firms to educate professionals about the drivers of profitability (see Figure 16.4). The acronym stands for:

Rates;

Utilization;

Leverage;

Expenses;

Speed.

Manage each of these drivers in the appropriate way and profitability will improve. Not all can be addressed equally and some PSF strategies will place greater emphasis on one or the other. Here are some of the key issues to consider:

- *Rates.* This is normally all about getting the rates as high as possible. Typically this means going for more complex or more strategic business or projects that allow for charging a premium. Note that firms focusing on 'commodity' business will not focus on this as much. Nevertheless, the higher the rates or fees the more profitable the project. Other issues associated with rates are all about charging what you are entitled to. Avoid double and triple discounting, eg not charging for all the work done and then giving an additional discount just because the bill seemed too high or the client growled a bit.

- *Utilization.* The busier the better is usually a reasonable guideline, but beware the utilization trap, ie taking on work just to be busy. If the work is unprofitable it will tie up resources better applied elsewhere. Also, if professionals are too busy they tend not to engage in sufficient business development to ensure that there is work after the big project has come to an end. Another issue to consider is effective time recording (particularly where the fee is based on day or hourly rates). No point being busy but not recording and charging this to the client. Looking for cross-selling opportunities would also come under this heading.

- *Leverage.* As discussed above, most PSFs are able to achieve additional profitability and effectiveness by applying leverage and using more junior professionals in project teams. Besides, professionals learn on the job and if the next generation of practitioners are not exposed to the work and the client the firm will not have much of a future. Another approach to leverage is to explore the use of IT and other technology to accelerate or optimize work flows. The use of precedent databases that allow complex issues that originally needed a partner to work on, but have been captured so that they can be handled by more junior members of the team, is an example of this.

- *Expenses.* Ensure that all relevant expenses (travel, accommodation, specialist resources, data, etc) are captured and where possible charged to the client. This will depend on the details of the fee agreement negotiated. Some firms apply a disbursement policy, others have a flat percentage for administrative overheads in their standard terms and conditions. I have seen examples of the latter ranging from 3 to 20 per cent of fees. Although they clearly don't include the same things I have also seen partners at these firms 'forgetting' to invoice for them, even though the fee agreement specifically calls for this. Where expenses cannot be passed to the client it makes sense to find ways of cutting expenses where such cuts do not cause either a fall in quality or an increase in workload.

● *Speed.* This is about getting bills out on time. The sooner the better, given the propensities for write-offs to increase with time outstanding for a bill. It is also about talking to clients as soon as possible after the successful conclusion of a project to capitalize on the feelings of achievement or euphoria. Sometimes the timing of such conversations can have a material impact on the likelihood of being mandated again or on the size of any possible performance bonuses.

As this chapter demonstrates, good project management lies at the heart of good fee management. I cannot over-emphasize how much of a contribution fee management and in particular the project management elements will make to both profitability and the quality of client relationships for PSFs and for professionals. It is a skillset well worth cultivating.

Having set out the key principles of effective fee negotiation and value managment, the following chapter provides evidence to illustrate the potential impact that good fee management can have.

Figure 16.4   The RULES of profitability

Realization +	Utilization +	Leverage +	Expenses +	Speed
Size/scope of instruction	Efficient/effective time recording	Exploiting 'efficiency'	Disbursements	Billing frequency
Avoiding 'write-offs'	Meeting deadlines for time recording	Managing expectations re use of partners, associates	Other services (printing, etc)	Billing processes (including compliance with client invoicing systems)
Managing 'add-ons', mission creep	Client agreement rework to be done		Other value added services	Payment terms
Cross-selling			Cost of added services	Payment 'incentives'

The impact of effective veto and target setting: research results

He uses statistics as a drunken man uses lamp-posts, for support rather than for illumination. (ANDREW LANG, SCOTTISH NOVELIST AND FOLKLORIST)

The book has so far provided a conceptual framework for effective fee negotiation. Chapter 8 provides guidance for setting effective vetoes and targets and highlights the central importance this has for preparation. This chapter provides statistical evidence to demonstrate the validity of our guidelines as well as a basis for estimating the economic impact that good preparation can yield for professionals and PSFs.

As the quote above indicates, I have a great degree of respect for the ability of statisticians to prove almost anything statistically. Nevertheless, I believe that the foundation of progress, especially with something as potentially important as negotiation, should be based on hard data, rather than feelings or wishful thinking. Given the direct impact on profitability from improving fees the data shows just how much value is at stake here.

The findings presented in this chapter are unique as our research and database are very much PSF focused and hence quite different to the other negotiation research that is out in the market.

Background to the research

My colleagues and I have been delivering a fee negotiation programme especially designed for the needs of professional services since 2010. Prior to this we were involved in various negotiation programmes but these were not specifically designed for PSFs.

The structure of the programmes is customized to the needs of our clients but typically includes several scenarios representing typical fee negotiations. Attendees are split into groups of usually two (allocated at random) to negotiate the scenarios. Each side is given a briefing which provides sufficient information for participants to set effective vetoes and targets. To illustrate the impact of preparation, attendees negotiate the first scenario relatively early in the workshop. This sets a baseline, reflecting their negotiation approach and competencies prior to our training.

After sufficient time for individual preparation, attendees are asked to negotiate the scenarios. Once these are completed we debrief attendees and construct the ALS (area of likely settlement), vetoes and targets for each negotiation. When we do this, attendees typically see strong patterns emerging, including:

- Almost all agreements fell within the ALS.

- Almost everyone left money on the table before starting the negotiation, as targets were rarely close to the other side's veto.

- There was usually a relationship between one side's veto and its target.

- The outcome of a negotiation could often be predicted based on the vetoes and targets. My colleagues and I are usually able to 'predict' negotiation outcomes within a 10 per cent error of margin on the basis of the numbers.

We started collecting data from 2012 onwards for the first scenario, ie the one that reflects attendees' pre-training competence and experience. To generate additional insights we also collected select background information on attendees: gender, self-reported cultural background and job description. The data was analysed by an independent statistician who is also a chartered and registered organizational psychologist. The analysis showed that the differences described below are statistically robust ($p<0.05$ for those with a background in statistics).

Size of database

The research data described in this chapter is based on data collected between 2012 and 2016 for a population of over 920 attendees from over 48 nationalities. The rough breakdown of participants by nationality is given in Table 17.1.

Table 17.1 Participants by nationality*

Country	Number of participants
UK	347
Germany	199
India	39
US	39
France	37
Australia	25
Ireland	24
Italy	23
Scotland	17
Eastern Europe	44
Other Western Europe	35
Asia	16
Other single nationality	20
Multiple nationalities	56
Total	*921*

*In some cases, negotiations were not conducted in pairs but in bigger groupings; in other cases, individuals self-reported their culture as mixed

A total of over 40 PSF firms were involved. The majority were law firms (over 70 per cent). Other sectors covered included: strategic communications, investment management, accounting, entrepreneurial, design, publishing, coaching, investment banking, consulting and 'other'. We also had a number of entrepreneurs attend our programme.

The functions covered were: private practice lawyers, consultants, HR, finance, banking, accounting, senior management, investment management and business development.

The majority of our participants were either at partner (or equivalent) level or one level below.

As this research is ongoing we expect to be able to grow the database over time and to be linking it to other diagnostic tools over time. Any reader interested in getting involved in the research can contact the author at www.psf-fees.com.

Although our statistical analysis provides fascinating insights into a broad number of issues I will focus on a small number of key questions:

- Are there any general patterns that our data shows?
- Is there a clear predictor of outcome?
- How well do attendees set vetoes and targets?
- Are there significant differences between cultures, gender or firms?

General patterns

The statistical analysis was able to confirm a number of basic patterns:

1 Ninety-six per cent of all negotiations reached outcomes within the range defined by the veto of the service provider (PSF) and the client. Where the outcomes fell outside this range, this was almost always when one of the vetoes was not real, ie when the person setting the veto did not 'really mean it'.

2 Seventy-three per cent of the outcomes fell within the range of the two targets. The reasons for the exceptions are more varied. The most common ones include one side not really having set meaningful targets, not being fully committed to the negotiation or one of the negotiators dropping a very effective anchor.

To help explain our other findings it is helpful to use the following definitions:

Ambition – the difference between veto and target.

Achievement – how close to their target they achieve.

Figure 17.1   Negotiation outcomes

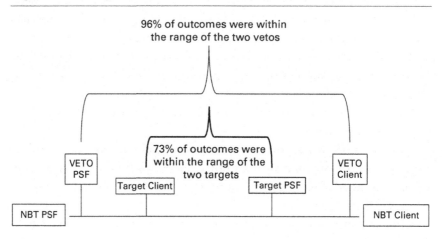

© Møller PSFG Cambridge 2017 – Ori Wiener

Veto estimate – how close to the other party's veto they aim.

Value claimed – how close to the other party's veto they achieve.

The impact of targets

The statistical analysis revealed a number of key insights:

1 The relationship between a negotiator's veto and target had some impact on the eventual outcome of a negotiation.

2 The single most important variable on outcome was the target.

3 For each 1 per cent of target set closer to the veto of the counterpart there was an improved outcome of 0.6 per cent, showing that the better a negotiator can estimate the other side's veto the better the outcome. In the past, with smaller samples, we found a higher improvement (0.8 per cent). The difference may either be due to the larger, more diverse sample size, or to the fact that delegates from firms that we have been working with for a longer time have, over time, started to negotiate harder

Figure 17.2   Distribution of target setting

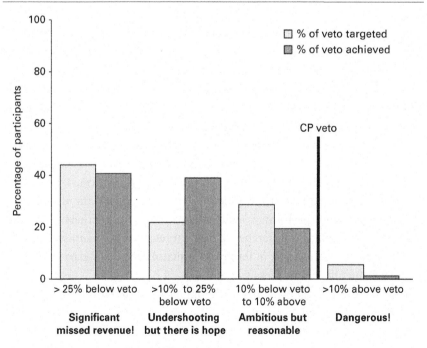

(and have therefore not been as influenced by an opening position as their predecessors). This may be an indirect effect of the workshops and changing behaviours in these firms.

4 Looking at our sample as a whole the data showed that:

a About 5 per cent of participants set a target that was greater than 10 per cent above the other side's veto. Such a high target is likely to contribute to an early breakdown on negotiation, especially if an opening number was quoted above the target.

b About 28 per cent of participants set a target that was within a 10 per cent range of the other side's veto. This is considered to be ideal.

c About 22 per cent of participants set a target between 10 per cent and 25 per cent below the other side's veto. This is likely to leave money on the table given the relationship between targets and outcome listed above.

d About 45 per cent of participants set targets that were 25 per cent or less, in some cases even 50 per cent of the other side's veto. These negotiators run the risk of significantly underperforming in the subsequent negotiation.

Other general patterns

Analysis of the data showed that generally speaking sellers outperformed buyers. This should not come as a surprise, as those in the seller's position typically feel under greater pressure and hence make a great effort. This view is supported by the fact that our data showed that those in the service provider (seller) role set higher targets compared to their vetoes than those representing clients (32 per cent vs 19 per cent).

Sellers also set better targets when compared to the veto of the counterpart (–19 per cent vs –37 per cent) than clients did. Consequently, sellers claimed more value than the clients (80 per cent vs 68 per cent).

Looking at the different job functions or sectors, the data also showed that lawyers underperformed against consultants and others. Although there was no significant difference in how targets were set against their own vetoes, lawyers were worse in terms of estimating the counterparty's vetoes and consequently claimed less value.

Our data did not show statistically significant differences in negotiation performance between men and women except for ambition, ie the difference between vetoes and targets. On this measure, women were less ambitious than their male or mixed group counterparts. This difference did not, however, translate into statistically significant differences in veto estimation or value claimed. This is quite at odds with the findings of other research studies. The reasons for this are discussed at greater length in Chapter 14. We suspect that one of the major reason for this absence of differences between genders, which is contrary to other findings, is that those attending our programme have gained sufficient experience and seniority that gender no longer has a significant impact on outcome. Any differences in initial ambition are offset by other factors.

Cultural differences

As we also collected biographical data we were able to look into potential differences due to culture and firms.

The data shows that German, US and Indian negotiators tended to be more ambitious, ie set relatively higher targets compared to their vetoes.

When we look at how well targets are set compared to the counterparty's veto and at the value claimed, we see that in fact US and Italian negotiators set more effective targets (relative to the other side's veto) and hence achieved better outcomes as determined by value claimed.

What this data is telling us is that the German and Indian negotiators in our client base may think that they are being ambitious when in fact they actually underperform on a relative basis.

Figure 17.3   Cultural differences – ambition

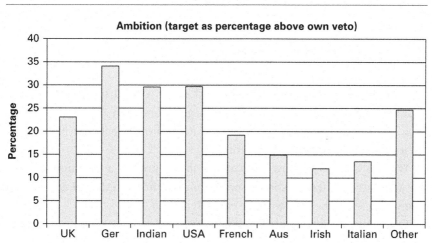

Figure 17.4   Cultural differences – veto estimation and value claimed

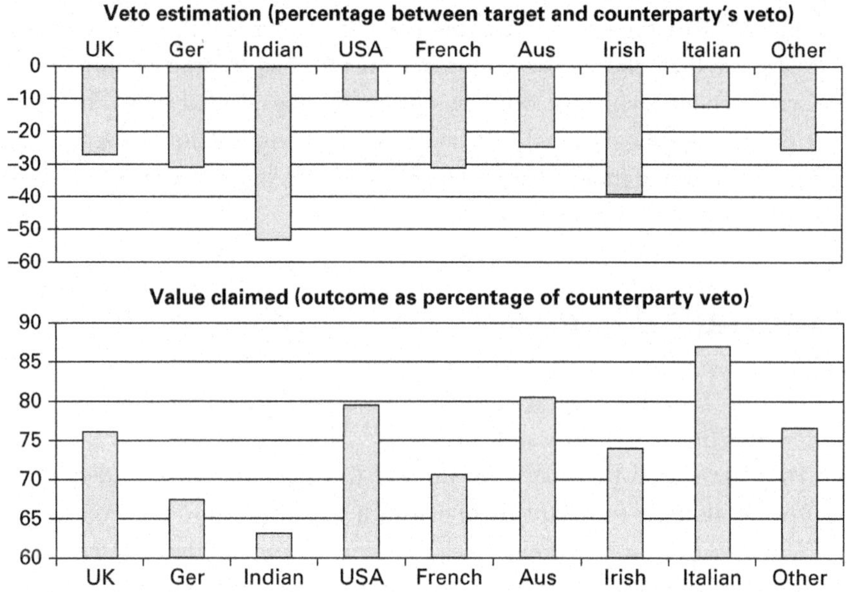

© Møller PSFG Cambridge 2017 – Ori Wiener

We do not at this stage have sufficient data to be able to explain the reasons for these differences. Some are no doubt due to differences in market practices, with the more competitive markets prompting 'better' negotiation behaviours. Other differences will, no doubt, be due to cultural differences, some of which I have outlined in Chapter 14.

The impact of organizations

One of the most interesting questions that we wanted to investigate was whether some firms produced better negotiators than others and, if so, which? Are participants from 'market-leading firms' generally better than their regional or boutique competitors?

We also wanted to know if it was possible to provide a quantitative basis for attributing differences in the profitability of firms to the fee negotiation competencies of their partners or equivalent staff.

Once the data was available and analysed we could see a pattern similar to the differences in cultures emerging.

The first pattern that was apparent was that partners from different firms, even within the same sector (eg law), had quite different levels of ambition (when targets are compared to vetoes). This is a particularly meaningful finding, as our negotiation scenarios are adjusted for each client so as to reflect the size of a typical fee negotiated in that firm. International, market-leading firms might be negotiating fees of several hundred thousand, or millions, whereas regional firms' scenarios would be focused on deals of several tens of thousands or a few hundred thousand.

Only when we look at targets in relation to the other side's vetoes do we see that many of the firms whose delegates appeared to be ambitious in fact underperformed on a relative basis. The relationship between effective target setting and value claimed can be seen in Figure 17.6. Those firms such as Firms C, D, E or W whose delegates on average set targets closer than other firms to the veto of their counterparty claimed disproportionally more value than other firms.

The impact in terms of profitability can be highly significant. In our dataset (for firms for which we had sufficient observations to be statistically significant) the difference in value captured between the best (85 per cent) and worst (57 per cent) performers was 28 per cent. Even if we were to use the average (74 per cent) as a reference point there is a 17 per cent difference. We think that our data suggests that many firms could improve their fee negotiation performance by between around 30 and 15 per cent. Even firms that perform above average could still improve performance by several per cent.

Figure 17.5 Firm differences – ambition

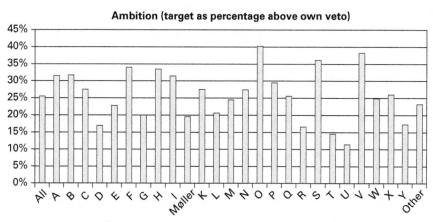

NOTE Møller refers to Møller PSF Group's Open Fee Negotiation Programme and reflects a broad range of firms.

© Møller PSFG Cambridge 2017 – Ori Wiener

Figure 17.6   Firm differences – veto estimation and value claimed

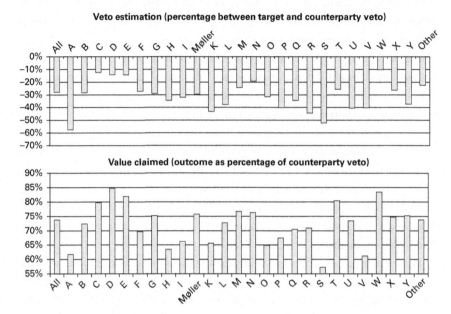

NOTE Møller refers to Møller PSF Group's Open Fee Negotiation Programme and reflects a broad range of firms.

We should not, however, over-interpret the results of our research but, given the statistical robustness of the data, we can be comfortable with the main conclusions drawn, which are:

- effective veto and target setting has a significant impact on profitability;
- the harder you try and the better you prepare, the higher will be your share of the value.

We look to continue to expand this research and would be interested to hear from readers who would like to participate either personally or who would like to determine how their firm compares to their competitors. For further details, please contact the author at www.psf-fees.com.

Summary
Value management: the critical skill set of the future

Insanity is repeating the same mistake and expecting different results.
(BASIC TEXT OF *NARCOTICS ANONYMOUS*)

Anyone who has never made a mistake has never tried anything new.
(ALBERT EINSTEIN)

This book started out with the premise that value management skills are a fundamental and critical skill set of the modern professional and that professional service firms need to raise and invest in the general level of fee management skills of their employees. Maintaining conventional approaches to handling clients and fees and expecting to improve profitability and generate sustainable growth is, as the first quote illustrates, illusionary.

It is a near certainty that the importance of fee management skills is set to rise even more. The previous chapter provides tantalizing evidence regarding the potential financial upside from improved fee negotiation capabilities. A failure to meet the challenges associated with setting, getting and keeping the right fees on the other hand, is likely to result in institutional and personal disappointment, if not ultimately failure.

Change is upon professional service firms

The 2008 financial crisis has prompted a review of many assumptions underlying our economic thinking, including demands to move away from a single-minded focus on pure profit motives (Sedlacek, 2011). It is more than likely, however, that the relationship between PSF firms and their clients will increasingly be characterized by greater attention to the economics of the relationships.

The increased focus on fees and value for money predated the financial crisis and was driven by developments over the last two decades in which globalization and advances in information technology prompted and facilitated increasing competition and benchmarking between service providers.

Information technology is also accelerating the commoditization of professional services in two ways. On the one hand the internet is allowing more providers, from a much larger geographic region, to compete effectively for, and deliver, PSF work. On the other hand, broader and easier access to information is reducing knowledge or know-how barriers of entry. This process is likely to be accelerating. John Kotter, one of the world's leading leadership and change management experts, wrote in 1996: 'the rate of change is not going to slow down anytime soon. If anything, competition in most industries will probably speed up even more in the next few decades.' (Kotter, 1996). It is more than likely that what held true for the last 15 years will apply even more so for the next 15 years. At the time of writing, a number of leading PSF firms have announced joint ventures or other projects involving the greater use of Artificial Intelligence (AI) to improve execution efficiencies.

PSFs and professionals can respond to this in one of two ways if they seek to preserve profitability. One alternative would be to adapt their business models to the commoditization and become more efficient, ie become low-cost providers. Alternatively, they can move up the value curve (see Chapter 3) and seek to win work and generate premium fees by developing specialist expertise, know-how or capabilities. The latter will become increasingly difficult to do successfully and will require increasingly sophisticated client management skills.

Either response will require much sharper pricing, negotiation and fee management skills. In particular those firms and professionals seeking to generate premium fees will have to become better at delivering value to clients. This may well require a more proactive and challenging approach than has been the norm to date.

Extensive research by the Corporate Executive Board (Dixon and Adamson, 2011) has shown that relationship-based sales representatives consistently underperform against those sales representatives who are able to challenge clients' thinking and who can provide their clients with new insights. Although most of the research was conducted with non-PSF firms, the key lessons apply to PSFs just as much, if not more so.

As outlined in Chapter 5, one of the best approaches to countering the use of procurement is to differentiate and offer clients something they cannot get elsewhere. Challenging the way that clients think about the way they work with their professional service providers and their selection processes may be part of this. This will also include more robust and creative approaches to fee negotiations.

As the book demonstrates, professionals and firms that continue to ignore fee management do so at their own peril. In fact, throughout this book, the reader should have found many ways of applying fee management skills to improve both the nature and quality of client relationships as well as their economic performance. One does not have to come at the expense of the other (love vs money fallacy).

Change is hard but easier than it at first appears

Professionals and PSFs are notoriously conservative; gaining technical expertise and know-how requires time and a certain degree of stability. It is no surprise then that PSFs and professionals are finding it difficult to adjust to the external changes that have taken place over the last decade or so.

To implement change it is best to get going fast, start with small things and monitor progress, making adjustments on the way. Useful hints and recommendations on how this can best be done can be found in a fascinating book called *Switch* (Heath and Heath, 2010).

Good fee management is about getting lots of small steps right. I do not advocate making wholesale changes to reporting or remuneration systems overnight or to go for big fee increases in one go. Rather, introducing small but continuous change is more likely to be accepted by professionals. Likewise, clients are unlikely to 'fire' a professional for a two or three per cent uplift during a project as a result of a change in scope. The professional, however, who can get such small changes through consistently during a project, will generate a significant premium by the end of it without risking the client relationship.

It is important, particularly for PSF management teams, to realize that small changes can have a big impact and that if a number of changes can be applied in an aligned manner these will generate major synergies. The beauty of fee management is that small changes in fees or reductions in costs (wastage) have a multiplier effect on profitability.

The book has provided lots of demonstrations of what can be done at both the individual and institutional levels with small changes such as trading concessions rather than giving them away or applying a well-thought-through anchor to improve the final outcome of a fee negotiation. Simply being more aware of scope creep and handling this constructively is likely to yield significant benefits to both professional and client.

Great negotiators and fee managers are made – not born

One of the central themes of the book is that everyone can improve their fee management capabilities. They need not all do it in the same way. After all, 3 per cent more revenue will have the same impact on profit whether it came from a better up-front negotiation, more ambitious pricing or better scope management. Different professionals will be more comfortable in different parts of the golden triangle. This should be recognized and capitalized on.

PSF management should also not yield to the temptation of labeling fee management for all partners as 'too difficult'. A number of my clients have been able to improve profitability consistently by providing all their professionals with the support needed to help them apply key fee management principles including training, peer-to-peer support and basic information on clients and profitability. The other critical element is the creation of a culture within firms that promotes and facilitates peer-to-peer exchange of views within the firms' professionals. Only when partners feel comfortable seeking each other's help will they feel comfortable engaging constructively with clients' constant demands for reduced fees.

The irony of professional service firms is that in theory PSFs ought to be in a strong position vis-à-vis their clients. After all, they have the specialist knowledge and qualifications that their clients lack but need. Their professionals are highly skilled and educated. In practice, however, we find that many PSFs and professionals remain stuck in a subservient mindset that significantly contributes to unhappy client relationships and lost fees. Professionals need to be better at understanding if a client is looking for a relationship or a deal and they need to deal with each differently.

When professionals are able to exercise this judgement, apply the appropriate approach and receive the support needed from their peers and organizations, they will deliver better work, have better client relationships and may enjoy the fruits of their professional careers more.

For more information see www.psf-fees.com

REFERENCES

Adair, W L and Brett, J M (2005) The negotiation dance: Time, culture, and behavioral sequences in negotiation, *Organization Science*, **16** (1), pp 33–51

Adair, W L, Brett, J M, Lempereur, A, Okumura, T, Shikhirev, P, Tinsely, C and Lytle, A (2004) Culture and negotiation strategy, *Negotiation Journal*, **20** (1) pp 87–111

Atkin, T S and Rinehart, L M (2006) The effect of negotiation practices on the relationship between suppliers and customers, *Negotiation Journal*, January

Babcock, L and Laschever, S (2007) *Women Don't Ask: The high cost of avoiding negotiation – and positive strategies for change*, Bantam Dell, New York

Babitsky, S and Mangraviti Jr, J (2011) *Never Lose Again: Become a top negotiator by asking the right questions*, Thomas Dunne Books, New York

Bacon, F (1597/1985) *Essays of Francis Bacon*, Penguin Classics, London

Baker, R J (2011) *Implementing Value Pricing: A radical business model for professional firms*, Wiley, Chichester

Barry, B, Fulmer, I S and Goates, N (2006) Bargaining with feeling: Emotionality in and around negotiation, in (ed) L L Thompson, *Negotiation Theory and Research*, Psychology Press, Hove and New York

Baumoel, D and Trippe, B (2015), Beyond the Thomas–Kilmann model: Into extreme conflict, *Negotiation Journal*, **31** (2), pp 89–103

Bazerman, M H and Gillespie, S S (1999) Billing on the future: The virtues of contingent contracts, *Harvard Business Review*, **77** (4)

Bazerman, M H, Magliozzi, T and Neale, M A (1983) Integrative bargaining in a competitive market, Working Paper, Alfred P Sloan School of Management, pp 1470–83

Bhappu, A D and Barsness, Z I (2006) Risks of e-mail, in (eds) A Kupfer Schneider and C Honeyman, *The Negotiator's Fieldbook*, 1st edn, American Bar Association, Washington

Bodine, L (2010) Alternative fee arrangements – ho hum, *Law Office Management and Administration Report*, **10** (12)

Bowles, H R, Babcock, L and McGinn, K L (2005) Constraints and triggers: Situaional mechanics of gender in negotiation, *Journal of Personality and Social Psychology*, **89**, pp 951–65

Bright, D and Parkin, B (1997) *Human Resource Management: Concepts and practices*, Business Education Publishers Ltd, Sunderland

Burcher, R (2012) I don't give a tinker's cuss about value – I just want the lowest price, in (ed) S Hodges, *Buying Legal: Procurement insights and practice*, Ark Group, London

Burns, D, McLinn, J and Porter, M, *Understanding Value: How to capture the pricing opportunity in chemicals*, Bain & Company website

Camp, J (2002) *Start with No*, Crown Business, New York

Cassell, J and Bird, T (2012) *Brilliant Selling: What the best salespeople know, do and say*, 2nd edn, Pearson Education, London

Ching-Chow, Y (2005) The refined Kano's model and its application, *Total Quality Management*, **16** (10), pp 1127–37

Cialdini, R (2007) *Influence: The psychology of persuasion*, Harper Collins, New York

Coates, J (2012) *The Hour Between Dog and Wolf: Risk taking, gut feelings and the biology of boom and bust*, The Penguin Press, New York

Collins, R B (2009) *Talking Your Way to What You Want: Negotiate to win!* Sterling, New York

Conti, G (2016) How women can demand a higher salary, *Financial Times*, 2 May, p 9, European Edition

Crocker, B, Moore, D and Emmett, S (2010) *Excellence in Services Procurement: How to optimise costs and add value*, Cambridge Academic, Cambridge

Curhan, J R and Pentland, A (2007) Thin slices of negotiation: Predicting outcomes from conversational dynamics within the first 5 minutes, *Journal of Applied Psychology*, **92** (3), pp 802–11

Curhan, J R, Neale, M A and Ross, L D (2004) Dynamic valuation: Preference changes in the context of face-to-face negotiation, *Journal of Experimental Social Psychology*, **40**, pp 142–51

Czerniawska, F and Smith, P (2010) *Buying Professional Services: How to get value for money from consultants and other professional services providers*, *The Economist* in association with Profile Books, London

Dawson, R (1999) *Secrets of Power Negotiating: Inside secrets from a master negotiator*, 2nd edn, The Career Press, Wayne, NJ

De Dreu, C K W (2003) Time pressure and closing of the mind in negotiation, *Organizational Behavior and Human Decision Processes*, **91** (2), pp 280–95

De Dreu, C K W and Carnevale, P J D (2003) Motivational bases for information processing and strategy in negotiation and conflict, *Advances in Experimental Social Psychology* **35**, pp 235–93

De Dreu, C K W, Weingart, L R and Kwon, S (2000a) Influence of social motives on integrative negotiation: A meta-analytic review and test of two theories, *Journal of Personality and Social Psychology*, **78** (5), pp 889–905

De Dreu, C K W, Koole, S L and Steinel W (2000b) Unfixing the fixed pie: A motivated information-processing approach to integrative negotiation, *Journal of Personality and Social Psychology*, **79** (6), pp 975–87

De Dreu, C K W, Beersma, B, Stroebe, K and Euwema, M C (2006) Motivated information processing, strategic choice, and the quality of negotiated agreement, *Journal of Personality and Social Psychology*, **90** (6), pp 927–43

DeLong, T J, Gabarro, J J and Lees, R J (2007) *When Professionals Have to Lead*, Harvard Business School Press, Harvard, MA

DeRue, D S, Conlon, D E, Moon, H and Willaby, H W (2009) When is straightfor-wardness a liability in negotiations, *Journal of Applied Psychology*, **94** (4), pp 1032–47

Deutsch, M (1958) Trust and suspicion, *Journal of Conflict Resolution*, **2**, pp 265–79

Diamond, S (2010) *Getting More: How you can negotiate to succeed in work and life*, Three Rivers Press, New York

Diekmann, K A, Tenbrunsel, A E and Galinsky, A D (2003) From self-prediction to self-defeat: Behavioral forecasting, self-fulfilling prophecies, and the effect of competitive expectations, *Journal of Personality and Social Psychology*, **85** (4), pp 672–83

Dixon, M and Adamson, B (2011) *The Challenger Sale: Taking control of the customer conversation*, Portfolio/Penguin, London

Dobrijevic, G, Stanisic, M and Masic, B (2011) Sources of negotiation power: An exploratory study, *South African Journal of Business Management*, **42** (2), pp 35–41

Dodds, S J T (2014) *Smarter Pricing, Smarter Profit: A guide for the law firm of the future*, ABA Publishing, Chicago, IL

Doolan, K (2015) *Mastering Services Pricing: Designing pricing that works for you and for your clients*, Pearson Education Limited, Harlow

Drucker, P F (1964) *Managing for Results*, HarperBusiness, reprint April 1993, London

Eagly, A H and Karau, S J (2002) Role congruity theory of prejudice towards female leaders, *Psychological Review*, **109**, pp 573–98

Englich, B, Mussweiler, T and Strack, F (2006) Playing dice with criminal sentences: The influence of irrelevant anchors on experts' judicial decision making, *Personality and Social Psychology Bulletin* **32**, pp 188–200

Epley, N, Caruso, E and Bazerman, M H (2006) When perspective taking increases taking: Reactive egoism in social interaction, *Journal of Personality and Social Psychology*, **91** (5), pp 872–89

Eriksson, K H, and Sandberg, A (2012) Gender differences in initiation of negotia-tion: Does the gender of the negotiation counterpart matter? *Negotiation Journal*, **28** (4)

Fassina, N E and Whyte, G R (2003) 'Quite frankly, this is an insult': The effects of strategic demurral in response to an opening offer in distributive negotiations, Paper presented at the meeting of the Academy of Management, Denver

Fassina, N E and Whyte, G R (2005) Strategic demurral in integrative negotiations: The mediating role of contentious behaviours and anger, *SSRN Electronic Journal*, January [online] www.researchgate.net

Fisher, R, Ury, W and Patton, B (2011) *Getting to Yes: Negotiating an agreement without giving in*, 3rd edn, Penguin Books, New York

Forgas, J P (1998) On feeling good and getting your way: mood effects on negotiator cognition and bargaining strategies, *Journal of Personality and Social Psychology*, **74** (3), pp 565–77

Fulmer, I S and Barry, B (2004) The smart negotiator: Cognitive ability and emotional intelligence in negotiation, *The International Journal of Conflict Management*, **15**, pp 245–72

Galinsky, A D and Mussweiler, T (2001) First offers as anchors: The role of perspective-taking and negotiator focus, *Journal of Personality and Social Psychology*, **81** (4), pp 657–69

Galinsky, A D, Maddux, W W, Gilin, D and White, J B (2008) Why it pays to get inside the head of your opponent: The differential effects of perspective taking and empathy in negotiations, *Psychological Science*, **19** (4), pp 378–84

Gates, S (2012) *The Negotiation Book*, 2nd edn, Wiley, Chichester

Giacomantonio, M, De Dreu, C K K and Mannetti, L (2010) Now you see it, now you don't: Interests, issues, and psychological distance in integrative negotiation, *Journal of Personality and Social Psychology*, **98** (5), pp 761–74

Gneezy, U, Leonard, K L and List, J A (2009) Gender differences in competition: Evidence from a matrilineal and a patriarchal society, *Econometrica*, **77** (5), pp 1637–64

Gottschalk, A (2008) The pharma negotiator: A style profile, *Business Development and Licensing Journal* [online] http://plg-group.com/wp-content/uploads/2014/03/The-Pharma-Neogitator-a-style-profile-Andrew-Gotschalk-PL.pdf

Guth, S R (2008) *The Contract Negotiation Handbook: An indispensable guide for contract professionals*, Lulu Press, Morrisville, NC

Hanohov, I (2008) It's about time, Challenging time based systems for pricing legal services and proposing changes to reform law firm pricing, MBA thesis, Cass Business School

Hardy, W (2008) The unhappy lawyer, at http://willhardy.com.au/legal-essays/unhappy-lawyers/detail/

Haselhuhn, M P (2007) Implicit negotiation beliefs and performance: Experimental and longitudinal evidence, *Journal of Personality and Social Psychology*, **93** (1), pp 49–64

Haselhuhn, M P (2014) Support theory in negotiation: How unpacking aspirations and alternatives can improve negotiation performance, *Journal of Behavioural Decision Making*, doi:10.1002/bdm.1823

Hazeldine, S (2014) *Neuro-Sell: How neuroscience can power your sales success*, Kogan Page, London

Heath, C and Heath, D (2010) *Switch: How to change things when change is hard*, Broadway Books, New York

Hill, P (2013) *Pricing for Profit: How to develop a powerful pricing strategy for your business*, Kogan Page, London

Hodges, S (2012) *Buying Legal: Procurement insights and practice*, Ark Group, London

Hodges Silverstein, S (2015) *Legal Procurement Handbook*, Buying Legal Council https://hbr.org/2013/04/common-language-doesnt-equal-c

Jarzabkowski, P and Balogun, J (2009) The practice and process of delivering integration through strategic planning, *Journal of Management Studies*, **46** (8), pp 1255–88

Kahneman, D (2012) *Thinking, Fast and Slow*, Penguin Books, London

Kano, N, Nobuhiku, S, Fumio, T and Shinichi, T (1984) Attractive quality and must-be quality, *Journal of the Japanese Society for Quality Control* (in Japanese) **14** (2), pp 39–48

Kennedy, G (1987) *Pocket Negotiator*, Basil Blackwell, Oxford and *The Economist* Publications, London

Kennedy, G (2004) *Negotiation: An A–Z guide*, *The Economist* Publications, London and Profile Books, London

Kim, P H and Fragale, A R (2005) Choosing the path to bargaining power: An empirical comparison of BATNAs and contributions in negotiation, *Journal of Applied Psychology*, **90** (2), pp 373–81

Kind, R (2007) *Negotiation Skills for Lawyers*, Ark Group, London

Kolb, D M and Williams, J (2003) *Everyday Negotiation – Navigating the hidden agendas in bargaining*, Jossey-Bass, San Francisco

Kotter, J P (1996) *Leading Change*, Harvard Business School Press, Boston

Kraljic, P (1983) Purchasing must become supply management, *Harvard Business Review*, September/October

Kray, L J and Haselhuhn, M P (2007) Implicit negotiation beliefs and performance: Experimental and longitudinal evidence, *Journal of Personality and Social Psychology*, **93** (1), pp 49–64

Ku, G, Galinsky, A D and Murnighan, J K (2006) Starting low but ending high: A reversal of the anchoring effect in auctions, *Journal of Personality and Social Psychology*, **90** (6), pp 975–86

Kwon, S and Weingart, L R (2004) Unilateral concessions from the other party: Concession behavior, attributions, and negotiation judgments, *Journal of Applied Psychology*, **89** (2), pp 263–78

Kwon, S and Weingart, L R (2005) Social motive expectations and the concession timing effect, Tepper School of Business, Paper 543

Lamb, P J (2010) *Alternative Fee Arrangements: Value fees and the changing legal market*, Ark Group, London

Larrick, R P and Wu, G (2007) Claiming a large slice of a small pie: Asymmetric disconfirmation in negotiation, *Journal of Personality and Social Psychology*, **93** (2), pp 212–33

Lawrence, J (2015) Why do I make less than my male co-stars, *Lenny*, Letter 3, 13 October [online] http://us11.campaign-archive1.com/?u=a5b04a26aae05a24bc4efb63e&id=64e6f35176&e=1ba99d671e#wage

Lax, D A and Sebenius, J K (2003) 3-D Negotiations: Playing the whole game, *Harvard Business Review*, November

Lax, D A and Sebenius, J K (2012) Deal making 2.0, A guide to complex negotiations, *Harvard Business Review,* November, p 11

Levy, S B (2009) *Legal Project Management: Control costs, meet schedules, manage risks, and maintain sanity,* DayPack Books, Seattle

Levy, S B (2014) *Legal Project Management: Field guide,* DayPack Books, Seattle

Lewicki, R J, Barry, B and Saunders, D M (2010) *Negotiation,* McGraw-Hill, New York

Lewis, R D (2005) *When Cultures Collide,* 3rd revised edn, Nicholas Brealey Publishing, London

Liu, B (2014) *Work Smarts: What CEOs say you need to know to get ahead,* John Wiley & Sons, Hoboken, NJ

Locke, J L (2011) *Duels and Duets: Why men and women talk so differently,* Cambridge University Press, Cambridge

Loomis, J L (1959) Communication, the development of trust, and cooperative behaviour, *Human Relations,* **12,** pp 305–15

Lorsch, J and Mathias, P (1987) When professionals have to manage, *Harvard Business Review,* July/August

Maaravi, Y, Yoav, G and Pazy, A (2011) Negotiation as a form of persuasion: Arguments in first offers, *Journal of Personality and Social Psychology,* **101** (2), pp 245–55

Maister, D H (1993) *Managing the Professional Service Firm,* Free Press, New York

Malhotra, D (2016) *Negotiating the Impossible: How to break deadlocks and resolve ugly conflicts (without money or muscle),* Berrett-Koehler Publishers, Oakland

Malhotra, D and Bazerman, M H (2007) *Negotiation Genius: How to overcome obstacles and achieve brilliant results at the bargaining table and beyond,* Bantam Dell, New York

Malhotra, D K and Ginges, J (2005) Beyond reactive devaluation: Implementation concerns and fixed-pie perceptions involving the Geneva Accords, IACM 18th Annual Conference

Malhotra, N, Morris, T and Hinings, C R (2006) Variations in organisational form among professional service organisations, in (eds) R Greenwood and R Suddaby, *Professional Service Firms: Research in the sociology of organisations,* vol 24, Emerald Group Publishing Ltd, Bingley, pp 171–202

Marcus, L J, Dorn, B C and McNulty, E J (2012) The walk in the woods: A step-by-step method for facilitating interest-based negotiation and conflict resolution, *Negotiation Journal,* **28,** pp 337–49

Mazei, J, Hüffmeister, J, Freund, P A, Stuhlmacher, A F, Bilke, L and Hertel, G (2015) A meta-analysis on gender differences in negotiation outcomes and their moderators, *Psychological Bulletin,* **141,** pp 85–104

Meehan, J M, Simonetto, M G, Montan, L Jr and Goodin, C A (2011) *Pricing and Profitability Management: A practical guide for business leaders*, Wiley, Chichester

Merrill, D W and Reid, R H (1984) *Personal Styles and Effective Performance*, CRC Press, Boca Raton, FL

Meyer, P (2010) *Lie Spotting: Proven techniques to detect deception*, St Martin's Griffin, New York

Miles, E W (2013) Developing strategies for asking questions in negotiation, *Negotiation Journal*, **29** (4)

Mintu-Wimsatt, A (2002) Personality and negotiation style: The moderating effects of cultural context, *Thunderbird International Business Review*, **44** (6), pp 729–48

Mnookin, R H, Peppet, S R and Tulumello, A S (2000) *Beyond Winning: Negotiating to create value in deals and disputes*, The Belknap Press of Harvard University Press, Cambridge, MA

Molinsky, A, (2013) Common language doesn't equal common culture, *Harvard Business Review*, April [online] https://hbr.org/2013/04/common-language-doesnt-equal-c

Morris, M, Nadler, J, Kurtzberg, T and Thompson, L (2002) Schmooze or lose: Social friction and lubrication in e-mail negotiations, *Group Dynamics: Theory, research, and practice*, **6** (1), pp 89–100

Mulqueen, C M and Collins, D (2014) *Social Style and Versatility Facilitator Handbook*, TRACOM Press, Centennial

Murray, B and Fortinberry, A (2015) Neurogenetics of pricing: Why fee discounts destroy client loyalty, *Managing Partner Magazine*, April

O'Brien, J (2013) *Negotiation for Purchasing Professionals*, Kogan Page, London

Ogilvie, D T and Simms, S (2009) The impact of creativity training on an accounting negotiation, *Group Decisions and Negotiation*, **18**, pp 75–87

Olekalns, M and Weingart, L (2008) Emergent Negotiations: Stability and shifts in process dynamics, *Negotiation and Conflict Management Research*, **1**, pp 135–60

Oliver, D (2011) *How to Negotiate Effectively: Improve your success rate, get the best deal, achieve win-win results*, 3rd edn, Kogan Page, London

Pecquet, A (1737/2007) *Discourse on the Art of Negotiation*, Peter Lang, New York

Phillips, R (2009) *Good Practice Guide: Fee management*, RIBA Publishing, London

Porter, M E (1990, 2003) *Competitive Strategy: Techniques for analyzing industries and competitors*, Free Press, New York

Pulido-Martos, M, Lopez-Zafra, E and Augusto-Landa, J M (2013) Perceived emotional intelligence and its relationship with perceptions of effectiveness in negotiation, *Journal of Applied Social Psychology*, **43**, pp 408–17

Raiffa, H (1982) *The Art and Science of Negotiation: How to resolve conflicts and get the best out of bargaining*, Harvard University Press, Cambridge, MA

Reilly, L (1994) *How to Outnegotiate Anyone (Even a Car Dealer)*, Adams Media Corporation, Avon, MA

Richardson, B (2013) *How to Sweet-talk a Shark: Strategies and stories from a master negotiator*, Rodale, New York

Riley Bowles, H and Flynn, F (2010) Gender and persistence in negotiation: A dyadic perspective, *Academy of Management Journal*, 53 (4), pp 769–87

Robertson, M A and Calloway, J A (2008) *Winning Alternatives to the Billable Hour: Strategies that work*, 3rd edn, American Bar Association-Law Practice Management Section, New York

Roch, M (2010) *Pricing and Profitability for Law Firms*, 2nd edn, Ark Group, London

Roche, H (2013) *Targeting Profitability: Strategies to improve law firm performance*, Ark Group, London

Rubin, J Z and Brown, B R (1975) *The Social Psychology of Bargaining and Negotiation*, Academic Press, London

Salacuse, J W (1999) Intercultural negotiation in international business, *Group Decision and Negotiation*, 8, pp 217–36

Sandberg, S (2015) *Lean In: Women, work, and the will to lead*, W H Allen, London

Sarkar, A N (2010) Navigating the rough seas of global business negotiation: Reflection on cross-cultural issues and some corporate experience, *International Journal of Business Insights & Transformation*, 3 (2), pp 47–61

Savage, G, Blair, J and Sorenson, J (1989) Consider both relationships and substance when negotiating strategically, *Academy of Management Executive*, 3 (1), pp 37–48

Schoonmaker, A N (1989) *Negotiate to Win: Gaining the psychological edge*, Prentice Hall, Upper Saddle River, NJ

Sebenius, J K (2013) Level two negotiations: Helping the other side meet its 'behind the table' challenges, *Negotiation Journal*, January, pp 7–21

Sedlacek, T (2011) *Economics of Good and Evil: The quest for economic meaning from Gilgamesh to Wall Street*, Oxford University Press, New York

Shell, G R (2006) *Bargaining for Advantage: Negotiation strategies for reasonable people*, 2nd edn, Penguin Books, London

Shenson, H L (1990) *The Contract and Fee-Setting Guide for Consultants and Professionals*, Wiley, Chichester

Sinaceur, M and Neale, M A (2005) Not all threats are created equal: How implicitness and timing affect the effectiveness of threats in negotiations, *Group Decision and Negotiation*, 14, pp 63–85

Sinaceur, M, Adam, H, Van Kleef, G A and Galinsky, A G (2013a) The advantages of being unpredictable: How emotional inconsistency extracts concessions in negotiation, *Journal of Experimental Social Psychology*, 49 (3), pp 498–508

Sinaceur, M, Maddux, W, Vasiljevic, D, Perez Nuckel, R and Galinsky, A D (2013b) Good things come to those who wait: Late first offers facilitate creative agreements in negotiation, *Personality and Social Psychology Bulletin*, 39 (6), pp 814–29

Slater, L (ed) (2014) *The Lawyer's Guide to AFAs and Value Pricing*, Ark Group, London

Sodhi, M S and Sodhi, N S (2008) *Six Sigma Pricing: Improving pricing operations to increase profits*, FT Press, Upper Saddle River, NJ

Sribna, T (2005) Creative thinking in negotiation. What is the challenge? Master Thesis, Department of Strategy and Management, Norges Handelshøyskole, Bergen, Norway

Tannen, D (1994) *Talking from 9 to 5*, Harper Collins, New York

Thomas, K W and Kilmann, R H (1977) Developing a forced-choice measure of conflict-handling behaviour: The 'mode' instrument, *Educational and Psychological Measurement*, 37 (2), pp 309–25

Thompson, L (2008) *The Truth about Negotiations*, Pearson Education, London

Thompson, L (2009) *The Mind and Heart of the Negotiator*, 4th edn, Pearson Education, London

Tolman, J L (1989) Learning from how others bill, in (ed) R C Reed, *Beyond the Billable Hour – An anthology of alternative billing methods*, American Bar Association, New York

Trötschel, R, Hüffmeier, J, Loschelder, D D, Schwartz, K and Gollwitzer, P M (2011) Perspective taking as a means to overcome motivational barriers in negotiations: When putting oneself into the opponent's shoes helps to walk toward agreements, *Journal of Personality and Social Psychology*, 101 (4), pp 771–90

Ury, W (1993) *Getting past NO, Negotiating in difficult situations*, rev edn, Bantam Dell, New York

Ury, W (2007) *The Power of a Positive NO: How to say no and still get to yes*, Hodder & Stoughton, London

Van Kleef, G A and Côté, S (2007) Expressing anger in conflict: When it helps and when it hurts, *Journal of Applied Psychology*, 92 (6), pp 1557–69

Van Kleef, G A and De Dreu, C K W (2010) Longer-term consequences of anger expression in negotiation: Retaliation or spillover? *Journal of Experimental Social Psychology*, 46 (5), pp 753–60

von Nordenflycht, A (2010) What is a professional service firm? Toward a theory and taxonomy of knowledge-intensive firms, *Academy of Management Review*, 35 (1), pp 155–74

Walton, R E and McKersie R B (1965) *A Behavioral Theory of Labor Negotiations: An Analysis of a social interaction system*, ILR Press, Ithaca, New York

Weiss, A (2008a) *How to Maximise Fees in Professional Service Firms*, Las Brisas Research Press, Costa Rica

Weiss, A (2008b) *Value-based Fees: How to charge – and get what you're worth*, 2nd edn, Pfeiffer, San Francisco, CA

Wheeler, M (2013) *The Art of Negotiation: How to improvise agreement in a chaotic world*, Simon & Schuster, New York

Wheeler, M (2013) The fog of negotiation: What negotiators can learn from military doctrine, *Negotiation Journal*, January

Wheeler, M (ed) (2015) *Negotiation Journal*, 31 (4), John Wiley & Sons

Wheeler, M (2016) Assessment: What kind of negotiator are you? *Harvard Business Review*, February

Wiltermuth, S S and Neale, M A (2011) Too much information: The perils of non-diagnostic information in negotiations, *Journal of Applied Psychology*, 96 (1), pp 192–201

Wong, E M, Haselhuhn, M P and Kray L J (2012) Improving the future by considering the past: The impact of upward counterfactual reflection and implicit beliefs on negotiation performance, *Journal of Experimental Social Psychology*, 48 (1), pp 403–06

Yeoman, I and McMahon-Beattie, U (2011) *Revenue Management: A practical pricing perspective*, Palgrave Macmillan, Basingstoke

Young, M and Schlie, E (2011) The rhythm of the deal: Negotiation as a dance, *Negotiation Journal*, 27, pp 191–203

INDEX

Note: **bold** page numbers indicate figures; *italic* numbers indicate tables.

CPSIA information can be obtained
at www.ICGtesting.com
Printed in the USA
BVOW06s1242090217
475769BV00001B/20/P

9 780749 477387